Beyond Yahweh
and Jesus

Beyond Yahweh and Jesus

Bringing Death's Wisdom
to Faith, Spirituality,
and Psychoanalysis

Robert Langs

JASON ARONSON

Lanham • Boulder • New York • Toronto • Plymouth, UK

Published in the United States of America
by Jason Aronson
An imprint of Rowman & Littlefield Publishers, Inc.
A wholly owned subsidiary of The Rowman & Littlefield Publishing Group, Inc.
4501 Forbes Boulevard, Suite 200, Lanham, Maryland 20706
www.rowmanlittlefield.com

Estover Road, Plymouth PL6 7PY, United Kingdom

British Library Cataloguing in Publication Information Available

Library of Congress Cataloging-in-Publication Data

Langs, Robert, 1928–
    Beyond Yahweh and Jesus : bringing death's wisdom to faith, spirituality,
and psychoanalysis / Robert Langs.
        p. cm.
    Includes bibliographical references and index.
    ISBN-13: 978-0-7657-0531-0 (cloth : alk. paper)
    ISBN-10: 0-7657-0531-1 (cloth : alk. paper)
    ISBN-13: 978-0-7657-0532-7 (pbk. : alk. paper)
    ISBN-10: 0-7657-0532-X (pbk. : alk. paper)
    1. Death—Religious aspects—Christianity. 2. Death—Psychological aspects.
3. Psychoanalysis and religion. I. Title.

BT825.L375 2007
236'.1—dc22
                                                        2007021620

Printed in the United States of America

To P. R.

Miracles happen.

Contents

Author's Note ix

Prologue: My Appointment in Samara xiii

1 The First Question and God's Answer 1

2 The First Question and Eve's Answer 19

3 Death Anxiety and Divine Wisdom 43

4 Augustine's Version of Adam's Sin 55

5 Eve's Motives 65

6 Cain and Abel 79

7 Augustine's Reliving of the Sin of Cain 91

8 The Failure to Master Death Anxiety: Yahweh 105

9 Resolving Death Anxiety: Jesus Christ 125

10 The Failure of Religious Beliefs 145

11 Why Psychoanalysis Failed Religion   155

12 The Future of Religious and Secular Spirituality   175

References   193

Index   197

About the Author   201

Author's Note

The recent acrimonious spate of antireligious writings offered by a quartet of self-styled rationalists (Harris 2004, 2006; Dawkins 2006; Dennett 2006; Hitchens 2007) move me to make clear from the outset that, to borrow a phrase from Shakespeare, I come not to bury religion, nor to praise it—I come to understand it.

I too am a rationalist, a biologically oriented psychoanalyst, but I have developed a new view of the human mind and emotional life that inevitably calls for a fresh look at religion and the belief in a supernatural God (Langs 2004c, 2006). As I shall soon explain, this innovative version of psychoanalysis is based on the disarmingly simple thesis that, like all species before us, we are first and foremost *adaptive organisms*. In the emotional realm, this means that we have *emotion-processing minds* that are designed to deal with and help us to survive physical and psychological dangers and thereby live satisfying, moral lives. Perhaps the most telling feature of this mental adaptive instrument—be it God-given, evolved through natural selection, or both—is that it copes with the animate and inanimate environments that impinge on us using two relatively independent operating systems, each with its own mode of perception, values, and adaptive resources. One system functions more or less with our full, direct awareness, but the other system goes about its business silently—unconsciously, if you will—entirely without our knowing what we have seen and heard, how it has impacted us, and how we are reacting to it. The coping activities of this second system are disguised in our dreams and daydreams, and these communications need to be properly decoded in light of the events that have stirred it into action—a process called *trigger decoding*. To do so is to access the human mind's most awesome emotional resources, a God-like adaptive wisdom system that stands well beyond anything that we can muster consciously.

Many of the unforeseen insights generated by the adaptive approach have come from mapping and understanding the distinctive sensitivities and coping strategies of this secret, deeply unconscious system. It took a long while, but it eventually became clear that on the deep unconscious level of experience, life is essentially about death. In contrast to conscious efforts at coping, which involve many different kinds of needs, issues, and triggering events, deep unconscious efforts at adaptation are always danger and death related. Death is with us each and every day of our lives even though consciously we are largely unaware of its persistent presence and pressures. Indeed, much like a ruling tyrant armed with secret service agents, *deep unconscious death anxiety* stealthily governs our lives.

Personally and professionally, my turn to religion and spirituality, while seemingly an inevitable outcome of my view of the mind, came about more through serendipity than a deliberate plan. A friend who was interested in helping me to find ways to present my new ideas to the general public urged me to read some of the books that had brought psychology to the masses. Abhorring vacuous clichés, I resisted at first, but gave in when I came across a review of Richard Bernstein's book *Ultimate Journey* (2001). I was fascinated by his efforts to duplicate the torturous journey of a seventh-century Chinese Buddhist monk who traveled from China to India to obtain some of the original Buddhist texts so he could generate new translations of these documents. To my surprise, I found that there were some striking parallels between my new version of psychoanalysis and Buddhist thinking about the design of the human mind. Sensing that there was some kind of broad and meaningful connection between my adaptive version of psychoanalysis and spirituality—as a classically trained Freudian psychoanalyst, spirituality and religion were not on my radar screen—I embarked on a new and unexpected adventure. And I must say that despite my reputation as a psychoanalytic tiger, I came to religion incarnated as a naïve and innocent pussycat.

I went from books on Buddhism and the Buddha to works about Muhammad and Islam, and then to readings in Judaism and Christianity, including the Old and New Testaments. I was stunned by the similarities and overlap between the ideas reflected in these spiritual writings and the observations and premises of my adaptive version of psychoanalysis. I came to appreciate that these reverent texts reflect a wide range of attempts to deal with the eternal, archetypal challenges inherent in human existence. My adaptive approach is similarly configured: It too deals with archetypal challenges and offers a variety of conscious and deep unconscious archetypal solutions to the dangers involved, many of them not unlike those proposed by religion. I began to reconsider and expand my psychoanalytic thinking in light of the revealed wisdom of the Bible even as I used my psychoanalytic insights to freshly illuminate the religious realm. I experienced a mutually enriching exchange of ideas between religion and psychoanalytic thinking that was as unexpected as it was transforming.

In the course of these investigations, I began to focus on a series of basic questions that I tried to answer using the fresh insights into the emotion-processing mind that I had forged through the adaptive approach:

- Why have so many humans, past and present, deeply believed in the existence of a supernatural God?
- What are the universal challenges with which this belief helps them to cope?
- What role do death and *unconsciously experienced death anxiety* play in this pursuit?
- What are the deep unconscious roots of good and evil—of human morality?
- To what extent have Judaism and Christianity succeeded or failed in their promise to make it possible for us as humans to live satisfying moral lives at peace with ourselves and each other?
- To the extent that they have failed, what are the reasons and how can the failures be rectified?
- And finally, how can adaptive insights into religion and morality be recruited as the basis for developing a more meaningful and constructive set of religious precepts as well as a similarly effective rational or secular spirituality?

Seeking answers to these questions, however preliminary and incomplete, inescapably fosters a measure of unity between faith-based thinking and its rational, nonreligious counterpart. This unification is grounded in the basic adaptive premise that surviving danger situations and dealing with the death anxieties that they evoke, much of this anxiety outside our direct awareness, places us all in the same ark afloat in a stormy sea foaming with threat. Both the belief in God in his two main Western incarnations as Yahweh and Jesus and the belief that God does not exist have been adopted and sustained in the service of surviving these treacherous seas. Much the same applies to psychoanalysis: It too should be—and should have been—crafted in ways that offer significant help to humans in their desperate effort to survive the threats that life inevitably presents to us.

With this in mind, let it be said once and for all: By whatever means you try to cope with these eternal human plagues, it is well to do so with a full measure of humbleness and modesty. I say this because the incontrovertible fact is that while your efforts to survive may well have their measure of success, they also most certainly will have their measure of failure—ultimately, death trumps all comers. In the course of my personal life and in my work as a psychoanalyst, this lesson has been etched in my mind, and as a writer, I have found it to be much the same. It is, then, with a strong sense of humility that I bring this book to you, offering it for your edification whatever your spiritual beliefs may or may not be.

Robert Langs, MD
New York City

Prologue: My Appointment in Samara

This book had its palpable origins some unthinkable fifty-three years ago when I was a medical student doing a clerkship in internal medicine at a private hospital in Chicago, Illinois. Quite by chance, I was instructed to work up the case of a man in his forties who had been given a diagnosis of "fever of unknown origin," which was a dignified way of saying that his doctors had no idea what was wrong with him. I was a bit anxious at being assigned a case of that kind. I would have been a lot more anxious had I known that, like Isaac as he accompanied his father to a mountain in the land of Moriah or Saul as he took to the road to Damascus, I had just embarked on a fateful journey that would forever change my life — and, I believe, the life of many others as well.

I went to my patient's bedside, took a detailed medical history, and conducted a careful physical examination. Like his primary physicians, I too had no immediate idea as to why his fever persisted despite his taking antibiotics and other medications that should have made him well. I was learning that God or the machinery of the miraculously complex human body works in mysterious ways that often defy the best medical minds.

My work-up finished, I went to a medical encyclopedia for help in making a differential diagnosis and listed just about everything except the common cold. But as I pondered these many possibilities, several of his symptoms — his fatigue, low blood pressure, slightly discolored skin — seemed to come together to suggest that he might have a syndrome called Addison's disease, a rare illness caused by an insufficiency of the adrenal gland.

That week, the American Medical Association was holding its annual meeting in Chicago, so I hurried down to the Steel Pier to see and hear what was new in medicine. At the time, I was in the throes of deciding on the specialty to which I would commit my medical career. The debate raged back and forth between internal medicine and psychiatry, which for me—this was the early '50s—meant psychoanalysis. Learning what was new in the world of "real doctors" might help me decide which way to go.

I got to the meeting and found that one of the poster displays was devoted to Addison's disease. To my astonishment, as I looked over the photographs I had the eerie feeling that my patient had posed for the pictures! Talk about coincidence or the invisible hand of God.

I raced back to the hospital to complete my write-up of the case, and with anxious anticipation, I presented it to my mentor. When I announced that I was convinced that this patient was suffering from Addison's disease, my overseer, who was quite stunned, soon entered a state of physicianly bliss. He quickly arranged for the necessary laboratory chemistries to be carried out, and they confirmed the diagnosis. Like a proud father, he had me present my patient to everyone within earshot.

Now you would think that this moment of seemingly unadulterated medical glory would have settled the debate as to my future as a physician—and it did. I decided to become a psychoanalyst! You see, I had reached the pinnacle of medical practice, had made a brilliant diagnosis that I could glory in for years to come, felt almost God-like, but there was no treatment for this illness. The man was going to die. And I had pronounced his death sentence. This was not how I wanted to spend my years as a physician.

I knew full well that I had chosen to run from death to the glories of life-affirming Freudian sexuality, to patients with unpalpable ills whose lives were not threatened. And most of all, as I later realized, I was running from grim realities to a fairy-tale world of fantasy and wishes. I had become a living example of the age-old adage that a psychoanalyst is a doctor who can't stand the sight of blood. As for underlying causes, all I could say was that my early-life experiences with illness and death—my father was a general practitioner who did tonsillectomies in his home office—had had a shadowy bearing on my decision.

Having made my choice, I pursued a career line that took me to a psychiatric residency and a psychoanalytic training institute. In time, I became a psychoanalyst with an avowed interest in the human mind, especially its enigmatic unconscious operations. I began to write books and have continued to do so ever since.

The Freudian psychoanalysis that I was taught was founded on the Oedipus myth, which was seen as a reflection of the universal unconscious wish of the young boy to sleep with his mother and do away with his father. Forbidden incestuous wishes and the sexual conflicts they caused were said to be at the heart of humankind's emotional problems. These same wishes were expected to emerge in the course of a psychoanalysis, disguised in patients' dreams and misdirected toward the analyst in lieu of the parent toward whom they were originally intended. In this way, these disruptive feelings and wishes—these so-called *transferences*—would become available for interpretation and renunciation, and the cure of the patient would soon follow.

I completed my training analysis and graduated from the analytic institute. I became skillful at interpreting my analytic patients' misplaced transferences and their unconscious sexual wishes toward me. They accepted my interventions either willingly or with a reluctance that was seen as an expression of resistance, something to be quickly interpreted away. Most of my patients stayed with me, spent four days a week on my analytic couch, and seemed to do better emotionally. My career as an analyst was blooming: I had a full load of analytic patients, was teaching at the analytic institute and writing books on psychotherapy, had become part of a cadre of fellow analysts, and very much enjoyed the satisfactions that all of this was affording me.

There was, however, one seemingly small fly in the ointment: I was bothered by the extent to which psychoanalytic thinking and practice gave short shrift to reality in favor of fantasy. The party line was (and still is) that reality is not the ultimate problem in human emotional life, it's what we make of reality that counts. Our imaginations trump our actual lives.

The problem was that I had been through some tough realities as a child, and I knew that without my imagining it, they had had a strong impact on me, much of it rather detrimental. But whenever I expressed my doubts about their way of thinking, my colleagues would tell me that they didn't ignore reality, they simply took it as a starting point for a sequence of inner mental events, some of them quite unconscious, that were the true source of emotional ills.

My concerns about the role of reality in emotional life prompted me to keep a watchful eye on what actually happened in the lives of my patients and in their interactions with me. I began to see how they dealt with reality and came to understand the workings of their minds in new ways. I'd been taught that patients disguise their forbidden, unconscious sexual fantasies in their dreams. But through my new-won eyes, I began to see that patients also disguise or encode in their dreams and daydreams many of their most disturbing perceptions of actual events—threatening perceptions of which they are quite unaware consciously. And one of the really disquieting aspects of these rather jaundiced *unconscious or subliminal perceptions* was that they pertained largely to my own interventions. Much of how I'd been taught to do psychoanalysis and psychotherapy, which was accepted *consciously* by myself, my colleagues, and my patients, was being experienced as harmful and unhelpful by my patients' *deep unconscious minds*.

It was becoming clear that while the unconscious mind may well be the seat of forbidden wishes and drives, it also contains a highly intelligent wisdom system that knows a lot more than the conscious mind does about reality, the meanings of events, how people behave, and even how to do effective psychotherapy. The conscious mind may be inclined to fantasize, but the deep unconscious mind is zeroed in on the real world and its often deeply upsetting impact on our lives.

A new, reality-centered, adaptive way of thinking about and understanding the human mind and of doing psychotherapy emerged from these unexpected clinical observations (Langs 1993, 1996, 2004c, 2005a, 2006). When it comes to emotional life, dealing with traumatic incidents rather than coping with our inner needs is the heart of the matter. It was as though a veil, placed there by my psychoanalytic training, had lifted: The idea that reality affects us far more than fantasy and that actual events are far more demanding of our coping skills than our secret wishes began to look like a much-denied no-brainer.

By decoding my own and my patients' dreams in light of the incidents that evoked our disguised dream imagery, I was able to see that the deep unconscious mind works much like the conscious mind—but does a far better job at it. Quite unexpectedly, I found that compared to our conscious resources, the deep unconscious system is wise beyond all conscious knowing and moral beyond all conscious morality. I came to think of the deep unconscious mind as an awesome *inner god* whose encoded revelations are truly divine and numinous.

There was a lot more that I discovered with my new version of psychoanalysis, but one of the last insights I developed brings me to the moral of this story. After overcoming my personal use of denial and avoidance, I finally was able to realize that the reality that most powerfully affects and drives our emotional lives is *the reality of death*. Once seen, there was no mistaking it: Death secretly empowers our lives, and having a good and satisfying, moral life depends on our mastering death and the deep unconscious death anxieties it arouses in us (Langs 1997, 2002, 2003, 2004a, 2004b, 2004c, 2005b).

I had come full circle: My escape route from the reality of death had brought me back to the reality of death!

Had I read Somerset Maugham's story "The Appointment in Samara," I might have spared myself the many years of effort that went into arriving at this astounding insight. In seeing death as an inherent part of internal medicine and fleeing to a supposedly death-free psychoanalysis, I had behaved like the manservant in Maugham's story who goes into town and sees Death looking at him askance. He promptly flees his home town for Samara. But when his master goes into town and asks Death what his odd look at his servant was about, Death explains that he was surprised to see him there because he had an appointment with the man that night in Samara.

As a writer personally familiar with death-related traumas, Maugham captured the essence of life in a single pithy paragraph, while it took me, a psychoanalyst who had suffered similar insults, more than twenty-five years to make the same discovery.

Death is what moved me away from Freudian psychoanalysis and toward a new way of understanding the emotion-processing mind and life itself. Death is what brought me to religion, and trying to solve the challenges posed by death is what unites my version of psychoanalysis with religion in common cause. Death is at the center of this book, and with it come the three forms of death anxiety that I have uncovered, each operating most of the time silently and unconsciously, yet with great power and influence: *existential*—the fear evoked by human mortality; *predatory*—the fear evoked when someone or an act of God or nature is trying to destroy us; and *predator*—the guilty fear of mortal punishment for having harmed others. Dealing with death and death anxiety are, then, at the heart of the new, adaptive psychoanalysis I have forged, much as it is the central feature of the revisions of religion and the secular-rational morality that I shall propose.

Having fully acknowledged that I—and you—cannot escape its visible and invisible clutches, it is time to let death have its say.

1

The First Question and God's Answer

We must read the Bible or we shall not understand psychology. Our psychology, whole lives, our language and imagery are built upon the Bible.

—Carl Jung, *The Visions Seminars*, vol. 1, p. 156

To gain an understanding of religious matters, probably all that is left us today is the psychological approach. That is why I take these thought-forms that have become historically fixed, try to melt them down again and pour them into moulds of immediate experience.

—Carl Jung, "Psychology and Religion," in *Psychology and Religion*, CW 11, par. 148

Once again, only religion can answer the question of the purpose of life. One can hardly be wrong in concluding that the idea of life having a purpose stands and falls with the religious system.

—Sigmund Freud, *Civilization and Its Discontents*, SE, vol. 21, p. 76

The richness of the wisdom of the Bible, so much of it secreted in its passages, is staggering to behold. We experience its divine mysteries from its opening pages. Where most books, like life itself, have but one beginning, the Bible has two distinctive moments of origination—the Old and New Testaments—and the first of these, also called the Hebrew Testament, has six inaugurals of its own. Four are in the opening chapters of Genesis. Two involve the creation of the physical world and the heavens, and the other two involve the creation of living beings, humans in particular. The remaining pair of creations comes much later and takes place after the flood that all but destroys the planet and its living beings and vegetation. One is the rebirth of the land and seas, while the other is the beginning of a new human lineage, the descendants of Noah.

All this is the work of the Hebrew God, Yahweh, who is variously alluded to as God, the Lord, or the Lord God. We cannot escape the impression that he who is supremely wise also is supremely uncertain—a point made by Miles (1995, 2001) in his books on the history of God and Jesus, and more recently by Dawkins (2006) in his assault on religious beliefs.

In any case, in the initial version of the first beginning, which is known as the *first creation*, God fashions *the overarching universe*. In his infinite wisdom he understands that before living beings can come to life, survive, and begin to act and interact, there must be a stable place where they can do so; before the action can begin and the inevitable satisfactions, conflicts, and issues arise, there must be a secured setting:

> In the beginning when God created the heavens and earth, the earth was a formless void and darkness covered the face of the deep, while a wind from God swept over the face of the waters. Then God said, "Let there be light"; and there was light. And God saw that the light was good; and God separated the light from the darkness. (Gen 1:1–4)[1]

Believers recognize this as God's first labor of love for humankind, the creation of a viable space and environment in which living beings can thrive. Nonbelievers see this as an intuitive description of the activities of some of the most basic principles of physical nature: the emergence of order out of chaos and the establishment of temporal and physical stability through boundary formations—for example, separating day from night, land from sea, earth from heaven. This is the first of many *archetypal moments* in the Bible in that it touches on and reflects the eternal laws and regularities, divine and natural, through which stable physical entities that support life on earth are and have been established since the beginning of time.

Archetypes, which the psychoanalyst Carl Jung described as representative, enduring inclinations and patterns of behavior that exist in the psychological realm (Jung 1958, 1968, 1972; Edinger 1987, 1992a; Maidenbaum 1998), play a significant role in both the Bible and religion. They are, in essence, universal templates and repetitive patterns, laws, and regularities that persist in timeless fashion in both the physical and psychological realms. The latter include recurrent and repetitive mythical themes, personality or character types, additional aspects of the human personality, and other similarly general and seemingly instinctive, persistent tendencies.

There is however a significant difference between physical and psychological archetypes in that the latter can be defied at times without necessarily causing havoc or harm. For example, as we shall see, both Jesus and Freud defied one form of the death-related, revenge archetype that is usually seen in response to early childhood, parental traumas. On the other hand, except for rare, transformative instances that bring new order into the universe, physical archetypes are difficult to establish and cannot be successfully defied—doing so almost always leads to chaos and devastation.

This may help to explain what appears to be God's first sign of uncertainty: In repetitively noting that the results of his creative efforts were good, God may have been indicating that he had tried to establish a stable universe countless times before and only now did he get it right. Today we know that it took—and takes—over twenty delicately fixed physical constants to fashion a reliable, secure universe that we can count on from one day to the next. From the very opening moments of creation, it can be said that God and nature are acting in consort.

Once an enduring universe that could support life was established, God populated the earth with the first living beings:

> So God created humankind in his image, in the image of God he created them; male and female he created them. God blessed them, and said to them, "Be fruitful and multiply, and fill the earth and subdue it; and have dominion over the fish of the sea and over the birds of the air and over every living thing that moves upon the earth." (Gen 1:27–28)

COMMENTING ON THE FIRST CREATION

There are several striking aspects to this initial act of biological creation. The first is that the living entities, including the two humans, are generic beings who lack individual identities. God will soon use a second creation to remedy this impersonal approach, but even so we may wonder why God did not create male and female as complete beings with strong identities from the very first moment. His hesitancy may have something to do with what the fact that once he did create well-defined humans, God experienced little else but grief and aggravation from them.

Also of note in light of the extent to which we presently value equality for all, God prefers to create a hierarchy of responsibilities that he evidently believes will help to maintain a sound social order among living beings. There is wisdom in such an arrangement, but problems can arise if those at the upper end of the hierarchy become exploitative or tyrannical, or fail to carry out their responsibilities in fairness to all. The extent to which humans have dealt fairly with so-called lower animals and beings, and behaved in ways that justify God's placing them at the top of the pyramid, is a matter open to serious question. Just as God has responsibilities to humankind, humans have responsibilities to God and to those whom God has placed under their care. Indications are that many humans have not as yet found a way to honor God's trust in them.

There are no signs of injustice to animals in the early chapters of Genesis: Eden is a paradise in which all manner of living beings live together in peace and harmony. Later on, at the time of the flood, Noah takes onto the ark he built two members of every living species. But then, beginning with the ram caught in a thicket by its horns, which Abraham sacrifices in lieu of his son, Isaac—an image that anticipates the human sacrifice of Christ with his crown of thorns on the cross—sacrificing animals to placate or please God is commonplace for a long period of time. Indeed, human cruelty and violent conduct toward others is directed not only toward animals and similar creatures, but even more so toward fellow humans. God may well have left out a significant set of instructions when he fashioned humankind and gave them major responsibilities for living on earth. That said, having planned to settle them in the paradise of Eden, he may have felt that there was no need to be more specific—but then again, shouldn't he have anticipated that their stay in paradise would be short-lived? There is much to ponder about the uncertainties of God's initial creative thrusts and how they set the future course of humankind on this planet.

There is another aspect to this first creation that is quite critical for the death-centered view of the psychological ramifications of the Bible that I will soon be espousing. Unlike the second creation, in this first effort God created humankind in his own image. Among the many implications of this decision, perhaps the most notable is that by design, male and female evidently were provided with both *eternal life and divine wisdom*. Acting as if this had been a grievous error on his part, God opts for a second creation so he can modify these crucial design features. As for his motives for making this change, possibilities include envy or jealousy of his own creations, not wishing after all to share his divine powers with humans, and wanting humans to be subservient to him. All we can say for sure is that it's a good thing that God did not make us of marble.

THE SECOND CREATION

God's first creation of the earth had left it arid, so he made a second effort to provide living beings with a life-sustaining physical environment and to then bring to that environment a refashioned man who could productively till the ground:

But a stream would rise from the earth, and water the whole face of the ground—then the Lord God formed man from the dust of the ground, and breathed into his nostrils the breath of life; and the man became a living being. (Gen 2:6–7)

This second creation of humankind initially lacks a woman who could be a partner and companion to the man, but equally telling is the fact that God has changed the features of the man and given him attributes that will characterize humans forever after. For one thing, he has now created a man with a definitive identity, Adam, so named because man (*adam*) comes from the earth (*adamah*). Thus, this time around, man has not been molded from the stuff that God is made from, nor does he descend from the heavens; instead, he is made from the dust of the ground, the natural substances of the earth. Adam is mortal rather than divine, that is, he no longer possesses divine wisdom, nor shall he, whether he's aware of it at first or not, be immortal and live forever. This is only the beginning of the troubles he will soon face.

Next comes the second physical creation, the fashioning of *the first sub-universe*, the Garden of Eden, a lush setting that is able to support life in all of its varieties and allow living beings to flourish, reproduce, and live with each other in peace and harmony. But the garden is not rent-free, so to speak, at least, not for humans. To have a place in Eden, humans must obey God's first commandment:

And the Lord God planted a garden in Eden, in the east; and there he put the man whom he had formed. Out of the ground the Lord God made to grow every tree that is pleasant to the sight and good for food, the tree of life also in the midst of the garden, and the tree of knowledge of good and evil. (Gen 2:8–9)

And the Lord God commanded the man, "You may eat freely of every tree of the garden; but of the tree of the knowledge of good and evil you shall not eat, for in the day that you eat of it you shall die." (Gen 2:16–17)

We can see then that within the span of the first few chapters of Genesis, issues related to humans possessing divine wisdom and immortality loom large. God first fashioned man replete with such wisdom and then gave him his second and enduring life without that gift. In addition, God took the trouble to deny Adam the opportunity to acquire that wisdom at risk of losing his life. And as if that were not enough ambivalence and waffling on the part of God, he places the tree of divine knowledge, the very tree he has forbidden Adam to eat from, smack in the middle of the garden! Now there's a test of frustration tolerance and restraint against temptation if ever there was one.

In respect to man's God-like immortality, that too was at first cheerfully given to him by God only to be taken away in man's creation from the dust of the earth. Still, Adam was not explicitly deprived of the possibility of eternal life; in fact, that possibility was open to him, as seen in the presence of a second special tree in the midst of the garden—the tree of eternal life. Oddly enough, despite their lack of immortality, neither Adam nor his soon-to-come-into-being wife, Eve, pay the least attention to this tree. This holds true until something untoward happens that convinces God that they will want to partake of its fruit, at which time he suddenly realizes that he had forgotten to forbid them to do so and makes amends for his lapse.

As for the opposite of immortality, namely death, God mentions death to Adam in forbidding him to eat from the tree of knowledge of good and evil, but for the moment death seems to be a fate that Adam only vaguely comprehends. Nevertheless, this stricture speaks for a connection between divine wisdom and death that for the moment takes the unusual (yet as we shall see, archetypal) form of the promise that acquiring such wisdom will lead to death. While the wisdom in question is said to involve knowledge of good and evil, the deeper symbolic and real-world meanings of this description are as yet quite uncertain, especially in regard to the question of what makes this knowledge divine and God-like.

Summing up, God's first concerns in fashioning man are centered on the evidently fundamental, archetypal problems of wisdom and death, with issues of morality—that is, knowledge of good and evil and the moral obligation to obey God's edict—linked to both of these concerns. For Adam, and soon for his wife Eve, the ideas of both wisdom and death are what the gifted psychoanalyst Wilfred Bion (1963) called *preconceptions*. That is, both are ill-defined, psychobiological states of expectation that await their realization, at which point the preconception will become a relatively fixed *conception*. In this way, a vague, basic need, idea, or reality is transformed into a well-defined experience and insight. The initial vagueness of both wisdom and death in the minds of Adam and Eve plays a crucial role in their story.

While not directly stating it, the Bible also implies that wisdom comes in two forms: *mundane* and *divine*. With the Lord's blessings, Adam and Eve evidently possess considerable mundane or ordinary knowledge, which they call upon to live well and in peace in Eden. This knowledge is reflected in their understanding of God's words and such practical skills as Adam's tilling the soil and reaping harvests. The couple does not, however, possess divine knowledge, because it can be acquired solely by eating the fruit of the forbidden tree—something that they have not done as yet. Even so, the story implies that this knowledge involves morality (good and evil) and death (the price for gaining such wisdom) in some yet to be determined manner.

It would appear, then, that the human possession of mundane knowledge is the universal norm, and that the acquisition of divine knowledge, which is forbidden by God, runs against this natural inclination. As for death, the archetype appears to call for a vague awareness or preconception of the idea of its existence as a possibility and actuality. This means that a sharper and more definitive awareness of death also runs counter to our natural or God-given human inclinations.

The archetypal qualities of these tendencies are confirmed to some extent by the fact that patients who enter adaptive psychotherapy are immediately faced with the same issues: whether to accept an Eden-like, safe, and secured framework and set of ground rules for their treatment experience; whether to strive to acquire divine wisdom or to restrict themselves to mundane insights; and if they so choose, whether to allow their pursuit of divine wisdom and morality to bring them face-to-face with the death-related, traumatic events that have caused them to suffer from the deep unconscious death anxieties that are the basic source of their emotional disturbances. Essentially then, there are striking parallels between the archetypal issues that arise in God's creation of a paradise in which Adam and Eve will thrive and the archetypal issues that arise in constructing an ideal therapeutic environment in which patients also may thrive. In both settings, the archetypal issues that follow pertain to knowledge acquisition, morality, and death anxiety.

To complete this part of the story, God brings every living being to Adam:

> So out of the ground the Lord God formed every animal of the field and every bird of the air, and brought them to the man to see what he would call them; and whatsoever the man called every living creature, that was its name. (Gen 2:19)

The role of *language acquisition* in humankind's dominance over other living entities is highlighted here (Langs 1996). God has already used language to pronounce his first commandment, and it is clear that Adam understood what God was telling him. Language will soon play a vital role in the drama that unfolds in Eden—the first and one of the most telling stories in the history of humankind.

For the moment, realizing at last that Adam lacked a helpmate, the Lord God creates woman, later named Eve, from Adam's rib. After Adam rhapsodizes over the birth of his companion it is said,

> Therefore a man leaves his father and mother and clings to his wife, and they become one flesh. And the man and his wife were both naked, and were not ashamed. (Gen 2:24–25)

With that, the backstory has been completed, and the dramatic action of life on earth and humankind's relationship with God is about to begin. I will take up what follows in the next chapter, but before I do so, a few additional perspectives on my approach to the Bible are in order.

PSYCHOANALYTIC APPROACHES TO THE BIBLE

Miles (1995) has persuasively argued that the stories in the Bible can be treated as passion dramas. Using that framework, it can be said that at this early juncture, the stage has been set for the drama of life on earth to begin in earnest, with the story possibly already written in the mind of God or about to unfold through natural causes. The players are present or about to appear — Adam, Eve, the serpent, and God — and the dramatic action is about to begin. It is a divinely archetypal tale, one that has been subjected to countless interpretations (see, for example, Pagels 1988; Miles 1995; Armstrong 1996; Shulman 2003). Still, we must continue to search for new ways of understanding the events that are about to take place because they set the course of humankind for ages to come. This is pertinent here because I am approaching the Bible with a new version of psychoanalysis in hand. Carl Jung, Freud's most gifted follower and one of the most ardent and incisive psychologically oriented interpreters of the Bible, suggested that new ideas about the human mind and the Bible are likely to arise when fresh historical material is unearthed or when a new depth psychology is developed. To quote him,

> These foreshadowings [Christ's flight into and call out of Egypt, as foretold in both Exodus and Jeremiah] illustrate the psychological fact that something new in the psyche can gain admission to consciousness only by following a previously established pattern. Thus it is, for instance, that the new discoveries of depth psychology find entry into the modern mind by the reinterpretation of biblical images. (*Mysterium Coniunctionis*, CW 14, par. 521)

Jung is alluding here to the discovery of ageless *archetypal patterns* — relatively fixed psychological needs, tendencies, and behavioral inclinations that can be thought of as fashioned by God when he designed man or as genetically programmed into the human mind through natural selection (Langs 1996). It was the recognition of the archetypes of the *collective unconscious* — that is, the universal aspects and psychological tendencies of the unconscious part of the human mind — that enabled Jung to transfer findings derived from his psychoanalytic work with patients to the narratives and figures in the Bible, and to the stories of Job and Christ in particular (Jung 1958; Edinger 1987, 1992b). While Jung turned to the Bible, and to myths and fables, to identify clues to modern-day archetypes that unconsciously drive human behavior — that is, he went from the *past to the present* — traveling this timeless trail in the opposite direction—that is, from the *present to the past*—can be equally rewarding. Journeys of this kind can bring present-day archetypes to the Bible and allow for fresh interpretations of the universal elements in its narratives. This is the main route that I take in this book—using archetypes that I have discovered in my adaptive psychoanalytic work with patients as a basis for reinterpreting the happenings in the Bible.

The likely success of these efforts arises largely because, ironically enough, the ideal place in which to discover the archetypes that are relevant to the Bible is *the psychoanalytic situation* that was created by none other than Sigmund Freud, the great nonbeliever. The psychoanalyst is in a unique position to observe emotion-related human behavior, its causes and underlying psychology, in ways that are not possible through any other means. But the kinds of observations that a particular psychoanalyst makes and the conclusions that he or she draws from them depend almost entirely on the framework and theory through which the analyst views and understands the workings of the human mind. Theory determines (and biases) observation, much as observation determines (and biases) theory. These are tools that must be used with utmost caution—and with as much effort at independent validation as possible.

Freud's sexual-conflict, wish-centered orientation led him to reject religion and the belief in a transcendental God because he saw these phenomena as little more than reflections of the infantile wish for an omnipotent father (Freud 1927). His thinking was buttressed by his model of the mind, his structural theory of ego, id, and superego in which each system was proposed to have conscious and unconscious aspects (Freud 1923). According to this model, the key to emotional life is to be found in the unconscious conflicts that arise when forbidden unconscious id drives are pitted against unconscious superego values, a struggle that is mediated by the ego, which also keeps in mind the demands of reality. Achieving peace between these warring factions was seen as the basis for emotional healing. In the world beset with neurotic wishes that Freud envisioned, the belief in the existence of God was simply another neurotic wish. On that basis, and with questionable logic as a psychoanalytic investigator who should have pursued the question as to why so many humans experienced such seemingly neurotic needs, he saw no reason to dig deeper into the belief in God or the Bible.

Jung's broader view, in which the quest for individuation is seen as the central struggle in emotional life (Jung 1968; Edinger 1986, 1996), facilitated a more open view of religion. This arose because the belief in God and an investment in the stories in the Bible were said to be based on timeless, archetypal needs that are pertinent to humankind's search for a mature, satisfying personal and spiritual identity. As was the case with Freud, Jung also saw both conscious and unconscious aspects to this ever-present quest. He called the conscious component the *ego* or *subjective psyche* because this part of the mind tends to adopt a highly individualized and often distorted view of life, while he labeled the unconscious component the *self* or *objective psyche* because it is the part of the mind where archetypes and the collective unconscious are located; it is here that universal rather than personal inclinations prevail.

The links that connect present-day longings and archetypes with the events connected with biblical figures like Adam and Eve, Abraham and Job, and Jesus Christ were the focus of much of Jung's religiously oriented writings. For him, the cure of patients' neuroses depended on their getting in touch with their unconscious selves and archetypes, which they needed to bring into conscious awareness in order to modify their infantile egos. As is characteristic of mind-centered theories of the human psyche and emotional life, however, exactly how a patient achieves this transformation was a matter of considerable uncertainty and was subjected to seemingly loose and arbitrary conjectures.

In crafting my own approach to the human mind, which, as I said, is called the *communicative* or *adaptive approach*, I stood on the shoulders of both Freud and Jung. In so doing, however, I have been afforded a field of vision that is more expansive and basically different from that seen by these giants of psychoanalysis. Both of these pioneers shared a similar way of listening to patients and formulating the meanings and implications of what they heard. Their view of the human psyche stressed inner mental tendencies, although they parted ways in defining their essential nature—that is, they were sexual issues for Freud (1917, 1924, 1925, 1940) and issues of individuation for Jung (1968; Edinger 1986, 1992a, 1996).

My own approach departed radically from their way of thinking. Instead of listening first and foremost for signs of inner mental conflicts, my attention was focused on how my patients were reacting, consciously and deep unconsciously, to emotionally charged, traumatic triggering events—that is, to troublesome external realities. My first concern, then, was to identify these events which were, as a rule, perpetrated by other humans or by natural upheavals. The human psyche was seen as fundamentally outer-directed and interactive, and to understand its responses, it was deemed necessary to identify the stimulus or triggering event that had evoked the response in the first place.

The situation is complicated by the finding that humans are unique among living beings in reacting to environmental incidents both consciously (knowingly) and deep unconsciously (unknowingly). These unconscious reactions are encoded in our dreams and stories, which have both *manifest contents* with their directly expressed meanings, along with *en-*

coded, latent contents replete with disguised, trigger-evoked meanings. In psychotherapy, then, it was only after I had identified the stimulus or event that had set the *emotion-processing mind* in motion that I could properly decode my patients' narrative imagery and determine what they had perceived unconsciously and how they had reacted and adapted to it (Langs 2004c, 2006). On that basis, I was able to account for what was going on in the patient's mind and what had triggered these mental activities—I could account for both reality and the psyche, or put another way, I could understand the psyche in light of the realities with which it was dealing. These are the stimuli that shape our most compelling mental responses and arouse our most powerful inner needs. Identifying impinging traumatic events provides the key that opens the locks within our minds.

Practically speaking, this means that whenever adaptive therapists look at emotionally charged behavior and symptoms, they do not, as did Freud and Jung, ask first and last what inner need, fantasy, or wish the person is trying to satisfy. Instead, they first ask, What has happened to stir up the patient's needs and fantasies? That done, they then look to see how much of the patient's reaction is expressed directly and manifestly in a straightforward, conscious manner, and how much is expressed indirectly and unconsciously, and encoded in the patient's dreams and daydreams. Thus, when we come to Eve's eating the fruit of the forbidden tree of knowledge of good and evil, I shall be asking a question seldom if ever asked before: "What happened to her that prompted her to do as she did?" Answering that vital question is essential to attaining fresh insights into her fateful act. In principle, reality comes first, inner motives and needs second.

A brief illustration will help to clarify these points. A depressed female patient in her midthirties reports a dream to her male therapist in which her butcher is overcharging her by keeping his finger on the scale as he weighs her meat. She associates to the dream by recalling her butcher's tendency to sell her extremely expensive meats and her mistrust of his scale. She then takes a check from her purse and pays the therapist his fee for the previous month's sessions. The therapist suddenly realizes that he had mistakenly billed the patient for a session that he had canceled by telephone without advance notice. The trigger-evoked, encoded meaning of the dream becomes clear to him—he is the thief whom the patient does not trust. He returns the check to the patient and interprets her dream accordingly. The patient then indicates that she had no conscious thought that the bill was in error. She goes on in the session to recall a newspaper story of a reformed thief who was now the head of a branch of Catholic Charities.

The manifest dream is about the patient's butcher, but with these very same images, the dream also encodes the patient's unconscious perceptions of her therapist in light of an unconsciously recognized error that he had made in filling out her bill. The trigger for the encoded meaning of the dream is the overcharge, and it had registered unconsciously rather than consciously because it was so anxiety-provoking for the patient. She had blocked the error from entering her conscious mind, or to put it another way, she had denied or obliterated the error consciously.

The trigger-decoded meaning of the dream is that the therapist had acted in a dishonest way in asking the patient to pay for a session that had not been held. This valid unconscious perception is encoded in the dream itself and in the patient's associations to the dream. Morally speaking, the therapist had been dishonest and immoral in rendering his bill. But once he had rectified his error and interpreted the patient's experience of the overcharge, the patient told a story that indicated that in her deep unconscious mind, the therapist had transformed himself from being a thief to becoming a moral, upright citizen. This is an encoded validation of the therapist's interventions—his rectification of the error and his interpretation of the patient's deep unconscious view of it. It seems clear that in the patient's eyes, he had atoned for his sinful mistake.

Such are the ways of the emotion-processing mind: a conscious system prone to denial and obliteration and a deep unconscious system that accurately perceives disturbing realities and nondefensively works them over accordingly. This system also seems to know exactly when a therapist has made an error and when he or she has set things right.

THE SYSTEMS OF THE MIND

The adaptive approach has forged a new model of the emotion-processing mind and has confirmed its propositions though deep unconscious, encoded validating imagery (Langs 2004c, 2005a, 2006). There is a *conscious mind* or *system* that is extremely fragile and easily disturbed. As a result, God or natural selection has favored minds that engage consciously in a great deal of self-protective denial and obliteration lest they be overwhelmed and malfunction. This means that aside from blatant traumas that insistently impact our conscious awareness directly, many of the most hurtful and damaging aspects of emotionally charged incidents fail to register in awareness, but instead, are perceived subliminally or unconsciously and processed by a *deep unconscious mental system. Perception without conscious awareness* is a basic capacity of the emotion-processing mind. By this means, many anxiety-provoking meanings of events are experienced outside of awareness. This mechanism enables us to survive and function in the face of countless emotionally trying and potentially disruptive events.

Once these unconsciously perceived inputs have been registered deep unconsciously, they are silently processed adaptively by the deep unconscious mind. The results of the entire unconscious experience are then encoded in dreams and other storied forms. Disguise is necessary because the implications of these triggering events would overwhelm the conscious mind, and the individual would be at sixes and sevens. This is the case because these incidents are always linked to the experience of death and evocative of one or more of the three kinds of disruptive death anxieties that we, as humans, experience—predatory, predator, and existential.

In defining the fundamental motivational forces of emotional life, Freud focused on sexual needs, Jung on maturational goals, and I concentrated on how we cope with the reality of death and the death anxieties it evokes at times of threat. I discovered that there is an enormous difference between our conscious and unconscious reactions to these death-related issues. By and large, the conscious mind is intent on avoiding the recognition and impact of these disturbing emotionally charged incidents. It denies and does not register much of the psychological harm that is caused by both those whom we love and those whom we hate. As a result, the conscious mind knows very little about the emotional world, understands even less, and suffers from a profound lack of adaptive intelligence and resources. These limitations are evident, however, only when the two systems are reacting to the same emotionally charged triggering event, which allows for a comparative study. The results of these comparisons are quite consistent: The perceptiveness and capabilities of the conscious mind pale by comparison with its deep unconscious counterpart. The conscious system has a very low emotional IQ, while the deep unconscious mind has an extraordinarily high emotional unconscious IQ—or "UIQ," as I term it. Indeed, the deep unconscious mind is very much like an inner god, while the conscious mind is much like an uneducated coward. We should keep in mind as we proceed that the thinking engaged in by both psychoanalysts and religious leaders has, until now, been based on extremely limited conscious-system efforts. There is, then, an evident need to recruit deep unconscious wisdom in carrying these endeavors forward from this time on.

The deep unconscious mind accurately perceives the all too threatening meanings of traumatic events and communications from others and, in addition, has an exquisitely sensitive and resourceful adaptive processing system and coping intelligence with which to deal with them. We actually learn a lot more about emotional life and how to deal with its dangers when the learning takes place without conscious awareness than we do when we consciously know what we are—or seem to be—trying to deal with. When the encoded insights and adaptive solutions arrived at by the deep unconscious system are decoded in light of their triggers, they almost always are surprising to an awe-filled conscious mind.

As humans, we possess a numinous inner god that sits on the throne of the unconscious mind and responds with profound wisdom to our death-related emotional challenges and dilemmas. This wisdom system, which is very sensitive to the death-related aspects of emotionally charged incidents, is aided by a unique deep unconscious system of morality and ethics that also is archetypal in nature. Its activities also are encoded in our narratives, and it is both a standard bearer and enforcer of sound morals. In contrast to our conscious morals, which are easily corrupted and compromised, this deep unconscious system possesses and operates on the basis of a set of universally embraced moral standards that are both pristine and unimpeachable. The system unconsciously orchestrates rewards such as enabling us to make sound and beneficial decisions when we adhere to its moral code, but it also silently directs us toward self-punitive, unsound choices and actions when we have violated its precepts. Tapping into these moral guidelines through trigger decoding offers us a fresh chance to establish a human morality that can be the basis for religious thinking as well as a means of creating an effective and peace-seeking rational spirituality for nonbelievers.

The central thesis of adaptive psychoanalysis is that death and death anxiety are the most powerful and fundamental determinants of human emotional life. In approaching the Bible, then, we will be alert to when these issues arise and how God handles them. But while death and death anxiety are our archetypal challenges, dealing with these basic, eternal concerns is a matter of experience and knowledge. We experience many moments of death anxiety entirely outside of direct awareness and therefore must turn to *trigger decoding*—deciphering the encoded aspects of narratives like dreams in light of their evocative triggering events—to realize that we are in the throes of such anxieties. But in addition, what we know and learn about death and its attendant anxieties is dependent on how we engage in the learning process. We may look death straight in the eye and consciously explore its effects using mundane wisdom. Alternatively, we can supplement these direct explorations by trigger decoding our reactions to death-related events. In this way we can make use of the far wiser and adaptively effective divine knowledge that is to be found in the deep unconscious mind. Indeed, the deep unconscious mind alone is the seat of divine wisdom, which means that this wisdom is built around the most disturbing and threatening events that happen to us in the course of our lives.

Be it God or natural selection, a supreme being or nature, some entity has played what seems to be a nasty joke on us. The offer of mixed blessings is characteristic of God's relationship with humankind, so it is not surprising to find that he has given us great wisdom but has hidden it from direct awareness where it can be used effectively on a day-to-day basis. It is only through the use of trigger decoding and thereby undoing the barrier that God—or nature—put between our conscious thinking and deep unconscious wisdom that we humans can gain the upper hand. Nevertheless, that barrier is merciful because it is the reason why the conscious mind is quite unaware of the subtleties of death and is ignorant of some of the more forbidding death-related meanings of traumatic incidents and of the pervasiveness of death anxiety in emotional life. However costly in loss of conscious knowledge and wisdom, only our deep unconscious minds know the extent to which death hovers over and threatens us each moment of our lives.

Dealing with death solely through conscious perceptions and thinking is a severely hampered approach to the human mind and to the study of the Bible and religion. By and large, the conscious mind does not recognize death as the central issue in human life, and when it does, the insight is either intuitively experienced and not realized consciously, or the system takes a relatively simplistic approach to the problem. Most students of the Bible also have not understood that death is the central theme and concern therein. This tendency is evident in the recent, thorough, and invaluable study of Christ penned by Wills (2006a), a book that I shall draw on heavily in exploring the New Testament. The subjects of death and death anxiety are almost entirely ignored in his book and are not placed in the center of Christ's story; they are dealt with in minimal ways and only when patently obvious as in his resurrection. This neglect is inevitable because the conscious mind can discern only trends and messages in the Bible that are somewhat obvious. It cannot detect some of the most powerful influences on biblical characters because they operate unconsciously and therefore can be discerned solely by the deep unconscious mind. Studies of the Bible that are guided by the deep unconscious system of the emotion-processing mind will take us to insights that could not be, and have not been, developed through conscious system explorations alone.

DEATH AND WISDOM IN THE BEGINNING

Having taken this hopefully informative detour, I return now to the opening chapters of Genesis for some final comments. I have said that from the perspective of adaptive psychoanalysis, dealing with the ramifications of death and acquiring wisdom are humankind's most fundamental, archetypal issues (see also Pagels 1988). What does the Bible tell us about this thesis in its opening pages? In the first creation, God makes male and female in his image. As I suggested, this implies endowing them with divine wisdom and immortality—that is, with perfect knowledge and an absence of death. In magnanimous fashion, God offers humankind relief from both ignorance and annihilation. But then, as I pointed out, God evidently has second thoughts about his grand and generous gesture, and in his second creation of man he withdraws both attributes. But knowing what we do about the present design of the emotion-processing mind, we can conjecture that while the Lord God never again made humans immortal—a most fateful decision that Jesus Christ in particular tried to rectify—he did keep his promise to give us divine wisdom, but located it in our deep unconscious minds—a forbidding place where few have dared to go.

The first order of business for God after his second creation and making Adam from the dust of the ground is the issue of a warning to Adam that he may eat from all of the trees in the garden except for the tree of knowledge of good and evil, that he will die if he does so. As the serpent later indicates to Adam's wife, Eve, this knowledge is divine and God-like, but it is, as I have emphasized, linked with death in some mysterious manner.

Notice too that God constructed Eden with two trees: One offers divine wisdom and is forbidden to Adam, while the other offers eternal life without restraints attached to eating its fruit. These archetypal trees also touch on matters of wisdom and death—the latter in its absence. The presence of the second tree implies that should he wish to do so, Adam could eat from the tree of eternal life and gain immortality. That he does not take this step suggests that he is not explicitly aware of death and that he is not suffering from any form of death anxiety—from its existential form in particular. These matters appear to be vague preconceptions rather than explicit conceptions. Because he—and more so, Eve—appears to understand the nature of the threat of death that God links with eating from the tree of knowledge, we may conjecture that Adam had a vague or instinctive awareness of death, but not one that was explicit and cognitive. This state of mind is not unlike the dim awareness of death that we often see in conscious minds today—knowledge of death mixed with the denial of its reality. From this it follows that a possible implication of God's warning that Adam will die if he eats from the tree of knowledge is that this act will bring him full force to an awareness of death and evoke in him one or more forms of death anxiety.

God's edict also offers Adam and humankind an archetypal choice: to eat or not to eat from the forbidden tree. Thus, Adam can decide to not eat the fruit and thereby choose to live his life on the basis of mundane knowledge that includes a dim sense of what death is about, but essentially is death-free. We may think of this as living in a state of divine but blissful ignorance. Or he can choose to eat the forbidden fruit and acquire divine wisdom, but he will then suffer from an acute awareness of death and experience disturbing forms of death anxiety—and possibly death itself.

As we shall see, it actually is Eve who makes this archetypal choice, but we can already recognize the similarity of this decision to the decision that I ask my patients to make when they first consult me for psychotherapy. While I do not specifically suggest that I am offering them the opportunity to eat from the tree of divine knowledge, my proposal to work with their narrative images is intuitively understood as just that. Broadly speaking, this is a fundamental decision that every human could make at some point in his or her life were it not for the fact that we generally are unaware of the existence of this particular archetypal choice. By nature, we are committed to conscious system thinking and mundane wisdom and are both unaware of, and disinclined to seek, divine wisdom. The Lord God makes this choice available to Adam and Eve in the Garden of Eden, but perhaps in anger over their defiance of his edict to not eat from that tree, he buries this wisdom in their deep unconscious minds where it is hidden to this very day. In so doing, God—or if you prefer, nature—has made the possibility of gaining further divine wisdom extremely difficult for humankind, and this may account for why, as we shall see, Adam and Eve do not seem to benefit from their hard-won acquisition.

The basic question of life on earth, then and now, is this: Do we endeavor to understand and deal with death based on the mundane conscious wisdom with which we are born, or do we take the trouble and risk inherent in both defying God and possibly facing death to deal with death with the help of divine wisdom?

God's position on this matter is clearly stated in his admonition to Adam, which is his first and most basic commandment: Do not access—that is, humans should not possess—divine wisdom. It is too dangerous to behold, and having it in our possession will be the death of humankind. At the very least, acquiring this wisdom will destroy humankind's blissful, seemingly everlasting days in paradise. God is so committed to this position that he makes it a sin to acquire such wisdom. He is, then, fully on the side of the conscious mind of most humans who, with rare exceptions, to this very day avoid gaining divine wisdom and live in dread of doing so. To turn this around, let it be said that today's humans consciously are very much on the side of the Lord God on this issue. Indeed, even those who decide to pursue such knowledge do so with enormously strong, unconsciously wrought resistances.

All in all, evidently hoping to spare humankind much emotional pain, God fully supports the idea of coping with life by means of mundane knowledge. His essential message is "Deny death and live in relative ignorance with blind faith in my pronouncements, and peace and the horn of plenty will be yours." God must have had good reasons to take this position. So let's go on with the story of Eden to see why he did so and what he was trying to offer to humankind to help them to cope effectively with death and death anxiety. His divine hidden motives are as illuminating today as they were at the beginning of time.

NOTE

1. For ease of reading, quotations from Genesis are taken from Armstrong (1996). Quotations from the New Testament are taken from the King James Version of the Holy Bible. Lk is Luke, Mk is Mark, Mt is Matthew, and 1 Cor is 1 Corinthians.

2

The First Question and Eve's Answer

The defining moment, the exciting incident of the first drama of life, is described in the Bible in the following manner:

> Now the serpent was more crafty than any other wild animal that the Lord God had made. He said to the woman, "Did God say, 'You shall not eat from any tree in the garden'?" The woman said to the serpent, "We may eat of the fruit of the trees in the garden; but God said, 'You shall not eat of the fruit of the tree that is in the middle of the garden, nor shall you touch it, or you shall die.'" But the serpent said to the woman, "You will not die; for God knows that when you eat of it your eyes will be opened, and you will be like God, knowing good and evil." (Gen 3:1–5)

It is now explicitly stated and unmistakable that the first drama of life as told in the Bible is centered on death and morality and the human acquisition of divine knowledge. Nevertheless, this first scene is beset with other issues of considerable importance. Acquiring divine wisdom has been cast as an act of defiance against God, which in strict religious terms, implies sinning against him. But to gain a full perspective on the situation, we need to understand why God is so opposed to this development and why the penalty for doing so is death. Then too, since divine wisdom also is linked with knowledge of good and evil, we also need to understand the nature of the connections between God-like knowledge, death, and human morality.

There is a lot at stake for humankind as Eve sits near the tree of knowledge of good and evil and contemplates whether she should partake of its fruit. It is evident too that the serpent is pitted against the Lord God on the question of whether Eve should eat the forbidden fruit and if she were to do so, what

19

the consequence would be. But the key adaptive question precedes this struggle: Why is she thinking of putting herself—and humankind—at such great
risk? After all, if she and Adam were to die, there would be no humans left on
earth. What has happened to motivate or drive her to do so—what is the triggering event that has prompted her to contemplate this monumental act?

The Bible is long on drama but short on triggers and motives. It has little
to say about human psychology, which is, by and large, starkly dramatized
and lived out without insight into the underlying causative events and the
emotionally charged psychological forces that are in play. Because of this, we
will need to draw heavily on our knowledge of eternal archetypes to discover
the vital secrets behind the story of Eve—and Adam—in Eden.

It is helpful to think of the beginning of Eve's story—and the story itself,
seeing that it is the first one in the Bible—as comparable to the first dream of
a patient in psychoanalysis or psychotherapy (terms I use interchangeably). In
so doing, we need to realize that the most compelling messages carried by
dreams are not contained in their manifest images (the dream as dreamt), but
are encoded and disguised in these surface elements and in need of proper decoding. The encoded meanings of first dreams of patients in psychotherapy
tend to portray the emotionally charged events in their lives that are being
triggered or activated by entering psychoanalysis under a particular set of
conditions—all of the dreams and stories told by patients (and by the rest of
us in real life) are responses to triggering incidents. These dreams tend to
dramatize the patient's biographical history, including his or her most influential death-related traumas, and as they encode these past incidents, they
also tend to foretell the course of the analysis.

In like manner, Eve's story can be thought of archetypically as speaking for
the past history of humankind as well as for her personal, evocative history
and its death-related traumas. In addition, the story foretells the future of humankind in respect to both its relationship to God and to the secular unfolding of the drama of life on earth. Oddly enough, using mundane wisdom, this
principle of prophecy has to some extent been articulated by Augustine and
others. It is based on a view of Adam as committing humankind's original sin
against God, a sin that will affect all future generations (Augustine 1958,
1961; Wills 1999, 2003). I shall have more to say about this idea as I proceed.

EVE'S DILEMMA

In terms of the biblical tale, it is, however, Eve who is making the archetypal
life decision, a first choice before all other choices. That is, to restate the plot

line in general terms, as soon as life on earth begins in earnest, humans must decide whether they wish to live their lives and survive, as God proposes, on the basis of the ordinary or mundane knowledge with which they are born, or alternatively, to do so on the basis of acquiring divine wisdom, which God evidently opposes. In this light, Eve's choice is a much like Sophie's choice as to which of her two children shall die, one that must be made between two extremely painful possibilities: A mindless, unarticulated, eternal life in paradise versus a well-defined life replete with divine knowledge lived under the cloud of death outside of paradise.

The first alternative is to live an evidently death-free life with absolute faith in God, under the protection of His blessings, using common sense to find limited satisfactions and a denial-based inner peace in harmony with others. The second alternative is a life that is sinful in the strictest sense of the term because it goes against God's edict and violates a boundary that he has set. But even so, it has the qualities of a blessing because it is based on a wisdom that embraces the richness and secrets of life—and death. Beyond that, there is the open question as to whether making the latter choice would lead to a life based on a deed that is evil or simply sinful, because it appears that no one would be harmed by the act—except, perhaps, for God, whose pride and self-esteem would be wounded. In any case, it would be a life that is either short-lived as predicted or one hovered over by death as a constant concern.

In this context, it is well for us to notice again that despite his injunction, the Lord God placed the tree of divine knowledge in the middle of the Garden of Eden and thereby made the choice of whether or not to eat the fruit of the tree available to Adam and Eve. This speaks for a measure of ambivalence in the Lord God regarding the question as to whether humans should acquire or be given divine wisdom. This uncertainty also is reflected in his first providing humans with this knowledge and then rescinding the gift. At the moment, then, God is against the human acquisition of this kind of wisdom, but even so, he apparently is leaving the final decision on this matter to his human creations.

As for the serpent, he is quite sure of his position on this issue. He stands squarely against God's stricture and the threat that accompanies it. He firmly assures Eve that not only will she not die if she eats the forbidden fruit, but that doing so will reward her with wisdom that is far reaching if not sublime, knowledge that goes well beyond the mundane knowledge that God gave to her on the occasion of her creation.

The tension between the Lord God and the serpent is both palpable and pivotal, but here too there are uncertainties. The strict religious view sees any opposition to the will of God as the work of the devil and a sin, but helping humankind gain divine wisdom and assuring Eve that she will not die in the doing do not, broadly speaking, appear to be inherently sinful or evil forms of support. More on this after we see how the story unfolds.

For the moment, then, the essential question is "To whom will Eve listen— God or the serpent?" Understanding in depth the choice that she makes depends in large measure on our discovering the triggering event that is driving her inner need for divine wisdom, and thus pressing her to go against God's will. Only the activation of a very intense personal, archetypal need could motivate her to accept the serpent's reassurances over God's warning of the dire consequences of eating the forbidden fruit. This is, then, an archetypal moment of personal and universal conflict in which humankind's quest for divine and moral wisdom is pitted against the threat of death, and the human belief and faith in, and obedience to, God are very much at issue.

MY PERSONAL DILEMMA

As I indicated in the first chapter, while few psychoanalysts know of the choice between mundane or divine wisdom for living one's life, I know it well because at one point in my professional career I had to make a similar, Eve-like decision. While this determination eventually centered on how I would do psychotherapy, it actually came up first when I experienced a need to engage in self-analysis or *self-processing*, as I prefer to call it (Langs 1993). This need arose after my so-called training analysis had been completed and I suffered from new emotionally founded symptoms. In trying to resolve them, I discovered that the analytic work that I had been trained to use—and had been used in treating me—was distinctly wanting. As a result, my efforts at self-processing moved from conscious system thinking to deep unconscious thinking, from intellectualizing to trigger decoding narratives, from mundane knowledge to what turned out to be divine wisdom as connected with my early-life, death-related traumas and the deep unconscious death anxieties that they had evoked in me.

I had eaten from the tree of knowledge of good and evil without knowing I was doing so, and I did it in the service of self-healing and thus without any sense of sinfulness. Making the choice for divine wisdom enabled me, in time, to insightfully resolve my symptoms. It also changed my personal life, expanded my understanding of the human mind (it was the basis on which I forged the adaptive approach—i.e., death driving creativity), and altered how I did psychotherapy—all very much for the better. No one, I learned, enters the grim world of death-related, deep unconscious experience and knowledge without dire personal need, and somehow I was able to endure the pain involved in doing so and benefit from its invaluable curative powers.

I began to offer every patient I saw in consultation a similar opportunity to heal his or her emotional wounds by acquiring personally shaped divine wisdom. Like me, they initially had no conscious awareness of what was at stake, but they did intuitively sense both the rewards and the risks—the latter often outweighing the former. Without realizing it, I was—and still am—taking on the role of the serpent in the Garden of Eden. And as was the case with the serpent, I made my proposals with full confidence that my patients could and would survive the ordeal involved, that they would not die in the doing. I found, however, that in most cases it was as if God had whispered his dire warning in their ears, because most of my patients thought otherwise (Langs 2004c, 2006).

There were indications that the struggle was not only between myself as the serpent and their god introject that spoke for avoidance, but that to some extent they too had an inner serpent that stood opposed to God's warning that divine wisdom must be avoided at all cost. In patients who stayed in adaptive psychotherapy, this archetypal battle was reflected in their encoded stories, which vacillated between expressing divinely meaningful encoded imagery and shutting off such imagery in evident efforts to avoid access to their deep unconscious, divine insights. It became clear that the natural state of mind, God-given or evolved, favors limiting or avoiding expression of the encoded themes that embody divine knowledge and that this avoidance is backed up with a turning away from trigger decoding as well. It requires both a strongly traumatic triggering incident and certain natural needs to go against the avoidance communicative archetype—that is, to follow the dictates of the serpent. Given that divine wisdom enriches a human life far more than divine ignorance, we must explain the paradox that God and human nature stand opposed to its acquisition. To find some tentative answers, let's move on.

IMPLICATIONS FOR ADAM AND EVE

There are two noteworthy points to be made about Adam and Eve on the basis of this discussion. First, it seems likely that before addressing Eve, the serpent already had eaten the fruit of the tree of knowledge of good and evil—and survived. In telling Eve that she will not die after eating the forbidden fruit and that she will thereby come to possess divine, God-like wisdom, he must, it would seem, have been speaking on the basis of divine insight of his own. Such insight can be gained only after surviving a death-related trauma and experiencing a strong need for divine wisdom, which in turn prompts an individual to act against God's edict and contrary to the avoidance archetype connected with possessing divine knowledge. Put another way, it seems likely that only someone possessed of such hard-won knowledge could successfully stand against God and human nature—and essentially be right in the position he takes.

The second point is an odd one, namely, that the Lord God's pronouncement that Adam and Eve will die if they eat the forbidden fruit appears to reflect a measure of unresolved death anxiety in God himself. As we soon learn, his prophecy does not come to pass—the couple learn about death but do not actually die. This means that the anxiety about their dying is his own and that we need to understand why this is the case. For the moment, based on latter-day archetypes, I would suggest as an initial possibility that the Lord God knew that he had not prepared humans to incorporate divine wisdom because he had failed to arm them with the means to face and cope with death and its attendant, often overwhelming anxieties. This likely lack of preparation suggests that the Lord God had not himself found a way to deal effectively with these issues. In addition, there are indications that despite his possession of eternal life, he lived in fear that should humans acquire the kind of wisdom that he alone was privileged to have, he would no longer be worshipped and obeyed by them, and that his own great creation would soon abandon him—a fate tantamount to death. This anxiety may well have found expression much later in the Bible, in Exodus, where we find that the opening words of the Ten Commandments are "I alone am your God." I shall return to this conjecture later on.

EVE'S CHOICE

We come back now to Eve and her transformational moment of decision making. Her conflicted choice is between a faith-based life of divine ignorance that will allow her to live endless years in paradise and a knowledge-based life that brings death down upon her along with the burden of going against God's edict and thereby sinning against him and inviting his punishment. Given her—and Adam's—loss of innocence inherent in her second choice, it also seems likely that they will be expelled from paradise if they eat the forbidden fruit. Unconsciously motivated by a triggering event about which the Bible is silent, Eve's decision is being consciously influenced by the opposing positions of God and the serpent. We can sense that God, in his infinite wisdom and kindness, is trying to offer humans eternal bliss based on blind but deserving faith in his words and creations, and that he sincerely believes that knowledge of good and evil, and in some way, of death, will be disastrous for humankind. This is not an unreasonable position to take in light of the havoc that death and death anxiety can wreak. Evidently, the Lord God wishes to spare humankind as much as possible of the suffering and emotional pain that comes about when death-related issues are a notable aspect of human awareness.

As for the serpent, the narrow religious view is that God's opponents are his enemies, that the ultimate enemy is Satan himself or a fallen angel who does his bidding, and that going against God's stricture is both a sin and an evil act. But there are biblical writings that portray Satan as God's helpmate, as the tester of humankind's faith in God and of each individual's moral position and morally tinged acts (Pagels 1996; Kelly 2006). There also are wise men and women who have believed and believe now that the serpent is the great healer and wise one, much of this belief reflected in the Gnostic Gospels (Pagels 1989; Barnstone and Meyer 2003). Others see Satan as the shadow side of God and believe that much like the humans whom he at first fashioned in his image, God is both supremely good and benevolent and most intensely bad and evil—both the highest of the high and the lowest of the low. All this should give pause for thought when we try to understand what follows in this story; so with this in mind, we come back to Eve's defining moment:

> So when the woman saw that the tree was good for food, and that it was a delight to the eyes, and that the tree was to be desired to make one wise, she took of its fruit and ate; and she gave also some to her husband, who was with her and he ate. (Gen 3:6)

Surprisingly, the only immediate consequence of the couple's acquisition of divine knowledge is this:

> Then the eyes of both were opened, and they knew that they were naked; and they sewed fig leaves together and made loin-cloths for themselves. (Gen 3:7)

Next, Adam and Eve hear God walking in the garden, and they hide from his presence among the trees.

> But the Lord God called to the man, and said to him, "Where are you?" He said, "I heard the sound of you in the garden and was afraid, because I was naked; and I hid myself." (Gen 3:9–10)

God asks who told him he was naked and if he has eaten from the tree which he commanded the man to not eat from. The man confesses that he did, and he blames the woman, who also confesses to the same defiant deed, but claims that she was tricked by the serpent. Nevertheless, because of what they have done, God curses them and the serpent, punishing each of them in a particular way.

THE MEANING OF THE COUPLE'S NAKEDNESS

Before we look at God's reactions to the couple's fateful act and speculate as to what drove them to do it, let's consider the immediate consequences—or should I say, consequence?—of their deed: their realization that they are naked and their covering themselves accordingly. Somehow this awareness is linked with divine wisdom and is so profoundly consequential for Adam and Eve and the future of humankind, so evocative of God's anger and beset with so many punishments that this sudden awakening to their nakedness must have some very powerful meanings and ramifications.

In trying to determine the essential meaning of the couple's nudity, then, I shall turn first to the Bible itself. Most of what follows the eating of the forbidden fruit involves God's discovery of their transgression and his punishing them and the serpent. It is often said that the punishment should fit the crime, but it also can be said that the punishment usually reflects the nature of the crime. This idea is a variation on the archetypal law of talion punishment—an eye for an eye, a tooth for a tooth. More broadly, it can be said that the consequences of a transgression tend to reflect the hidden nature of the boundary-violating deed, including the evocative trigger that motivated the action taken.

The Bible says little about the underlying meanings of Adam and Eve's conscious and self-conscious realization that they are naked. However, their acute sense of exposure and embarrassment does stand in contrast to their reaction to their nakedness immediately after Eve was created from Adam's rib:

And the man and his wife were both naked, and were not ashamed. (Gen 2:25)

As the essence of divine knowledge, the couple's present realization of their nudity must be more than a simple allusion to their dawning, conscious awareness of their sexuality; it must have additional symbolic meanings and encode some type of forbidding perception of reality as well. Indeed, their nakedness may have several mutually compatible meanings even though none of them are explicitly spelled out in the biblical story. Each implication is likely to have a grain of truth to it, and each should tell us something about the significance of their recognized nudity and its connection to the acquisition of divine wisdom. But these various implications do not appear to be of equal weight and consequence. Therefore, in identifying what I consider to be the main possibilities, I shall move from the least to the most compelling of the likely significances of this newly experienced sense of exposure.

SEXUAL AWARENESS

The first possible meaning of Adam and Eve's need to cover themselves—their seeming embarrassment in recognizing their nudity—is that it alludes to a dawning of their dormant sexual needs and feelings, and an explicit recognition of their physical sexual differences—a position that most likely would be adopted by Freud and his followers, among many others. This possibility is connected with another aspect of the mindlessness on which living in Eden was based—the relative absence of sexual yearnings and conflicts. While it may be difficult for us to imagine such innocence and an absence of active sexual feelings, we can appreciate that the blunting of sexual drives would be a mixed blessing. On the one hand, it precludes sexual conflicts, but on the other, it does not allow for sexual satisfactions of a kind that would promote interpersonal bonding, nor would it provide a basis for the sublimation of sexual needs and their transformation into creative channels and personal growth. Nevertheless, just as there is awareness without conscious registration, there also may have been instinctive sexual activities in Eden without explicit, conscious sexual wishes and feelings.

There are, however, indications that sexual awakening facilitates the transformation of humans from an essentially instinctive state of being in which they are dimly aware of themselves and their environments to one in which they are sharply cognizant of themselves, others, and the world around them. In the world's first recorded epic, the tale of Gilgamesh (Mitchell 2004), the humanization of his companion, Enkidu, from his animal-like state to the human condition is accomplished by his having intercourse with the goddess Shamhat for seven days. A similar awakening, configured rather differently, is implied in the incestuous outcome of Oedipus's search for his biological parents, and it also will be evident in the story of Augustine's repetition of Adam's sin, which I shall discuss in chapter 4. The adaptive study of archetypes suggests that these sexual awakenings presage and prepare humans for their eventual confrontation with death and its attendant anxieties and issues—a point I shall soon make regarding Adam and Eve.

The sexual meanings of the nakedness of Adam and Eve find support in the punishment that is meted out to Eve by the Lord God for her having eaten the forbidden fruit:

> To the woman he [the Lord God] said: "I will greatly increase your pangs in child bearing; in pain you shall bring forth children." (Gen 3:16)

This punishment is, of course, related to the consequences of sexual intercourse, but there are several other implications to this penalty. For one, it pertains to bringing life into the world, which God now makes more painful than before. As an archetype, it suggests that divine wisdom involves an awareness of the process of giving life and that this wisdom also makes life giving especially difficult to bear. The question then is why such wisdom, which should be a great asset in dealing with life's challenges, nonetheless is the cause of considerable pain as well. That said, we should make note of the often overlooked words "greatly increase," because they imply that Eve may well have already experienced labor—another point to which I shall return momentarily.

The chapter in the Bible that follows the subsequent expulsion of Adam and Eve from Eden also touches on a sexual implication of the couple's nakedness. It begins,

> Now the man knew his wife Eve, and she conceived and bore Cain, saying, "I have produced a man with the help of the Lord." Next she bore his brother Abel. (Gen 4:1–2)

Procreation is the event that follows the expulsion of the couple from the Garden of Eden—awareness of their sexuality has led to the first conceptions in the Bible. We should note, however, that there is nothing untoward or inappropriate about this development, and it therefore does not speak for sexual embarrassment or shame. Indeed, if the conception of two sons is linked with divine wisdom, it speaks for an effect that is positive and certainly not deserving of punishment from God. Thus, there are strong reasons to doubt that the couple's sexual embarrassment is the essential meaning of their acquiring forbidden divine knowledge about good and evil. Adam and Eve were marital partners for whom sexual exposure and contact would be a natural, expected event—hardly evil, sinful, or punishable. There is nothing sexually forbidding about an intensification of their awareness of their nakedness and no compelling reason for their covering their genitals in sexual discomfort.

All in all then, the idea that acquiring divine knowledge was intimately connected with the couple's intensification of their sexual urges and identities seems to be at most an introductory, secondary meaning of this profoundly affecting biblical incident.

INDIVIDUATION AND ESTABLISHING SEPARATE IDENTITIES

As Jung has stressed (Jung 1968; Edinger 1986; Maidenbaum 1998), Adam and Eve's sudden realization that they are naked may imply that with their newly acquired knowledge of good and evil, they have become distinctive individuals in their own right, that having been previously merged, each of them has gained an individual identity. As a result, they feel embarrassed in the presence of the other and have a need to cover themselves.

This line of thought finds support in the prior sections of Genesis that begin with the Lord God's making Eve from Adam's rib. The very derivation of Eve from Adam's body speaks for their unity and oneness. In addition, it is then written,

Therefore a man leaves his father and his mother and clings to his wife, and they become one flesh. (Gen 2:24–25)

In this context, divine knowledge appears to be linked with an understanding of who we are vis-à-vis others and a recognition that others are not us. As is true of virtually every development in this story, this sense of individual identity also is a mixed blessing. On the downside, it entails the loss of security, protection, and support that is gained by being at one with another human being. This sense of unity is, however, grounded in a costly blunting of self-awareness, a muted degree of self-motivation, a relative diminution of personal resources, and a reduced awareness of the external world and of the exigencies of life. Oddly enough, this last group of blunted attributes nevertheless appears to sustain the idyllic life found in an undisturbed Eden. The disadvantages of individuation may provide a clue as to why the Lord God wanted humans to avoid the acquisition of divine knowledge: Such an acquisition involves leaving a protective unity and safe bubble and thereby giving up one means through which humans can live in peace with each other in a world that might otherwise be fraught with almost constant danger.

In addition to its drawbacks, however, achieving an individual identity also has its advantages. It would enable Adam and Eve to become relatively independent human beings who are able to develop their own adaptive strategies so they can deal with life's adversities in effective ways that are best suited to their personal needs. This change also would facilitate their efforts to satisfy their particular wishes for companionship and gratification and would enhance their sense of self and personal growth through both self-discovery and the satisfactions that come from finding their own way in the world. While the development of these capabilities would enable Adam and Eve as separate individuals to cope better with life's adversities, it nevertheless entails the entry into a painful state of relative isolation and vulnerability.

All in all, the idea that acquiring divine insight is a means of gaining personal autonomy and relative independence as a well-functioning human being has merit. We can see that acquiring this kind of knowledge can cause a measure of anxiety even as it becomes the means through which human beings are able to experience a richer state of existence and cope better with life's inevitable challenges. The anxious, archetypal quest for separation and individuation is as much a part of today's life as it was a part of the implied struggles of Adam and Eve ages ago. How many of us, in fear of the threats posed by relative independence, choose to remain merged with a parent or with others who cause us undue pain for the seeming protection so gained? Perhaps if we can understand what drove Eve to seek her own identity, we can find a better way to do the same for ourselves. But to properly answer this question, we will need to know the event that triggered her act of defiance — a challenge we shall get to in due course.

DEATH AND DEATH ANXIETY

A third meaning of Adam and Eve's recognition of their nudity is that it alludes to a newly experienced sense of vulnerability, that it essentially reflects a distinct awareness of their vulnerability to death and thus pertains to a recognition of their personal mortality. This interpretation, which appears to be the most compelling of the three possibilities that I am presenting, finds considerable support from the biblical story. In addition to the Lord God's warning that Adam — and by implications, Eve — would die if he ate the forbidden fruit, among God's punishments of Adam, there is this:

> By the sweat of your face you shall eat bread until you return to the ground, for out of it you were taken; you are dust, and to dust you shall return. (Gen 3:19)

This is a death sentence, and it seems likely that Adam now understands exactly what these words mean. With his acquisition of divine wisdom, we would expect to find that his vague preconception of death becomes a fixed and powerful conception (Bion 1963).

There also is the fact that, after meting out his punishments to the three sinners, the Lord God covers the devastated duo. This act of compassion implies that the Lord God knows how difficult life will be for the vulnerable couple from here on in. This grand gesture speaks more strongly for the Lord God's wish to offer them a measure of protection against the scourge of death than it does for his wanting to cover over the couple's nakedness; indeed, their dawning sexual needs are appropriate and soon to be properly satisfied. The biblical word for naked (*arum*) shares a root with the word for death and is generally "used to describe someone stripped of protective clothing and naked in the sense of being without defenses" (Armstrong 1996, p. 29). The nakedness that Adam and Eve are aware of, then, seems to allude to their human vulnerabilities and to the inadequacy of human protection against harm and death, natural and otherwise.

There are in addition rather direct indications in the Bible that recognizing their vulnerability to death was the main consequence for Adam and Eve in acquiring divine wisdom, and that the Lord God knew this to be so. This evidence is found in what happens after the Lord God has meted out his punishments to all concerned:

> Then the Lord God said, "See, the man has become like one of us, knowing good and evil; and now he might reach out his hand and take also from the tree of life, and eat, and live forever." (Gen 3:22)

It is for this reason that the Lord God drives the couple from the garden, and for good measure,

> at the east of the garden of Eden he placed the cherubim, and a sword flaming and turning to guard the way to the tree of life. (Gen 3:24)

It appears then that while Adam and Eve did not die as promised and foretold by the Lord God—and as rightly contradicted by the serpent—death nevertheless played a significant role in the consequences of their acquisition of divine wisdom. Indications are, as I said, that in their relatively mindless innocence, the couple was only dimly aware of death and of their own mortality—aware enough to vaguely understand the nature of the punishment that the Lord God promised them if they ate the forbidden fruit, but not explicit enough to evoke acute personal death anxieties. As soon as they acquired divine insight, however, they evidently were shocked to realize that this knowledge centered on the incisive fact that they were mortal and would die someday.

This idea finds support in the Bible in that Adam and Eve paid no attention to the tree of eternal life before they acquired divine knowledge, implying that they had no need to eat from that tree, that is, that death and dying were not an active issue for them. But now, even though they did not make a move in that direction, the Lord God knows that, having acquired divine wisdom and having become sharply aware of their mortality, Adam and Eve will have a strong need to undo or deny the inevitability of their own demise—that is, to eat from the tree of eternal life.

This suggests that the first form of human death anxiety to appear in the Bible is *existential death anxiety*—the anxiety evoked by the recognition that human life always ends in death. Here too Adam and Eve share with us an archetype that is active to this very day—that is, that the dawning of self-awareness is accompanied by an acute appreciation of one's personal mortality. The writers of the scripture, possibly God or guided by God, intuitively appreciated that this archetype is fundamental to human life. That said, we must reserve final judgment on this matter because a different form of death anxiety may well have motivated Eve to eat the forbidden fruit.

Also pertinent to these happenings are questions pertaining to the ideal ground rules, strictures, and moral code within which we, as humans, should and can best live our lives in peace and comfort and in harmony with others. By eating the forbidden fruit, Adam and Eve violated a boundary set by the Lord God, and as a consequence, they appear to have been confronted with the boundary that divides their lives from their deaths—in thought although not as yet in fact. As a result, the Lord God establishes a new set of boundaries, however limiting and punitive: The couple is expelled and banned from Eden, and their path to the tree of eternal life is blocked. Boundary issues are prominent in this archetypal tale.

Clinical studies based on the adaptive approach indicate that on the deep unconscious level of experience, there is an ideal, universally sought set of ground rules and boundaries—both physical and interpersonal—that are experienced as morally sound and both supportive emotionally and healing. These archetypal rules pertain to matters like appropriate respect for privacy and confidentiality when called for, lawful behaviors, fulfilling commitments, and religiously, actions and thoughts sanctioned by God—and much more. Some of these rules are made by humans, others are God-given or products of nature. The most basic of the natural ground rules is called the *existential rule of life and death*—namely that a human life must always end in death. This rule, which is invoked here by the Lord God and evidently recognized by Adam and Eve in their nakedness, is the source of human existential death anxieties. In light of his actions, we can see that the Lord God knew that this anxiety would impact Adam and Eve after they acquired a measure of death-related, divine wisdom. He knew too that most surely, they would therefore want to eat the fruit of the tree of eternal life to alleviate the terrible dread associated with this kind of death anxiety. But the Lord did not grant them relief from these anxieties; he insisted that only he can be eternal, so he blocked their way to that tree. Boundary-wise, it appears that there was, then, a shift from a stricture that gave Adam and Eve an immortality of which they were not especially mindful to a pair of strictures that took this immortality away from them and left them in the throes of existential death anxiety.

This is a most fateful decision on the part of the Lord God because from that day on, humans have spent enormous amounts of time and energy—some of it creative and much of it the source of damage and harm to themselves and others—in a never-ending quest for the illusion or delusion of immortality. Many of these efforts are denial based and reflected in religious beliefs of eternal life in heaven, as well as in everyday secular behaviors like the search for undue power and wealth, unnecessary death-defying acts, and violent actions directed against others as a way of creating the belief that the perpetrator will not die even as others do so. Most of these motives operate unconsciously and without the awareness of the person so engaged. In this context, even though it is a weak connection and an evidently constructive means of dealing with existential death anxiety, we may think of Adam and Eve's turn to having children, which immediately follows their expulsion from Eden, as their way of trying to lessen the impact of their mortality by creating heirs. However it is done, dealing with death and death anxiety is the core issue at the beginning of life on earth—as it is to this very day.

DEATH ANXIETY AND GOOD AND EVIL

God characterizes divine wisdom as becoming aware of good and evil. Yet my analysis of the story and of present-day archetypes sees divine wisdom as becoming aware of death and suffering from the consequent death anxieties. Both of these consequences of divine wisdom appear to have validity, so there must be a link between evil and good acts and the three forms of death anxiety. Here too, the divine intuitions of God and the writers of the Bible are in sync with present-day archetypes that can help us to define this connection. To begin with, our deep unconscious minds universally indicate that there is indeed a strong tie between the mastery of death anxiety and being able to carry out good or moral acts, and between failures of such mastery and evil acts and deeds. It seems, then, that while divine knowledge is manifestly described as becoming aware of good and evil, this most likely is an allusion to a deeper truth, namely, that the awareness of death and the anxieties it engenders have enormous consequences for the morality of how we live our lives.

Death rather than money—and rather than jealousy, envy, lust, or pride, as have been claimed (Pagels 1996; Kelly 2006; Langs 2006)—and death anxiety are the roots of all evil. Turning this around, evil acts against others are, at bottom, efforts to deny death by violating interpersonal boundaries, breaking ground rules, disobeying laws, ruthlessly trying to gain death-defying power and wealth, and harming others. As seen in encoded stories, ground rule violations and defiance of the law are experienced deep unconsciously as inherently immoral and evil, but they are invoked to deny the fundamental existential rule of life—that it ends in death. Harming others in evil ways allows the unconsciously experienced belief that proving that others are vulnerable and can be made to die magically renders the perpetrator invulnerable to death. The evil quest for power and wealth also is carried forward because quite unconsciously, there exists a universal, illusory belief that extremes of power and money can ensure oneself against harm and death. Evil acts are in their deepest roots attempts to deny death and to create the illusion or delusion of personal immortality.

God's stricture against eating the fruit of the tree of knowledge suggests that he understood full well that acquiring divine wisdom was tantamount to becoming incisively aware of death. And he also knew that because of the unmanageable anxieties this causes, this awareness would open the door to evil in this world of ours and wreak havoc for humankind. He knew too that he hadn't provided humans with an effective means through which they could cope with death and its array of anxieties, experienced both consciously and more devastatingly, deep unconsciously. He understood that being unaware of death was vital in allowing humans to live and flourish in Eden and that his obliteration of death could keep Satan and evil acts at bay. The position of the Lord God on this matter is very much related to the secular, adaptive realization that for many humans, despite the unfortunate cost involved in ignorance and harm to oneself and others, denial of death is their only recourse in dealing with the issues that death raises. The hope is to invoke benign and creative forms of denial instead of the far more common devastatingly destructive forms.

While it may seem, then, that the Lord God was being cruel and selfish in insisting that humans avoid acquiring divine wisdom, his heart was in the right place—he had the best interests of humankind in mind. There is something to be said for blind faith and the denial of death. Were it not for the fact that the use of denial is extremely costly in causing us problems in coping with the harsh realities of life, we would have to say that God had it right and Eve had it wrong. But the problem is that denial precludes awareness of and the adaptive use of many important facts of life and living. As a result, it is responsible for much physical and mental suffering, as seen, for example, in the denial of illness and the turning away from the realization that loved ones whom we revere are trying to harm us emotionally or murder us psychologically. In addition, denial is one of the basic causes of the violence that permeates the world today. As matters stand, then, the truth of the matter seems to be that after all, Eve was on the right track and the Lord God, however well meaning, was leading her—and us—astray because ultimately, denial is too costly a defense, and its use and overuse have failed to bring us personal or collective tranquillity.

God's closing off the path to the tree of eternal life also offers some additional clues to the connection between death, death anxiety, and evil acts. Evil is unheard of in Eden, which implies that a blind belief in God—that is, sustaining a state of *divine ignorance*—is one basis on which humans do not experience a need to behave in evil ways. Strictly speaking in religious terms, Eve and Adam's acquisition of divine knowledge was a sin because it violated the Lord God's commandment. Yet even though it seems likely that this act was motivated by a need to resolve a death-related conflict, it also was intended to bring freedom and a new level of integrity and coping abilities to humankind. All things considered, it may not have been the eating of the forbidden fruit that was the sin that caused the fall of humankind as argued by Augustine and others (Augustine 1958, 1961; Wills 2003, 2006b); the more important cause of our downfall was the acquisition of a sharpened awareness of death and the extent to which this awareness, which is so difficult to master, can when unresolved cause humans to act in sinful, evil ways.

Adam and Eve do not appear to have acted out of malice, and no one was harmed by what they did. Nevertheless, they did open the door to evil, which is at the heart of the very next story in the Bible, that of Cain's murder of Abel. There we find evidence that the killing was indeed motivated by Cain's unconscious experience of unresolved death anxieties, and it is there too that the first allusion by God to sin—that is, to sin lurking at Cain's door—is made.

In this light we can more fully understand why the Lord God issued his first commandment to Adam, and we can appreciate the compassion and worry for humankind that lay behind his injunction. While divine knowledge is vital to a productive human life and personal growth, it is an extremely dangerous acquisition fraught with potentially damaging consequences—it is the ultimate double-edged sword. Divine wisdom is the greatest adaptive, psychological resource available to humans in coping with life's exigencies, but its effective use requires the mastery of death and death anxiety, something that neither the Lord God nor natural selection have prepared us for. The Lord God was trying to protect us from these sequelae through avoidance of the issues. Evidently he knew that, as has proven to be the case, the destructive consequences of this attainment would far outweigh its positive results—that is, that humans would not be able to cope effectively with death-related threats, in part because he himself had not found a way to do so. Thus I again suggest that God was acting on the basis of his own unresolved death anxieties and his personal inclination to try to cope with these disruptive feelings through denial and avoidance—a heritage that he passed on to humans. We shall soon see that there are other signs of unresolved death anxiety in Yahweh, and I shall trace its effects on his actions in both the Hebrew and New Testaments—and on us today. This is a dysfunctional heritage that we need to recognize and overcome.

GOD'S PUNITIVE MEASURES

God's ambivalence and uncertainty as to whether humans should possess divine wisdom is seen first in his arranging for humans to possess this wisdom but then taking it away from them in his second creation. To emphasize the uncertainties of his position, he then forbids Adam to try to acquire this kind of knowledge, but places the tree bearing it in the center of the garden. Talk about divine teases—and mixed messages! Then, after the forbidden deed was done, God punishes the serpent by making him crawl on his belly, where he will eat dust for the rest of his life, and he puts enmity between the serpent and the woman and their respective seeds, thereby bruising the serpent's head and the heel of her seed. For the woman there is an increase in pain in childbearing and submission to her husband, while for Adam, the Lord God curses the ground and promises him sorrow as he eats of it all the days of his life.

> Thorns and thistles it shall bring forth for you; and you shall eat the plants of the field. By the sweat of your face you shall eat bread until you return to the ground, for out of it you were taken; you are dust, and to dust you shall return. (Gen 3:18–19)

As harsh as the Lord God is at this punitive moment, he then reverses himself again and makes coats of skins and protectively covers Adam and Eve. It's as if God feels guilty for allowing the couple to become so helplessly aware of death, so he provides them with a modicum of temporary protection from this scourge by clothing them. That done, but still unsettled, he then blocks their access to the tree of eternal life, which could be their salvation, and expels them from Eden to make sure they will not seek the fruit of that divine tree with its supreme gift.

Death and death anxiety appear to be overwhelming issues for the Lord God, much as they are for us today. It seems fair to say that there are indications in his first appearance to humans that he is so beset with uncertainty and guilt in regard to the human possession of divine wisdom and their awareness of death that he is unable to be of any real help to humankind in respect to these archetypal issues. His own unresolved death anxieties seem to be getting in his way, and as a result, he passively allows Adam and Eve to become more sharply aware of death, to suffer the attendant anxieties, and then, rather than giving them a means of finding relief, exiles them from paradise, sending them into a most difficult world of dangers poorly armed to cope with what will befall them.

In the end, God has designed us, as humans, in a way that has left us in a helpless position in respect to existential death anxiety—and as we shall see, in respect to the other two forms this anxiety takes as well. In so doing, he created a situation in which humans would turn to their faith in God and his power over matters of life and death and to the power of prayer to alleviate these anxieties, and he thus would live on—as he has. Other than creating delusions of personal immortality or finding a much-needed way to adaptively come to terms with death, there appears to be no other palpable solution. God set things up so he himself would not have to suffer from existential death anxiety, so he was assured of his continuing existence, while humans would have to fend for themselves. This arrangement did not augur well for the future of humankind—or for that matter, the future of religion either.

THE CHOICE OF WISDOM

More can be said about the first fundamental archetype in human life, which involves choosing, as did Eve and Adam, between living one's life based on common, mundane knowledge and living on the basis of uncommon divine wisdom. In the first case, the unwitting choice is made to live unknowingly in a state of divine ignorance, thereby siding with the Lord God, while in the second case, one chooses to cope using God-like knowledge and sides with the serpent. This knowledge resides today in the deep unconscious wisdom system of the human emotion-processing mind as encoded in narrative responses to death-related triggering events. The conscious mind dreads becoming aware of the death-related experiences to which such wisdom is attached, and as I said, I have seen the effects of this dread, unconsciously experienced, in most of the patients to whom I have offered the possibility of accessing this kind of highly effective set of adaptive insights.

God or nature provided our conscious minds with a storehouse of mundane wisdom and an array of defenses designed to keep our minds from accessing deep unconscious experiences and knowledge. As a result, all but a handful of humans are unconsciously convinced, as God warned Adam and Eve, that they will not survive if they gain access to divine insights. In keeping with God's advice, they prefer to live in divine ignorance and in most cases to rely on faith in God or some form of secular thinking to deal with their death-related issues. These archetypal tendencies are so ingrained in the emotion-processing mind that they characterize and have limited the efforts of Freud and his followers to understand the emotion-related mind and emotional life. Their pursuits have been restricted to the use of mundane wisdom and have been affected by the unwitting use of conscious system denial of death; trigger decoding seldom if ever is invoked. Quite unconsciously, then, despite his best efforts to be otherwise, Freud was on the side of God in this matter.

Eve is a striking exception to the avoidance-of-divine-wisdom archetype. She consciously chose to taste the fruit of divine knowledge, which Adam only passively accepted. Even so, it appears that neither of them was able to use this wisdom in their subsequent lives. This implies that except for their sharpened awareness of death, God saw to it that the wisdom that they had taken in was set down in their deep unconscious rather than conscious minds, where it has remained undecoded and unrealized for centuries by their (and Noah's) heirs. This conjecture may explain why Adam and Eve showed no signs of extraordinary wisdom after they had eaten the forbidden fruit. To this day, humans do not as a rule have divine wisdom at their conscious beck and call; many extraordinary factors have to come together and culminate in the use of trigger decoding for this to happen.

Choosing between the Lord God and the serpent would not be easy for anyone, but ultimately the choice is not under a person's conscious control. Much depends on the severity of his or her history of death-related traumas and the extent to which the person automatically and unconsciously invokes the use of denial mechanisms—the more pervasive the traumas, the greater the inclination to side with the Lord God and the lesser the inclination to encode and access deep unconscious knowledge. The basic archetype or default position is, as I have said, for humans to operate on the basis of common wisdom, which, except for major, manifestly experienced, death-related incidents, is only rarely and vaguely death related. The spiritual wisdom generated by religious figures and others from biblical times down through the ages tends to involve matters of faith, belief in God, and the offer of conscious moral guidance—a chancy set of values at best. However profoundly configured, these pronouncements are the products of mundane, conscious system thinking and not based on the otherworldly, superbly gifted wisdom of the deep unconscious mind. These efforts are therefore greatly limited by the effects of unmastered death anxiety and the pervasive use of denial, and they leave room for the creation of another set of insights and moral guidelines based on the workings of our inner god of wisdom, which resides in the deep unconscious mind.

Divine wisdom is encoded, unconscious knowledge that is activated and evoked by emotionally charged, traumatic triggering events. It is adaptive wisdom wrought by an inner god that possesses an awesome array of perspectives and insights that stand well beyond all conscious understanding. And as I have been emphasizing, we can access this knowledge only by decoding narratives like dreams, daydreams, and stories in light of their evocative triggers. These decoded narratives convey archetypal knowledge that is very different from conscious knowledge, which not only is beset with denial, but also strongly affected by deep unconscious guilt and the need for punishment for past harmful deeds against others.

Deep unconscious wisdom is surprising and awesome to the conscious mind, remarkably effective adaptively, and entirely devoted to our best interests. Be it God-given or the result of natural selection, this kind of knowledge emanates from a divine realm—from a world of deep unconscious experience that is both heaven and hell in one. Heaven because the knowledge involved embodies unfathomable but sound solutions to our emotional woes that the conscious mind cannot even imagine, and hell because it is knowledge built around our personal traumas and the death-related terrors that they have evoked in us.

As I have indicated, I know a fair amount about this divine hell because I am, as an adaptive psychotherapist, the gatekeeper and guardian of its realm. I have for some time understood that I am one of those exceedingly rare modern-day serpents who knows and tries to reassure my patients that they will not be annihilated if they engage in the search for divine solutions to their unrelenting death anxieties and come face to face with their death-related traumas (Langs 2004c). To shift analogies, I am in a way a modern-day Chiron, the ferrier to the underworld where death and death anxiety pervade the realm. My interventions—the things I say and do, especially in connection with how I handle the ground rules of their therapy and in my asking them to communicate through narratives like dreams and stories—provide my patients with the vehicles they need to take them to this awesome land. It is there and only there that they can begin to deal with their death-related ghosts of time past as they are awakened by recent triggering events, many of them my doing—ghosts that keep them from sleeping peacefully at night and living happily by day. And make no mistake about it, sitting next to their ghosts is my own collection of ghosts who have been activated by my patients' stories and by the traumatic incidents in my personal life. These are the activated ghosts with whom I must deal silently and privately as I struggle to decode my patients' imagery in order to interpret the nature of their grim struggles and the solutions to these travails that are encoded into their narratives by their deep unconscious wisdom systems. In the end, much of what unfolds is about how my ghosts are unconsciously affecting their ghosts and how my ability to make peace with the incidents that haunt me makes it possible for me to help my patients to make peace with their own death-related phantoms—and how through it all, their deep unconscious wisdom system is showing them fresh pathways to inner and outer peace.

We can see another reason why the serpent is often seen as the devil: He opens a pathway to each person's inner hell, though please note, with nothing but true healing through genuine insight in mind. We can see too once more why God wanted humans to avoid this terrible struggle, why he advocated divine ignorance and the avoidance of this shadow realm. He wished humankind well even though it meant depriving us of divine wisdom, a sacrifice that comes at the price of never making true inner peace with oneself and being left to try to gain emotional relief and peace through self-deceptions or by shoring up denial-based defenses. Either choice you make, for or against gaining divine insight, it is a matter of choosing your poison and trying to keep the dosage at a homeopathic level so that it heals rather than destroys.

SUMMING UP

In bringing this chapter to a close, I want to identify some of the more unusual adaptive conjectures about the story of Eden. They are offered in part as a way of suggesting that it will be of great value to reconsider many biblical shibboleths in light of the adaptive understanding of the human mind and its core challenges, and to begin to point to ways in which this understanding can provide a sound basis for fresh religious perspectives and a viable secular spirituality.

Going over this chapter, it is striking to see the extent to which the adaptive orientation, with its stress on coping with death and death anxieties and on the kind of wisdom with which one adapts to these issues, unites rather than separates religious thinking and the belief in God on the one hand, and secular thinking and atheism on the other. Again and again I have tried to show that the ways in which the human mind deals with these problems can be thought of with equal cogency in terms of how God has shaped the human mind and its behaviors, or by pointing to the powers of natural selection in passively designing the emotion-processing mind. While the religious explanation relies on faith and belief, and the natural explanation depends on indirect evidence and belief, each approach both offers and fails to offer a measure of relief from the underlying death anxieties with which all humans suffer to some extent. Whatever or whoever the designer, we must face the fact that either God or nature has done a poor job in fashioning the emotion-processing mind. This mental entity surely is one of the most compromised, dysfunctional adaptive structures in the history of living organisms on this planet. Both disciplines need to recognize its flaws and seek ways to repair them.

Along different lines, there are a number of implications of this story that pair up opposite possibilities. Archetypically, the conscious mind tends to envision a single likely cause for a given piece of behavior, while the deep unconscious mind tends to think simultaneously of several different possible causes—often, they are contradictory in nature. This latter situation seems to apply to the tales in the Bible. Thus, the question as to whether Adam and Eve sinned or did not sin in eating the forbidden fruit can be answered with both a yes and a no. Focusing on Eve for example, it can be said that in defying God's edict, she was committing a sin, yet in trying to make peace with an unknown death-related trauma and to develop a fuller life for herself and humankind, she was not acting in sinful fashion. After all, the Lord God himself did not accuse her of sinning when he punished her for violating his commandment.

Much the same applies to the question of whether the serpent is the devil or was acting under his influence. While we may think of anyone who stands against God's words as Satanic, this view needs to be tempered by the fact that the serpent speaks the truth to Eve and is helping her to gain her autonomy. We may wonder if the serpent knew that gaining wisdom would open the door to existential and other forms of death anxiety and thereby to human acts of evil and sin in efforts to deny one's vulnerability to death. In any case, given the complexities of the situation, we may well need to rethink our view of the players involved. This reevaluation apparently needs to include the Lord God in that the opening passages of the Bible that we have been exploring raise questions about both his level of unresolved death anxiety and his fallibility.

God is a never-ending enigma, and so, as Jung pointed out, when new ways of understanding cosmic interactions arise, we may well find it necessary to revise our view of his psychology and actions. In this sense, there needs to be a set of core religious beliefs around which revisions are made, thereby allowing them to better fulfill the human needs that they are designed to satisfy. This calls for a reexamination of religious values, which I will undertake in more detail in chapter 12. Such efforts are in keeping with the tradition of reinterpreting the Bible set by the rabbis in the Talmud, and as seen in Christianity in the Catholic ecumenical councils and the writings of revisionists such as Paul, Augustine, Thomas Aquinas, Martin Luther, John Calvin, and many others.

The archetypal struggle between God and the serpent has generally been thought of as a battle between good and evil. Based on a version of Freudian psychoanalysis, Shulman (2003) has suggested that this conflict reflects an inner struggle within Eve between obedience to and defiance against God. Adaptive studies indicate that there is a more basic inner mental conflict reflected in this conflict and that it is fought around the issue of knowledge acquisition. Every human being has an antiwisdom, unconscious system that takes form and operates in keeping with the stricture made by the Lord God to avoid the acquisition of divine wisdom. It is a mental system that advises the nonexpression of the encoded images that convey active forms of that wisdom. It is, then, a system that sees to it that in times of adaptive need, such narratives are suppressed or silenced. The nondreamer is a prime example of an individual under the dominant influence of this part of the mind. But people who dream or tell stories also are affected by this noncommunicative system; while they do encode adaptively, they do not trigger decode the resultant imagery. Thus, we humans have two opposing communicative systems, one that speaks for the serpent and encourages the turn to narrative expressions and another that speaks for the Lord God and advocates the avoidance of narrative communications and their decoded meanings. As was true in Eden, to this very day, with fascinating rare exceptions, the Lord God has the final say in this matter.

In this light, we see again that Eve was an extraordinary woman. But then too she must have had extraordinary reasons to do what she did. We are, I confess, still without knowledge of the triggering event or events that drove her to act as she did. But before I turn to the question of her motives, I want to provide further evidence that death and death anxiety are the basic archetypal problems for humankind and that the challenges they pose compel us deal with the equally basic issues of finding the adaptive wisdom and knowledge with which to cope with them.

3

Death Anxiety and Divine Wisdom

I have offered the thesis that the basic archetypes of human life, emotional and spiritual, involve an individual's selection of his or her knowledge base for coping with death and its attendant anxieties. The choice is between its *mundane* form, as given to us by God or nature, and its *divine* form, which is acquired at great emotional cost. Having the wherewithal to cope with the threat of death is humankind's basic challenge, much as dealing adaptively with the danger of annihilation is a basic task for all living organisms—it is the key to organismic survival as reflected in the biology of creation, adaptation, and evolution. The fundamental problems in life lie with danger situations and death, a basic principle that is reflected in the story of Eden, where God himself made it the first danger faced by humans, largely as the price to be paid for acquiring divine wisdom.

Several paradoxes arise in this regard. For one, adaptive studies show that while divine wisdom is far more effective and healing than mundane wisdom in trying to cope with death and death anxiety, the need for and turn to divine wisdom are motivated by these very same death-related experiences and the anxieties they arouse. Another paradox is that death anxiety, especially when it is overly severe because of intense or multiple past traumas, is also the basic cause of the turn away from divine wisdom and toward mundane efforts at coping with these threats. The Bible does not explicitly indicate that Eve was being affected by these issues when she ate the forbidden fruit, but I shall soon suggest that such was the case—these are archetypes that hold as much for her in the past as for ourselves in the present. The relevant death anxieties most often are experienced deep unconsciously and without direct awareness, but at times of acute stress and distress, they may be felt consciously as well.

Nevertheless, because this anxiety so often operates outside of direct awareness, its presence and effects on our lives are difficult to identify—a turn to
trigger decoding is essential in this regard.

DEEP UNCONSCIOUS DEATH ANXIETY

In this chapter I try to garner convincing evidence from a variety of sources
within and outside of the Bible that indicate that death and death anxiety are
the basic emotional issues in human life. But before I turn to the relevant writings, I want to offer an illustration of deep unconscious death anxiety to provide a sense of this elusive but enormously powerful hidden experience. Suitably disguised, this is the story:

God or coincidence sat me at a table at a dinner party with a man in his early
sixties, with whom I struck up a conversation. He told me that for years he had
owned a small art gallery and that when he turned fifty, he switched careers
and became a teacher. He spoke at length of the difficulties he had faced in
making the change and ended by saying it had been a very satisfying move.

He then asked me what I did, and I told him that I was a psychoanalyst and
that my recent focus was on issues related to death and death anxiety. In response, he told me that he had once suffered from a cardiac arrest when he
touched some live wires and that he was fortunate that a doctor was nearby
who was able to resuscitate him. Strangely enough, he knew as he passed out
that he might die, but he hadn't felt any anxiety, nor did he feel any during
the aftermath, when he was subjected to some rather dangerous therapeutic
interventions. In fact, he could talk about it now with great equanimity. With
that our exchanges ended.

Some time later, I heard the woman seated on the other side of this man ask
him about himself. He proceeded to tell her about his career change, but this
time he added an incident he hadn't mentioned to me. It involved 9/11 and the
fact that the school in which he was teaching was quite near the World Trade
Center. When the planes hit the buildings, an effort to evacuate the school was
initiated. And when the first building collapsed, he was convinced he was going to die; at one point, with the shock of it all, he had nearly passed out in
fear. Fortunately, he added, everyone was safely evacuated from the school.

The triggering event for the man's unconsciously driven need to add the
9/11 incident to the story of his career seemed clear to me: It was his recollection in talking to me of his near death from cardiac arrest. While he denied experiencing any form of (conscious) death anxiety then or now, the
added story clearly conveyed a powerful deep unconscious experience of
both existential and predatory death anxiety. The man had no conscious

awareness that this was the case, but these deep unconscious anxieties are expressed in a seemingly coincidental manner by his adding a story about another death-related incident that encodes his terror of being assaulted and dying. The theme of nearly passing out links the cardiac arrest story to the one about 9/11, as do the happy endings to each tale. Deep unconscious experiences of death anxiety are conveyed in this manner: In reaction to a death-related triggering event, somewhere in the narrative that is being told about the incident another powerful incident is mentioned, one that encodes the death-related aspects of the triggering event that have been experienced and processed outside of awareness.

To summarize, deep unconsciously experienced death anxiety is a reaction to a death-related triggering event (or its recall) in which the trauma is mentioned in one part of a story and the death anxiety is expressed in another part—the conscious link between the two having been severed. There is no conscious experience of the anxiety in connection with the key trauma; it emerges in connection with some other incident. Nevertheless, it is clear that the two incidents are linked. This proposition finds ample support in the psychotherapy situation where patients unconsciously support interpretations fashioned on this basis with affirming encoded (deep unconsciously created) images (Langs 1997, 2002, 2003, 2004a, 2004b, 2004c, 2005a, 2006).

GILGAMESH

There are countless examples of death-related archetypes in the Bible as well as in epics, novels, plays, and myths—including the myth of Oedipus, which Freud took as the basic paradigm for the unconscious conflicts that drive human emotional life. Just about every major epic tale affords a central role to death and death anxiety in its story line. This is the case in the first known written epic, the story of Gilgamesh, and it holds true for the classics such as the *Iliad*, the *Odyssey*, the *Aeneid*, *The Divine Comedy*, Shakespeare's tragedies, countless fairy tales, and so on. Indeed, all manner of historical epics and fictional writings are death centered, a fact that speaks to the realization that life is at bottom about death—an insight known to just about everyone except psychoanalysts despite this rare quotation from Freud's address on thoughts for the times of war and death:

> We recall the old saying: *Si vis pacem, para bellum.* If you want to preserve peace, arm for war.
> It would be in keeping with the times to alter it: *Si vis vitam, para mortem.* If you want to endure life, prepare yourself for death. (Freud 1915, p. 300)

Most certainly, I am not the first person to place death in the center of life. To cite some prominent writers among many others, Heidegger (1962) built his very convincing and profound existential philosophy around issues related to death and dying, Gilbert (2006) described modern ways of dying and how we express grief, and Harrison (2003), building in part on the work of the eighteenth-century Italian philosopher Vico, who convincingly argued that all civilizations are founded on three institutions—religion, matrimony, and burial of the dead—presents an extensive study of the crucial role the dead play in the lives of the living and the as yet unborn.

As an initial demonstration of the archetypal link between death anxiety and the need for divine wisdom, I turn to the epic of Gilgamesh (Mitchell 2004), the king of Uruk, which was written about 2100 BCE. There are notable sexual elements to the first part of this tale in that Gilgamesh exercises his droit du seigneur—his claim to first intercourse with the brides of the land. In addition, Enkidu, whom the gods send to tame the tyrannical side of Gilgamesh, is transformed from his animal-like state into a human being by having sex for seven days with Shamhat, a female goddess. The tie between sexuality and the dawning of consciousness and sexuality as a prelude to an individual's struggle with death and the anxieties it arouses is a basic death-related archetype. It has, as I already indicated, some pertinence to the story of Adam and Eve in Eden—and to many other epic tales as well as Augustine's story of repeating the sin of Adam (see chapter 4).

As for Gilgamesh, his story turns grim after a physical struggle for dominance between himself and Enkidu, in which Gilgamesh triumphs. The incident is followed by Gilgamesh's observations of the dead floating down a river outside the confining city walls, an experience that prompts him to decide to go on a journey with Enkidu to kill the sacred monster, Humbaba, who guards the cedar forest from human entry. Some writers see Humbaba as the epitome of evil, but most commentators see him as a protector of the forest and an innocent victim of Gilgamesh's need for lasting fame. In any case, in response to the goading of Enkidu, the hesitant Gilgamesh kills the monster. The killing is punished by the gods, who cause Enkidu to die. Gilgamesh is bereft over his great personal loss. He longs to know if he too must die or if he can join his friend without dying—if there is a way for him to become immortal. He seeks out his uncle, Utnapishtim, who, having survived the Great Flood, has been granted immortality by the gods. He hopes to learn the secret to immortality from him only to discover that it is impossible for humans to achieve that state. Gilgamesh is left to face his fate, and in time, he succumbs to death.

These first known written words indicate that humans have intuitively realized that sexuality brings life to humankind in a variety of ways. It prepares them for both their awareness of death and the consequent need for divine wisdom and immortality. Gilgamesh's search for wisdom is driven by the existential death anxieties that were evoked by observing the dead, much as the Buddha began his search for inner peace after seeing a man die. Gilgamesh's death anxieties are intensified by the death of his friend, Enkidu, and possibly by the predator death anxieties and deep unconscious guilt he experienced as a result of his killing of Humbaba to achieve fame. Another source of this form of anxiety may well have arisen because of his belief that he in some way was responsible for the death of Enkidu—a death-related archetype that I shall discuss when exploring the story of Cain and Abel. As for the nature of the wisdom achieved, as with Adam and Eve, it appears to be quite limited and lies with the grim realization that a central reality of life is that immortality is unavailable to humans. As Harrison (1992) points out, Gilgamesh's realization at the dawn of civilization that death is an ineluctable and non-negotiable condition of life is called "wisdom." Archetypically, then, the first recorded epic links death and existential death anxiety to what I am calling "divine wisdom." From this we may infer that this archetype played a role in Eve's quest for such knowledge as well.

A MODERN-DAY TALE

A passage from a novel by the contemporary Japanese writer Haruki Murakami, *The Wind-Up Bird Chronicle* (1998), is illustrative of the intuitive wisdom shown by many present-day writers in regard to the effects of death anxiety on human adaptability. The central character in the book, a man of twenty or so named Toru Okada and nicknamed "Mr. Wind-Up Bird," has found a dry well in a closed-off back alley behind his house in Tokyo. He buys a ladder, descends into the well, and spends the night there. When he awakens in the morning, the ladder is gone. After a while, a teenager named May Kasahara, whom he has befriended, shows up; evidently she is the one who removed the ladder. She checks to see if Toru is alive and after he speaks up she teasingly reassures him that it will take a while before he starves to death.

May then ponders the subject of death, suggesting that if people could live forever and not face dying, they wouldn't bother to think about serious matters as she and Toru are now doing. Thoughts about all sorts of important subjects—philosophy, religion, logic, and literature—would never come into existence. Without knowing that they are going to die some day, people would also have no need to think about what it means to be alive. She then suggests that death makes us evolve and the more intense the image of death seems, the more we're compelled to drive ourselves crazy thinking about all kinds of things.

In this pithy passage, Murakami places the wisdom of the ages into the mouth of a somewhat lost teenager. While his message is expressed directly through the character of May, it nevertheless is archetypal and touches on the sources of divine wisdom. Murakami intuitively appreciates that the prospect of death engenders the need to acquire knowledge and divine-like wisdom, and that death is the driving force behind human creativity and the evolution of knowledgeable life on earth as well. He also understands that the acquisition of this deeper kind of wisdom is a terrifying experience that can drive a person crazy. These revelations, uplifting and growth-promoting on the one hand and anxiety-provoking on the other, are experienced unconsciously by all who search for this kind of death-related insight.

THE SECOND COMING OF HUMANKIND

The Old Testament tells two tales that involve acquiring divine wisdom, and each follows a beginning of life on earth. The first is the story we have been exploring, that of Adam and Eve in Eden at the dawn of life on earth. The second follows the flood, which God, to his later regrets, brought down on humankind because of its wickedness and evil ways. God wiped out all living beings except the family of Noah and matched pairs of the other living creatures that Noah took with him on the ark he built based on God's instructions. The Bible details the reactions of Noah and his sons when the flood recedes, and speaks of their descendants—Noah has often been thought of as the second Adam. This second beginning of life on earth is soon followed by the story of Babel, which begins,

> Now the whole earth had one language and the same words. . . . Then they said, "Come, let us build ourselves a city, with a tower with its top in the heavens, and let us make a name for ourselves; otherwise we shall be scattered abroad upon the face of the whole earth." The Lord came down to see the city and the tower, which the mortals had built. And the Lord said, "Look, they are one people, and they all have one language; and this is only the beginning of what they will do; nothing that they propose to do will now be impossible for them. Come, let us go down, and confuse their language there, so they will not understand one another's speech." (Gen 11:1–7)

The flood is the basis for another moment of creation, a new world in which the descendants of Noah will populate the earth. And the first dramatic incident—and it is quite reminiscent of the situation with Adam and Eve—takes shape as his descendants try to acquire divine knowledge and God-like capabilities by building a tower that reaches into the heavens. And once more, God objects to their gaining a measure of Godly omnipotence. This time he defeats their effort by confounding their tongues—confusing their languages—and scattering them about so they are unable to work together to achieve their lofty goals. In essence, then, once more, the gift of life is followed by a human quest for divine wisdom that is opposed by Yahweh.

While the Bible continues to be sparse on motives, on this occasion the triggering event seems to be quite evident: These efforts take place after humans have suffered from a catastrophic death-related trauma, which at first threatened the end of life on earth and actually entailed the eradication of almost all living beings that existed at the time. This is a dramatic, death-related triggering event that would arouse both existential and predatory death anxieties—anxieties over one's personal mortality and fears that God would wreak havoc and devastation again.

As was true in some sense with Adam and Eve, God is once more, and this time unmistakably, the primary enemy of humankind—he is the predator against whom the humans are trying to defend themselves. God, their greatest defender and protector, has once again assumed the role of their greatest threat. It appears that God feels threatened and preyed upon by the human quest for divine wisdom, and possibly by their wish for eternal life as well, so he draws on his greater powers to prey on humankind first. This is an archetypal response to a death-related threat, and it is an early example of a very common, fateful predator-prey arms race that involves a competition for survival. God's action has been triggered by the human effort to share in his divine powers; his death anxieties—his fear of annihilation—seem to have been mobilized again and to have led to a violent reaction on his part.

As for the human side of this story, their motivation seems to stem from the annihilatory death anxieties triggered by the flood. Knowing that they cannot defeat God as they now stand constituted and not wanting to engage in a hopeless effort to destroy God before he destroys them—which is the archetypal reaction to predation—the people of Babel conspire to capture some of God's power and wisdom. This evidently is their way of preparing to fight God on his own terms. The hope seems to be that by acquiring some of his unique strengths they will be able to prevent him from creating further death-related catastrophes. Here too, then, death anxieties, mainly existential and predatory in nature, are the motivating forces behind the human quest for divine wisdom. Oddly enough, it would seem that these anxieties are being experienced on both sides of this struggle—in the humans as well as in God. We also can see that in addition to predatory death anxiety, existential death anxiety seems to be empowering the turn to predation. This too is a common death-related archetype.

Also of note is the sense that God realizes that language acquisition, which is his or nature's most telling gift to humans, gave humankind its most extraordinary powers—creative as well as destructive. The Lord God evidently

attacks humans where their greatest strength lies. By confounding human languages, God also has destroyed one of humankind's most powerful weapons
against the threat of death—the use of language to avoid or cope with dangers, think out strategies, join forces with allies, and the like. Paradoxically,
then, the attempt by humans to acquire divine wisdom to better alleviate their
death anxieties seems to lead to an intensification of these anxieties instead.
This paradoxical outcome is due in large measure to their trying to combat
death anxiety with frame-violating, exploitative, immoral pursuits. In essence
this is seen in their efforts to violate the boundary between heaven and earth,
God and humankind, in their efforts to steal God's wisdom and immortality.
The inclination to cope with death anxiety in this kind of sinful and immoral
way is with us in full force to this very day. The time has come for humans to
acknowledge these tendencies and face the dire consequences of these desperate and self-defeating efforts at coping with the threat of death—and to
modify their hapless, denial-based, harmful ways of trying to do so.

THE MYTH OF OEDIPUS

Greek myths also are replete with stories that describe human efforts to acquire the divine wisdom of the Greek gods. Prometheus tries to trick Zeus by
giving him bones to eat while giving humans edible meats. In his anger, Zeus
withholds fire from man, but Prometheus steals the fire and gives it to
mankind. He is punished by being chained to a rock, where a vulture tears at
his liver each day and he is healed each night. Somewhat like Adam with Eve,
Prometheus's innocent brother, Epimetheus, also is punished by Zeus, who
sends him Pandora, from whose box emerge all the plagues of humankind.

There are moral issues here of deception and theft, but in addition, Zeus is
opposed to humans acquiring the power inherent in fire, a symbol for both life
and divine wisdom. Zeus responds ambivalently to Prometheus's doing so by
giving him a near-death punishment and then healing him as well. This response is not unlike the Lord God's reaction to Eve's comparable acquisition
in that he both punishes and protects her from harm. In addition, Prometheus's
brother is punished in a way that releases plagues and evil into the world—
the brother is treated as if Prometheus's sins were his. Here too, the human
gain of divine wisdom is linked to both death and the onset of evil in the
world—archetypes seem to be in play once more.

Another Greek myth of relevance is the tale of Oedipus, which Freud saw
as the most fundamental story of human emotional life. Based on his wish-
centered paradigm of psychoanalysis, Freud claimed that the heart of the
myth lies with the incest that Oedipus commits with his mother, Jocasta. Also

important, but secondary to the incestuous liaison, is Oedipus's murder of his father, Laius, which was carried out unwittingly and resulted in Oedipus's unknowingly marrying and bedding his mother.

I shall have much to say about this myth in chapter 11 when I discuss the question of how classical psychoanalysis has dealt with religion and death. For the moment, I want to briefly examine the highlights of the myth to see if, despite Freud's focus on incest, it too indicates that death, death anxiety, and the acquisition of divine wisdom are first-order, archetypal human concerns.

As portrayed in Sophocles' play *Oedipus the King* (D. Taylor 1986), a drunken friend attending Oedipus's twenty-first birthday party tells Oedipus that the king and queen of Corinth, who brought him up and whom he believes to be his mother and father, are not his biological parents. This is the exciting (triggering) event of the myth, and it clearly is a matter that pertains to divine knowledge: Who are Oedipus's parents? It also is a death-related trigger because it implies that Oedipus's biological parents are either dead or have abandoned him and possibly left him to die, which we later learn to be the case.

In the course of searching for his biological parents, Oedipus leaves Corinth for Thebes. Along the way he murders a man who insults him and later turns out to have been his father. He moves on toward Thebes only to find that his path is blocked by a monster, the Sphinx. Travelers going to or from Thebes must solve the riddle she poses to them, or she will kill and devour them. The question she asks is this: "What walks on four legs in the morning, two legs at noon, and three legs in the evening?"

Oedipus is the first traveler to solve the riddle and thereby free the city from the Sphinx's grasp. His answer is "Man, who crawls on all fours in infancy, walks upright on two legs in adulthood, and uses a cane as a third leg in old age." In response, the Sphinx commits suicide by throwing herself from the city walls.

Finally, Oedipus is rewarded with the hand of the queen of Thebes in marriage. When she discovers that she has been sleeping with her son, she commits suicide, and Oedipus blinds himself with her pins.

Oedipus escapes death by being able to solve the riddle of the Sphinx, and he evidently does so by possessing something more than common or profane knowledge, something akin to divine wisdom. While we are not told how Oedipus had gained this measure of divine wisdom, present-day archetypes indicate that this kind of knowledge is always death related and that it is acquired in the process of dealing with death-related traumas—for Oedipus, this seems to have been his father's (and mother's) maiming him and abandoning him to die.

The pain of acquiring divine wisdom is pitted against its life-saving qualities. Divine knowledge holds the key to coping successfully with death and death anxiety, which in the case of the Sphinx is predatory in nature. At its core, and well before the incest issue arises, the foundational myth of Oedipus involves both death anxiety and knowledge acquisition.

Adaptive studies of death-related archetypes indicate that Oedipus was living out the archetype of the damaged or abandoned child in which the overriding deep unconscious need and intent is the murder of the offending parents in talion revenge. He accomplishes his mission by murdering his father and causing his mother to kill herself. In this way, his story is one of divine knowledge acquisition in which the wisdom cuts both ways—it is both illuminating and devastating. The myth also is a story of the mastery of a childhood death-related trauma, which, when it fulfills the vengeance archetype, is largely destructive to all concerned. There are, by the way, eight acts of violence and murder to one act of incest in this tale, a ratio that supports the thesis that its central theme is death related rather than sex related.

Finally, it is noteworthy that Oedipus does not turn to divine wisdom in dealing with his father on the road to Thebes. This too is characteristic of the acquisition of divine wisdom: One minute it is accessible and ready for adaptive use, the next minute it has disappeared and is not available for coping with death-related threats. Divine wisdom is hard-won and easily lost.

All in all, the myth indicates that death, death-related traumas, and the acquisition and adaptive use of divine wisdom are intimately linked. I shall make ample use of these archetypal configurations when I return to the story of Eve and try to fathom what drove her to eat the forbidden fruit.

FREUD'S INTUITIVE LINKING OF WISDOM AND DEATH

While Sigmund Freud consciously offered several ways for psychoanalysts and the world at large to avoid death and issues pertaining to death anxiety, he nevertheless unconsciously expressed the archetypal connection between death and death anxiety on the one hand, and the quest for divine wisdom on the other. The first of his own personal dreams that he describes in his letters to Fleiss (Freud 1892–1899, p. 233) is a dream that he dreamt the night after his father's funeral, a dream in which he is asked twice to close his eyes. Because I will comment in chapter 11 on the alternative and more complete version of this dream, which he reported in *The Interpretation of Dreams* (Freud 1900), I note here only that this inaugural dream is clearly death related and that it suggests that such issues played a significant role in the origins of Freud's pursuit of psychoanalytic wisdom.

This point is made even more explicitly in Freud's choice of dreams for his dream book. His specimen dream, which is known as "the Irma dream" and is the first dream in his dream book, is his own dream, and it is striking for its sexual symbolism. The dream also brings forth from Freud a series of death-related associations, several to patients who died or nearly died while under Freud's care and one to the near-death of his daughter Mathilde. Freud dreamt this dream a few days before his wife's birthday, at a time when she was pregnant with their daughter Anna. Thus both life and death are in the air in connection with this inaugural dream.

There is another dream, perhaps of greater importance than the Irma dream, that has a bearing on this discussion. The dream is presented as the prelude to Freud's well-known chapter 7 in the dream book, which is devoted to some highly original writings on the psychology of the dream process—at bottom, to the architecture and workings of the human mind. Freud made the odd choice of using a dream reported to him by a woman patient who had heard the dream in a lecture on dreams and who had redreamt aspects of the dream herself. The dream was dreamt by a father whose young son had died and who, with the help of an old man, was keeping vigil with the body. The father had gone into an adjacent room, left the door open, fallen asleep, and dreamt that

> *his child was standing beside his bed, caught him by the arm and whispered to him reproachfully: "Father, don't you see I'm burning?"* (Italics in the original; Freud 1900, p. 509)

The father awoke to find that the old man he had hired to watch his son's body had fallen asleep, and the wrappings and arm of his child had been burned by a candle that had fallen on them.

Freud raises the question as to why the father had had a dream rather than awakening immediately to the glow of the fire, which he could see through the door opening. He also suggests that the wish behind the dream—that the son be alive—and the dream's meaning and interpretation are obvious. Freud recounts that previously in the dream book he had been concerned with the secret meanings of dreams, the methods of discovering them, and the means by which the dream work conceals these meanings. But now he claims that none of this is at issue. It is this realization that led Freud to acknowledge the incompleteness of his understanding, and the general psychology of dreams—which he then undertakes to develop.

Freud's conscious logic here is shaky and questionable. It suggests that the choice of the dream that he used to announce his psychology of the mind was driven by unconsciously experienced triggers and needs of which he was quite unaware. It also suggests that the archetype that links wisdom with death was driving this selection process. Whatever the deep unconscious motives, this material is one more way of showing that even though the conscious mind often misses the point, the deep unconscious mind fully appreciates the connection between death, death anxiety, and divine wisdom. This was especially true of Freud.

That said, I shall now return to the path that is taking us to a final study of the story of Adam and Eve in Eden. I must, however, request your patience because I find it necessary to take one more detour—a look at Augustine's *Confessions* (Augustine 1961). I do so because Augustine reveals there that he had repeated the sin of Adam—that is, that he too had stolen some forbidden fruit. There is much to his personal story that illuminates the archetypal aspects of the biblical events in Eden, so it will be worth our while before returning to the garden to see what Augustine was up to and what he revealed—consciously and unconsciously.

4

Augustine's Version of Adam's Sin

My ideas about the implications and meanings of the transactions in Eden were based largely on the discovery of relevant, timeless, wisdom- and death-related archetypes in my clinical practice. I was, however, on the alert for other tests of the propositions that I had begun to generate. In the course of these pursuits, I came across a series of books written by Garry Wills on Augustine's *Confessions* (Augustine 1961; Wills 1999), of which I shall focus on one: Wills's presentation of Augustine's sins. I was pleasantly surprised to discover that Augustine had described in his book two Bible-related sins that he had committed. The first was a repetition of the sin of Adam, and the second was a replay of the sin of Cain (see chapter 7). It turned out that the descriptions of both incidents were accompanied by nuanced supplementary narratives that lent themselves to in-depth exploration and understanding. Indeed, Augustine had the extraordinarily intuitive wisdom not only to describe the manifest nature of his sins, but also to produce a series of unwittingly encoded, storied associations to each of his biblical reenactments. It could be said, then, that quite unconsciously Augustine had put himself on an archetypal analytic couch and had generated dream-like narratives that are open to trigger decoding and interpretation. One of the world's first psychologists appears to have been one of the world's first psychoanalytic patients as well.

In addition to providing us with an opportunity to explore the unconscious archetypes associated with these two biblical tales, Augustine also offers us a chance to make comparisons between his conscious, mundane interpretations of both tales and his deep unconscious, divine efforts along similar lines. This prospect arises because, remarkably enough, Augustine offered direct interpretations of what he had done, while his associations provide us with his encoded, deep unconscious view of these same happenings. In a way then, we will be completing a task that Augustine initiated when he penned his extensive study of Genesis, which he titled *First Meanings in Genesis* (J. Taylor 1982). To his first meanings, I shall try to add his own second meanings, of which he was quite unaware consciously. Hopefully the two-paneled picture, profane and divine, will provide us with a more enlightened understanding of Augustine's behavior and thereby of the two biblical tales to which he linked his actions.

SETTING THE STAGE

Given that the Bible deals with archetypes and humankind's most fundamental challenges, it seems clear that all of us redream and relive the Bible over and over again. Augustine's dream-like story takes place in his home city of Thagaste. The defining action, which is comparable to a manifest dream—the conscious story, if you will—occurs in a local grove from which he and some adolescent male friends steal some inedible pears. The associated material, which is not directly about the pear incident and thus an encoded reflection of the deep unconscious experiences that underlie the surface incident, involves a diversity of subjects. By discovering the triggering event for the theft and decoding these associated incidents in light of the trigger, I shall try to ascertain Augustine's unconscious motives for what he did and his unconscious perceptions and reactions to it as well. It is here, on the deep unconscious, archetypal level that we can expect to find clues to the triggering event that motivated Adam and Eve to eat the forbidden fruit and to their unconscious view of what they had thereby enacted.

As background, Augustine believed that there are three founding or original sins, and that in hierarchical fashion, each sin prepared the way for the next one. He was convinced that these sins had been passed down to humankind from generation to generation, inherited from father to son, and that it fell to Christ to make reparation for these sins on behalf of all humans.

The first sin was committed by the fallen angels who, for no known reason, brought evil into the world in the form of disorder and the unmaking of beings—this is Satan's self-seduction. The second sin was committed by Adam in eating the forbidden fruit, while the last sin was the antisocial act that took form as Cain's murder of Abel.

Consciously, Augustine traced Adam's transgression of God's edict to Eve's seduction by Satan in the guise of the serpent, through which he moved her to eat the forbidden fruit and gain forbidden knowledge. Adam's sin is different from Eve's, who acquired knowledge of good and evil from her act, while Adam did not. Nevertheless, Adam sinned and he did so because he could not allow Eve to suffer the consequences of her fall without his company. Adam's sin is, then, based on a need or compulsion for solidarity—a sin that was triggered by Eve's going against God's stricture and eating the forbidden fruit. In addition, while the fallen angels' sin was an indefensible rejection of God and therefore irredeemable, the sins of Eve and Adam are lesser sins that are redeemable and were, indeed, redeemed by Christ.

AUGUSTINE'S MUNDANE INTERPRETATIONS

This is the story of how Augustine relived Adam's sin: He is sixteen years of age when he and several male friends steal some inedible pears from a local orchard. No sooner are the pears taken than they are thrown away.

Like the stories in the Bible, this is a tersely told narrative. It lends itself to mundane interpretations, inspired or otherwise, that we may arrive at by examining the story's manifest contents and proposing a number of possible implications. Augustine himself engaged in extensive efforts along these lines in the form of a conscious analysis of the incident, doing so in ways that are typical of biblical scholarship and commentary. As is usually the case, his thinking tends to be highly speculative, relatively simplistic, and overly intellectualized. But in addition, Augustine departs from these scholarly efforts and from the Bible itself by providing us with a narrative introduction to the story of the theft and with a supplementary series of associations that arise as he tells his tale and in his afterthoughts as well. In that way he opens a window into his deep unconscious experiences and accesses a kind of wisdom that is not available in his conscious thinking or in the Bible as manifestly revealed.

Augustine's own direct commentary on what he did is quite straightforward. He was, he tells us, in his home town of Thagaste, resting between studies that he carried out away from home, and was bored. One day he and a few male friends decided to have some fun stealing some pears—which they then did under the cover of nighttime.

Augustine attempts consciously to analyze his motives for, and the meanings of, the incident. He begins with the thought that he had repeated the sin of Adam, one of the founding sins of humankind. He notes that much as Adam's eating the "apple" [sic] defied God's commandment against eating from the tree of knowledge, his own act of stealing the pears defied God's commandment against theft. To some extent, Augustine saw this reliving as the result of Adam's sin being handed down by means of male inheritance to the generations that followed him—including Augustine himself.

Augustine could find only two (conscious) motives for his theft. First, there was a wish to commit a sin for sinning's sake, to act in a way that expressed pure evil. As he put it, he feasted on the sin rather than the pears. Second, there was his need for the good of companionship—he was certain that he would not have acted alone. He then interprets the story of Adam and Eve on this basis, arguing that Adam "yielded to Eve in breaking God's law, not because he believed she was telling the truth, but out of a compulsion to solidarity [with her]" (cited in Wills 2003, p. 13).

This, in substance, is Augustine's intellectual, mundane or profane, conscious assessment of the theft of the pears: doing evil for evil's sake (a religious root for the act) and for the sake of companionship (a social root for the act).

THE PRELUDE TO THE THEFT

As for his associations to the incident, Augustine offers a prelude to the theft that alludes mainly to the dawning of his adolescent sexuality. This introductory narrative segment begins with his mentioning the interruption of his studies in Carthage and his living at home again. It quickly moves to an incident in which Augustine's father observes his son in the baths and sees that his son is no longer a child. In his joy over the prospect of becoming a grandfather, the father then tells Augustine's mother about his discovery. She becomes fearful that her unbaptized son will sin sexually, and she urges Augustine to refrain from illicit sex, especially from relations with married women. Augustine notes that she did not actually try to check, let alone repress, his pernicious and potentially fatal conduct. He then implies that he did not stray from the path set for him by his mother, but instead, took to feigning deeds never done, so his friends would think him outrageous sexually.

(Some historians [e.g., Brown 1967] have speculated that by the time of the theft, Augustine may have already met and slept with his unmarried concubine—an acceptable sexual partner at the time—and that she may have been pregnant as well.)

Taken at face value, the prelude to the theft suggests that there was a sex-related triggering event and unconscious sexual motive for Augustine's act. In this regard, we might conjecture that in stealing the pears, Augustine was unconsciously acting out a sex-related sin. The triggering event may have been his having had intercourse with his concubine and possibly impregnating her—or some other boundary-violating sexual or pregnancy-related incident like a miscarriage. It is possible that even though sleeping with a concubine was socially acceptable at the time, it was experienced deep unconsciously by Augustine as a sinful sexual contact. The theft of the pears has a clear predatory meaning, so it seems likely that it encodes a harmful act abetted by others whom Augustine recruited. If so, there also would be evidence of deep unconscious guilt and predator death anxiety for causing this harm, with a resultant deep unconscious need for punishment, ultimately by being put to death.

There is another possible interpretation of this material, which involves Augustine's more disguised, unconscious perceptions of his mother. Here the triggering event would be his mother's incestuously tinged, sinful seductiveness toward him, which may have aroused his unconscious incestuous wishes toward her. The mother's unconscious seductiveness is encoded or implied in her warning to her son against illicit sexual activities and against having relations with a married woman. It is well known that Monica was overinvolved with her son. In this light, Augustine would have been dealing with predatory death anxiety based on his mother's psychologically harmful seductiveness, and he would have been likely to seek ways to combat his sexually intrusive mother.

Augustine's thought that engaging in illicit sex would be "fatal conduct" suggests two additional possible deep unconscious meanings. The first is the commonly held idea that illicit sexual acts (and wishes), such as adulterous or incestuous engagements, are forbidden, punishable, sinful acts of predation. The second is based on the finding that sexual dreams, while they may touch on unconscious guilt for forbidden sexual wishes and transgressions, almost always serve the additional purpose of denying death and the death anxieties aroused by death-related triggering events. For example, the father of a woman patient being seen by a therapist whom I was supervising was seriously ill. The patient dreamt of having an illicit affair with one of her father's friends. Associations were about the friend's sixtieth birthday party and his being in excellent health; "Everyone else will die and he'll live forever," was the patient's comment. The sexual contact was serving as a way of denying death and creating the illusion of immortality in the face of a death-related trauma—the anticipated death of the patient's father.

Using this as our archetype, we can apply it to Augustine's prelude. As such, it suggests that in addition to his evident unconscious incestuous conflicts, Augustine was, at the time, also dealing with death-related issues—and thus his allusion to fatal conduct. As I said, the most likely death-related trauma would have been a miscarriage by his concubine or another woman, but as far as I have been able to determine, there is no record of such an event—nor would we expect such a record to exist. That said, it is well to appreciate that the sexual aspects of the prelude to his sinful theft of the pears lend some support to the thesis alluded to earlier that the nakedness of Adam and Eve had forbidden sexual meanings—and possibly death-related sexual meanings as well. As we saw in the epic of Gilgamesh, sexual awakening often is the prelude to a confrontation, consciously or deep unconsciously, with a death-related trauma and the death anxieties it evokes. As we shall see, this seems to hold true for Augustine as well.

All in all, then, these initial fragments of narrative tend to speak for strong sexual and death-related triggering events and deep unconscious motives for Augustine's theft of the pears, motives of which Augustine had no conscious awareness. In this light, his conscious, mundane analysis of the incident appears to be unwittingly defensive and naïve—essentially a reflection of how the denial-prone, poorly equipped, conscious system of the emotion-processing mind operates. Such analyses typically have a grain of truth to them, but in important ways, they serve as unconsciously wrought and unrecognized ways of avoiding and bypassing the most compelling and awful meanings of emotionally charged incidents. More broadly, this is a frequent but hidden dynamic in mundane readings of the Bible—formulating obvious implications while unknowingly avoiding and covering up deeper, empowered meanings.

THE POSTSCRIPT TO THE THEFT

The initial hint that death-related issues played a significant role in the theft of the pears finds considerable elaboration in the stories that came to Augustine's mind after he presented the details of the incident. At first, his thoughts extend the theme of incest and its connection to death by likening the theft to an act of murder, with the intention to steal another man's wife or wealth, or to snatch the necessities of life. The act, he adds, may be carried out to satisfy a variety of other reasons, but he rejects the idea that murder can be an evil without a motive.

Here the death-related meanings of the theft, albeit shaped around sexual boundary violations, become much clearer. Stealing the pears is experienced deep unconsciously as the frame-violating, adulterous act of murder—a predatory act of violence that is, as noted, likely to evoke predator death anxiety, deep unconscious guilt, and needs for punishment. In light of the probable trigger of his mother's intrusive seductiveness, this deep unconscious view of the theft may reflect Augustine's divine deep unconscious perception of the violence that lay behind his mother's sex-related warnings. The tie to the trigger of his possibly having impregnated his concubine is less clear, but the imagery suggests that Augustine felt seduced by her and that he may have been reacting violently to either the experience of a miscarriage or the prospect of having a child.

The punishment called for by the predator death anxiety archetype appears in Augustine's next associations, in which his thoughts revolve around the idea that murder is a motivated evil act. His thoughts then turn to Catiline, an ancient Roman leader who loved crime, not for its own sake, but for the objects to be gained by it. The reference, he explains, is to Catiline's attempted coup d'état, which was thwarted by Cicero in the year 63 BCE—an event that Augustine connects to Adam's fall. The link to the theft of the pears is found, he adds, in the belief that Catiline augmented his forces with youth gangs who performed acts of violence and murder on the streets. Cato had called for their execution as killers. Some Romans believed that these youths were acting without a motive or from the simple motive of keeping in practice and preparing for larger crimes. Augustine concludes that false and sinful companionship in acts of evil is the theme that unites his group's theft of the pears, Catiline's murderous rowdies, and Adam's fall.

These associations to the theft, replete with allusions to murder, death, and punishment by execution, bring death-related issues full force to the theft of the pears and suggest the presence of unmentioned, archetypal, death-related triggering events and unconscious motives. Augustine makes his analogies to Adam's sin, and the sexual issues soon give way to death-related conflicts of great intensity. The imagery seems to encode Augustine's unconscious perceptions of the theft as an act of wanton violence, murder, and rebellion directed against existing laws. This is a prime example of how a seemingly innocuous or minor incident can be experienced deep unconsciously in raw, violent, primitive ways that have strong effects on our thoughts, feelings, and actions. In keeping with this principle, the theft of the pears also is characterized deep unconsciously as a sin against God and humankind that has incestuous roots (the allusion to committing murder to take another man's wife), but basically it is seen as starkly predatory in nature—preying on and doing violence to others for the sake of murder itself. The call for the execution of the street murderers seems to be a disguised call for self-punishment from Augustine's own deep unconscious inner god and system of morality and ethics—it is the result of the predatory qualities of his action and the guilt-ridden predator death anxiety that he seems to have experienced as a result of it.

In a striking analogy, Augustine also likens this kind of violence to a "prisoner's maimed freedom." This allusion to combating entrapment anxieties with murder suggests that the theft of the pears also was a frame-violating, unlawful act that was unconsciously motivated by claustrophobic, existential death anxieties. These anxieties are triggered archetypically on occasions of impregnation and are even more common when the pregnancy leads to the death or destruction of the fetus. In these cases, the fetus is seen deep unconsciously as trapped and being destroyed in the mother's womb.

IMPLICATIONS OF AUGUSTINE'S STORY

There are several as yet unmentioned but noteworthy implications of this analysis of Augustine's narrative associations to his theft of the pears. The first is to appreciate again that the divine, narrative experience and interpretation of this event are very different from and far more powerful and meaningful than the mundane, intellectual analysis offered by Augustine and far more telling than anything that can be gleaned from examining the event itself. The idea that the theft was carried out for the sake of doing evil and maintaining a social bond pales next to the trigger-decoded narrative material that indicates that the theft was deep unconsciously and rightfully perceived as an incestuous or otherwise sexually illicit, frame-violating, unlawful, sinful act of murder. The divine reading is far more cogent and affecting than the mundane assessment. Indeed the two formulations touch on two very different worlds of experience: a mundane world that is easy to grasp and deal with, even though it is not especially meaningful or emotionally affecting, and a divine world that is awesome and awful to behold, but most certainly the hidden basis for the unfolding of much that is significant in regard to both human creativity and human madness—and for emotional life in general.

It also is of interest that, in addition to whatever God may have decreed, adaptive research into the biological evolution of the emotion-processing mind has produced strong evidence that as humans, we actually do, as Augustine postulated, inherit an archetypal, deep unconscious system of highly principled morals and ethics—although contrary to Augustine's belief, this inheritance applies to both men and women. There is, then, a distinctive set of universal standards against which we deep unconsciously evaluate our choice of actions and respond accordingly. Thus it appears that, as suggested by A. N. Wilson in his book on human morality, natural selection has influenced the evolution of the human mind and has favored minds with well-formed, ideal, deep unconscious moral codes. This implies that minds with these ideals survive better than minds lacking in these values. It seems then that Augustine, who had the genius to think of the human mind as structured at birth and of language acquisition as programmed genetically into the human mind, also correctly intuited that the human sense of morality and ethics has an inherited component that is, however, carried by both sexes rather than by males alone.

CONNECTIONS TO THE STORY OF EDEN

The archetypal unconscious equation between the theft of the pears and acts of murder that are punishable by death resonates with the warning made by God that eating from the forbidden tree of knowledge will cause Adam and Eve to die. Archetypically, Augustine's story also suggests that Eden was entrapping for Adam and Eve. It was indeed, as we eventually learn, a bounded paradise that provided them with security even though it restrained their mobility. Augustine was trapped in Thagaste, where his education languished and ignorance prevailed. In addition, he also may have felt trapped in the situations with both his parents and his concubine. The crime of stealing the pears and its associations with murderous violence suggest that the theft of the pears was unconsciously viewed as a frame-violating effort by Augustine to break out of his state of entrapment. The associations to murder and death, and their evident criminal and evil qualities, also lend further support to the idea that the forbidden knowledge of good and evil is linked to both death anxiety and sinful acts. Augustine's entrapped, existential death anxieties seem to have deeply motivated his evil, frame-violating theft of the pears — a relatively innocuous consequence of such anxieties, which quite often are the basis for far more damaging, frame-violating behaviors.

We can see too that this exercise in identifying archetypes shows how important these eternal configurations are in enabling us to gain fresh understanding of biblical tales. For example, Augustine's encoded narratives seem to pertain primarily to his unconscious motives for the theft and to the unconscious meanings of the theft itself. Deep unconsciously, then, the theft was experienced as a sinful act of murder, and the ultimate victim was God. Archetypically, this suggests the previously unrecognized possibility that Eve's eating the forbidden fruit had similar meanings. Thus, the threat of death that God alluded to may well have encoded his own fear of being destroyed by Eve's defiance and by her gaining divine wisdom. God promised death to Adam for his participation in the deed, and he also, once and for all, cut off the couple's path to eternal life after they ate the forbidden fruit. In talion fashion, then, the death threat from Adam and Eve may well have prompted God to make a death threat against the couple by making sure that they clearly understood that they themselves will die — not he.

Augustine's material also suggests archetypically that Eve was experiencing some kind of deep unconscious predator death anxiety and a need for punishment for an act of harm that she had perpetrated. In this context, her defiance of God could have been her deep unconscious way of inviting God's condemnation and chastisement. I shall return to this conjecture in the next chapter, but wish to point out here that present-day archetypal studies indicate that blatantly murderous themes of the kind that Augustine offers near the end of his associations to the theft of the pears almost always arise in response to violent, death-related triggering events. Indications are that in Augustine's case, the most critical act of violence was perpetrated by himself with the aid of others. Since we can be fairly certain that he did not commit an act of murder against a living person, we need to speculate on other possibilities. Given the allusions to sexuality, children, and uncontrolled violence, we come back to the possibility that Augustine was party to a pregnancy and miscarriage. But given that this is a highly speculative conjecture, we can only treat it as a rather tentative clue to what happened to Eve in Eden. Even so, this thought brings us back to the Bible and to the task of trying finally to solve the mystery of what moved (triggered and deep unconsciously motivated) Eve to make the monumental decision to eat the forbidden fruit.

5

Eve's Motives

While the Bible does at times present us with self-evident triggering events and offers an occasional insight into the apparent motives of its characters, including God himself, it does not deal in depth or thoroughness with causative incidents and the most powerful forces that drive the behaviors of those who are party to some of the most telling incidents in its sacred texts. Nevertheless, human behavior is driven by the interaction between external circumstances and active triggering events on the one hand, and on the other, the inner needs and propensities they arouse and with which they are consonant.

In principle, the personal, inner motivating forces involved in those who are party to significant happenings in the Bible are quite complex and ultimately very powerful. But as I have been stressing, what is done and said is triggered by external happenings—so-called *environmental events*, broadly defined—fraught with consciously and deep unconsciously experienced meanings. These evocative events arouse conscious and deep unconscious needs, evaluations, and morally colored adaptive responses that come together in behavioral responses in thought, feeling, and action. The central insight is that human behavior is not, as once thought, merely or primarily the result of some personal inner drives, needs, or wishes. Instead, we now know that needs and wishes are aroused by external events and that a full understanding of an emotionally charged incident requires recognizing its activating stimulus—that is, *the triggering event*—and its most telling meanings, and then determining which aspects of the stimulus have been experienced consciously and which, because they are more threatening, have registered deep unconsciously and been processed accordingly. This is especially the case with inexplicable or paradoxical actions and reactions because they are driven by traumatic events whose most critical meanings impact us and are processed outside of awareness—deep unconsciously. It is here that death-related archetypes play a crucial role because archetypal reactions tend to be activated by paradigmatic situations and events—they are timeless, universal responses to timeless, universal traumas and their timeless, universal meanings. They are individualized, collective experiences and reactions.

In returning to the story of Eden, then, the fundamental question we need to answer is this: What was the incident (or incidents) that triggered Eve's— and Adam's—need to eat from the forbidden tree of knowledge? The answer to this question is the key to this archetypal act, which was—and is—of such enormous consequence for humankind.

Focusing primarily on Eve because she is the prime mover, based on clues in the biblical tale itself and on present-day dreams and archetypes that seem pertinent to her story, I shall consider two possible triggering events for her fateful act. The first and less likely of the two is a prior traumatic confrontation with God, while the second is some kind of actual death-related experience that she endured in the course of her life in Eden. I make this proposal because, as I have tried to show, archetypal studies show that death and death anxiety alone drive the need for divine wisdom, so a death-related trauma must be our basic consideration in trying to identify the missing trigger for her fateful act.

EVE AND GOD

The first possible trigger for Eve's act is entirely religious and rather straight-forward. It pertains to Eve's relationship with God, about which the Bible tells us very little. God had issued only one edict in Eden, a stricture that he conveyed to Adam, who evidently passed it on to his wife. A prior confrontation between Eve and God would, of necessity, have involved that edict. It might well be that Eve was awakening to the confining and limiting conditions of her life in Eden and the emptiness and mindlessness of her existence there. This sense of deadness would cause her to see God as a stultifying predator and prompt her to resent his trying to prevent her from gaining the divine knowledge she needed to oppose him and come into being. God's prohibition against acquiring divine knowledge therefore would be the death-related trigger for Eve's action.

The issue of disobedience to God seems to be reflected in one of the three punishments meted out to Eve by God after the forbidden act:

Yet your desire shall be for your husband, and he shall rule over you. (Gen 3:16)

The subjugation of Eve to her husband may have been God's response to her defiance. But even as we try to make a case for this kind of triggering event, we would have trouble identifying or speculating about an immediate incident along these lines that would have been powerful enough to prompt Eve to do as she did—acts of this kind are always caused by recent or immediate triggering events. In addition, this line of thought is not supported by the answer Eve gave God as to why she ate the forbidden fruit:

"The serpent tricked me, and I ate." (Gen 3:13)

Eve's problem here is with the serpent, not with God.

Perhaps more importantly, the proposition that Eve felt predated in being kept from acquiring divine wisdom goes against present-day archetypes. Universally, short of an acute death-related experience, conscious minds dread and avoid the search for divine wisdom—that is, they do not naturally seek such knowledge and are content to do without it. In addition, the present formulation does not entail the kind of death-related trauma that would have made the serpent's reassurances so appealing to Eve. It appears then that we need to find a more compelling death-related incident to account for Eve's contra-archetypal pursuit of God-like wisdom.

A DEATH-RELATED TRIGGERING EVENT

A more compelling triggering event that could have driven Eve to seek divine wisdom and knowledge of good and evil would have taken shape as an experience with death itself. There is, of course, no direct mention of such a happening in the biblical text. In fact, as I suggested earlier, prior to their eating the forbidden fruit, Adam and Eve seem to have had only the dimmest sense that death exists, and indications are that neither death nor illness was experienced consciously in Eden.

In searching for a death-related incident, there are three possibilities, each corresponding to one of the forms of death anxiety. It is quite unlikely that Eve had experienced *predatory death anxiety* because Eden was a segment of the world in which all living beings were well supplied with nutriments and lived in full harmony with each other; there was no cause for predation of others. While this type of death anxiety might have arisen from the experience of a natural disaster, this too is extremely unlikely because Eden was a perfect, natural paradise, and there are no hints that a physical catastrophe had struck the realm.

Existential death anxiety is ruled out because there is no indication that Eve was acutely aware of personal death before she ate the forbidden fruit. There are, as I said, indications that she, and possibly Adam, had a sense of what God meant when he warned them that they would die if they ate the prohibited fruit and that she also understood the nature of the serpent's reassurances that this would not be the case. But these allusions to death seem to have registered only vaguely in the couple's minds and were without substantial impact because the concept of death seems to have been quite undeveloped in their thinking. Then too there is the aforementioned absence of illness and death in paradise, rendering the possibility of active existential death anxiety highly unlikely.

This leaves us with *predator death anxiety*, that is, with the proposition that Eve had in some manner harmed another living being. We must reject an act of violence against Adam because the couple showed no sign of conflict and he willingly took the forbidden fruit from Eve and ate it. The idea that the target of her destructiveness was someone else in Eden is eliminated by the absence of others to this point in the story, and the serpent also is excluded because he shows no indication of being damaged in any way, and he allies himself with Eve rather than seeking some kind of revenge against her as he would have if she had caused him death-related harm.

This narrows down the field, I believe, to only one other possibility, namely, that Eve had become pregnant and had suffered a spontaneous miscarriage—the first of its kind in human history. Her need for divine wisdom and knowledge of good and evil would have been quite intense after such a death-related incident. She would have desperately needed to gain this wisdom to fully understand what had happened to her and the fetus. She also would need to find divine answers to questions related to whether she had done something good or evil, whether death and harm were involved in any way, and whether she should or should not be punished by God or herself for what she had done. And behind these grave personal concerns would lie a series of gnawing fundamental, archetypal questions: What is life, what is death, what is murder? Is murder a sin, an evil act, a punishable crime? None of these vital questions could be answered using mundane or ordinary knowledge; only divine wisdom could help her to understand these conundrums, personal and universal as they were. This wisdom alone could bring her inner peace in the face of these awful threats.

This, then, is my proposal: that Eve suffered a death-related trauma in the form of a spontaneous miscarriage, and this is the event that triggered her deep unconscious need to seek divine wisdom despite all of the risks that this pursuit entailed. In a few words, it is death that brought Eve to life!

BIBLICAL EVIDENCE

There are no allusions to miscarriages or abortions in Genesis—or for that matter, anywhere else in the Bible. There are, however, several indications of the possibility that pregnancy and miscarriage may have played a role in human life from its very onset. There also is a clue that Eve herself may have miscarried and thus been driven to seek divine wisdom.

Of all of the possible blessings that God could have offered to humankind, one is emphasized more than any other. In the course of the first creation, we read:

> So God created humankind in his image . . . male and female he created them. God blessed them, and God said to them, "Be fruitful and multiply." (Gen 1:27–28)

The blessing is for fertility and offspring, and while it is a stretch, God may have felt a need to stress successful procreation as a counter to the threats of infertility and miscarriage that existed in these early days. More telling is one of the ways that God punished Eve after she and Adam had eaten the forbidden fruit. Of all of the possible curses, God says to the woman,

> "I will greatly increase your pangs in childbearing; in pain shall you bring forth children." (Gen 3:16)

And finally, after Adam and Eve were expelled from Eden, as another small hint, we read,

> Now the man knew his wife Eve, and she conceived Cain saying: "I have produced a man with the help of the Lord." Next she bore his brother Abel. (Gen 4:1–2)

This emphasis on fertility is likely to have made childbearing a prime concern for Eve—and Adam—and as a result, any disturbance in this area would be a major disaster for Eve, the bearer of children. Because much of this thinking is indirect and tangential, I turn now to more compelling evidence for my thesis, beginning with a study of relevant present-day archetypes.

ARCHETYPAL EVIDENCE

There are two other avenues of corroboration that seem to be more substantial, one of them an astounding surprise. The first line of support comes from the study of universal archetypes. As I said earlier, the conjecture that a miscarriage was the triggering event that moved Eve to seek divine wisdom is in keeping with the finding that archetypically, humans are motivated to overcome their natural resistance to seek such wisdom only when they have suffered from a death-related trauma. This is a most compelling archetype, and the clinical evidence for its existence is overwhelming. The power of this archetype is the basis on which I proposed in the previous chapter that the deep unconsciously experienced "crime" that prompted Augustine to steal and throw away the pears also may have been a miscarriage by his concubine.

If predator death anxiety and deep unconscious guilt are the issues that propelled Eve to seek divine wisdom, we would conjecture that she needed this wisdom to deeply understand her most unexpected and terrifying experience of miscarrying. But in addition, in going against God's edict and eating the forbidden fruit, Eve may have been implicitly asking God to punish her because on some level she felt guilty over having destroyed her fetus. That said, it also is possible that her search for divine enlightenment about good and evil, and life and death, was carried forward as a more creative, adaptive quest to better understand what she had done so she could find ways to atone for the harm she had caused and make peace with herself—and possibly Adam.

In my therapeutic work with patients, I have found that many women who have had miscarriages or elective abortions have only the slightest awareness that a living being has been destroyed. While they suffer deep unconsciously from severe predator death anxiety and thus with deep unconscious guilt and needs for self-punishment that ultimately are suicidal in nature, they are consciously oblivious to both the nature of their deed and the plight that they are in. Condemned by their archetypically severe and unforgiving deep unconscious system of morality and ethics, which brooks no moral failure, these patients tend to act out in unconsciously driven, self-destructive ways in both their work situations and social lives. They repeatedly make poor job-related and other personal decisions and select inappropriate and hurtful partners, only to blame bad luck for their seemingly endless suffering. They tend to live lives fraught with consciously unrecognized, deep unconsciously orchestrated self-punishments. And because they eschew or have no way of accessing divine insight into the trigger for, and deep unconscious sources of, their difficulties, their troubles go unabated. Their defensive, denial-prone conscious minds are not motivated to seek deep unconscious wisdom, and thus, they are unable to make reparation and to atone for what they have done so they may live in peace with themselves—and others.

In consultation with me, most of these women consciously decide against seeking trigger-decoded, divine wisdom in fear, deep unconsciously, that such efforts will activate their deep unconscious guilt and move them to suicide—suicidal themes abound. Nevertheless, some of these women do enter the Eden-like, secured psychotherapy situation that I offer them and proceed to discover their personal version of death-related divine wisdom by accessing the workings of their own deep unconscious god of wisdom. With much effort and in the face of strong resistances, they are able to awaken to the reality of death and of the death that they have caused, and to thereby open pathways to deep insight and lasting relief from the deep unconscious guilt with which they suffer. They are able to make genuine, deep unconsciously directed efforts at atonement and self-forgiveness, however painful the realities and truths may be. In this way, they revitalize their lives, make peace with themselves, and live far better lives for having done so. They are Eve's true heirs and they are extraordinarily heroic. And like Eve, all of this comes to pass because they have been able to defy the denial-of-death archetype that drives humans away from seeking divine wisdom and toward either divine ignorance or blind faith in God.

EVE'S PARTNER

Before I turn to a final piece of evidence for my thinking about Eve, I want to ask another vital question: If Eve had indeed been pregnant and miscarried, who fathered the fetus? Leaving God aside (as a father, he comes up solely in the story of Jesus Christ), there are only two possibilities: Adam or the serpent. And there are clues that support each of them as the father of the lost fetus.

The first hint that Adam was the father is that he too eats the forbidden fruit along with Eve. While he is silent on the matter, this may well represent his own need for divine wisdom following a death-related trauma in which he played a part. Present-day archetypes indicate that men who are party to miscarriages and abortions, even when they play no other role than having impregnated the woman, deep unconsciously see themselves as having a full share of responsibility regarding what has happened—they tend to suffer in much the same way that the aborting woman suffers.

When the Lord God discovers that Adam and Eve have transgressed, he asks Adam if he had eaten from the tree of which he commanded him not to eat. Adam replies,

> "The woman whom you gave to be with me, she gave me fruit from the tree and I ate." (Gen 3:12)

Adam blames Eve for his transgression, and this could well imply that he is holding her responsible for the miscarriage to which he had been a party.

(But then again, Eve turns around and blames the serpent, so we must wonder if he is the culprit after all.) Further support for the idea that Adam is the father of the lost fetus is suggested by the sudden shift in both himself and Eve from an absence of shame over their nakedness to the need to cover themselves after they ate the forbidden fruit. This speaks for the likelihood that they had shared a traumatic, sexual triggering event that had evoked in both of them a sense of embarrassment and feelings of vulnerability to, and the need to know about, death. In addition, Adam is punished with a kind of future barrenness (which does not fully prevail, as he soon will impregnate Eve and have children) and with a return to the dust from which he was created and born.

All of this adds up to an admittedly tentative case in the Bible for Adam being the father of the child whom Eve may well have lost. There is one more clue to his paternity, but before I bring it up, let's look at the case for the serpent having impregnated Eve.

First, there is the serpent's role in assuring Eve that she will survive acquiring divine wisdom; he seems to have a personal stake in her doing so. Comments that fly in the face of God's pronouncements tend to be personally and deeply motivated and triggered by being party to a death-related trauma. Then too Eve blames him for her transgression, suggesting that he was a party to the triggering event that moved her to act as she did. In addition, the surety with which he reassures Eve that she will not die if she eats the forbidden fruit suggests, as I commented earlier, that the serpent himself had already done so. If this is the case, his participation in a miscarriage by Eve could account for his need for this kind of wisdom. Beyond this, all we have to go on are his punishments from the Lord God:

> Upon your belly you shall go, and dust you shall eat all the days of your life. I will put enmity between you and the woman, and between your off-spring and hers; he will strike your head, and you will strike his heel. (Gen 3:14–15)

While these punishments could simply be the serpent's due for having reassured Eve that she could survive gaining divine wisdom, there are allusions here to eating dust, becoming enemy to the woman, and to the enmity between their offspring. In addition, God's punishment of Eve includes her being subservient to Adam, which may have been a reaction to her having been disloyal to him. This would imply that Eve had participated in a first sin by being unfaithful to Adam—to which she added so-called sins of violating the boundary set by the Lord God regarding the tree of divine knowledge and, as she deep unconsciously experienced it, the sin of destroying her fetus.

While incest is ignored in such edicts as the Ten Commandments but forbidden in Leviticus, it goes unpunished in Genesis, as seen in the story of Lot and his two daughters, in which incest is committed twice and ignored by God after each of the deeds is done. On the other hand, the threat of adultery does appear in Genesis, and God treats it as a sexual sin—the first of its kind. The possibility of adultery is the trigger for the first dream in the Bible, which is dreamt by King Abimelech while Abraham's wife, Sarah, is in bed with him. In fear of being executed if it were known that she is his wife, Abraham tells a half lie to the king by informing him that Sarah is his sister—actually, she is his wife and half sister. In the king's dream, God appears and warns him that he will die if he has sex with Sarah—which he has not as yet done, and with that warning, forgoes. Clearly, the warning is against an act of adultery. Given that here too we are dealing with archetypes, it may well be, then, that God's severe punishments of the serpent and Eve had to do first and foremost with their having committed the unmentioned sin of adultery.

These conflicting clues as to the paternity of the hypothesized fetus and the lack of a basis for a definitive conclusion would compel us to keep an open mind on both issues: Did Eve suffer a miscarriage, and if so, who in her small world was the father? However, there is one last piece of evidence that re-markably seems to answer both questions, so let's get to it at once.

THE TALE OF LILITH AND ADAM

Months after I had formulated the thesis that Eve had suffered a miscarriage, I found unexpected support for my thinking in the Midrash and Talmud, the books that record elaborations on the stories in the Bible made by early-day rabbis. Based on the Bible's two allusions to God's creation of men and women, several of these rabbis believed that Adam had two wives, that is, that he had a wife before he married Eve. His first wife's name was Lilith, and the story is told that when she refused to lie beneath Adam in intercourse and then abandoned him, he complained to God about her behavior. God responded by punishing Lilith by making her kill one hundred newborn children each week, including some of her own.

In a few words, then, Adam's first wife was the killer of newborn babies!

Lilith can be taken as a representation of the shadow side of Eve. As such, this tale is a stunning validation of my proposal that Eve suffered a miscar-riage, which created her need for divine, death-related wisdom. In addition, since Adam is Lilith's partner and the serpent is not part of the story, this ad-dendum supports the idea that he, rather than the serpent, was the father of the fetus whom Eve miscarried. That said, however, his lack of motivation re-garding the quest for divine wisdom immediately comes to mind and raises fresh doubts regarding Eve's hypothesized pregnancy and miscarriage. As

Freud (1918) said on closing his discussion of whether his patient's—the Wolf Man—primal scene memories were real or fantasied, about the paternity of this hypothetically aborted fetus I must conclude for the moment, *non liquet* (it is not clear).

LAST WORDS ON EDEN

I have taken a long, hard look at the stories of creation and Eden in order to establish some basic ideas regarding human nature and the transcendental God, whom the Bible tells us created the universe and its subuniverses, and humankind, and all other living beings, a God who then participated in the first drama of human life on earth. My central concerns have been identifying the archetypal dangers humans face as they move through life, the kind of knowledge that they need to deal most effectively with the challenges that inevitably arise in the course of this journey, and the role that God plays in assisting or opposing them in this crucial pursuit. The opening chapters of Genesis are focused on these archetypal issues.

As for danger situations, it seems clear from the story of Eden that the prospect of death and the three kinds of death anxiety it evokes are what most threaten human life and drive both human creativity and human madness, as well as our inclinations to act morally or immorally as the case may be. Death and death anxiety create a fundamental need for the acquisition of divine knowledge in order to understand and cope with the deepest intricacies of life and death. However, satisfying this need meets with unforeseen, natural, denial-based defenses that unconsciously determine which kind of knowledge a person will seek—mundane or divine. Naïvely, we would have expected that humans would insist on gaining the most profound and effective adaptive wisdom available to them. But because divine wisdom is linked to terrifying death-related traumas, this seldom turns out to be the case. Instead, the prevailing archetype is in keeping with God's first commandment to not seek divine wisdom lest it cause you to die—or to be painfully aware of death. It is only the rare Eve who will, in the face of a death-related trauma, defy this avoidance-of-divine-wisdom archetype and seek out such gifted and sacred, unequivocally healing, knowledge.

The serpent is the advocate for acquiring divine wisdom, and he speaks for the belief that humans can deal deeply and incisively with death without succumbing to the anxieties and pressures this causes. He is joined in this belief by Eve and by a very passive Adam. And yet, because the serpent offered advice that prompted Eve to go against God's edict and commit a sin, he is seen as the devil or the devil's disciple. This view is reinforced because gaining divine wisdom brings death full force into human life, ends our stay in paradise, and by virtue of the unmanageable death anxieties that humans then experience, motivates and brings evil actions into the world, actions designed at bottom to deny one's personal vulnerability to death.

In this context, we need to appreciate that countless people have lived their lives without acquiring divine wisdom. More often than not, however, this lack of wisdom has been responsible for much devastation and suffering—past, present, and most likely future as well. Mundane wisdom offers little or no protection against deep unconscious death anxiety and enables us to cope in only very limited and generally inadequate ways with consciously perceived, death-related experiences. This type of wisdom is conscious system–based and as such is grounded in defensiveness and denial; it thereby is the cause of many death-defying, evil, and sinful actions enacted in the service of such denial. All in all, awareness of death has opened the door to evil in the world, but that door can be shut, even if partially, only through the acquisition of divine wisdom—short of that, evil easily dominates the world at large.

We need to realize, then, that while Eve went to the tree of knowledge to gain divine wisdom, what she got—and we may think of it as what God granted her—was an acute, conscious awareness of death and her mortality. This is not unlike what happened to Oedipus went he went to the oracle of Delphi to learn the identity of his parents—all he got was the prediction that he would murder his father and sleep with his mother. This knowledge unconsciously drove his actions for the rest of his life. This was true of Eve as well in that, while the Bible does not spell out the happenings of the rest of her days, we can suspect that in being given an explicit awareness of death, she had been gifted with the source of divine knowledge, but most probably, as present-day archetypes tell us, deep unconsciously rather than consciously. God did not present a detailed compendium of divine insights to her in a manner similar to his delivery of the Ten Commandments, which define aspects of an archetypal moral code. Instead, he gave Eve deep unconscious divine wisdom and a life with a well-defined identity. She may or may not have subsequently accessed this wisdom, although given that her son murdered his brother, it seems likely that she quickly succumbed to the avoidance archetype—a common regression among divine wisdom seekers to this very day. On this basis, Eve would represent the rare human who seeks and acquires a measure of divine wisdom only to typically retreat from the quest soon after this happens.

The serpent's advocacy for the human acquisition of divine wisdom opened the door to the human awareness of death, which in turn is the root cause of sinning and engaging in evil acts. The realization that death-related divine wisdom is healing and the basis for a truly moral life on the one hand, while on the other, that the death anxiety to which it is linked is the root source of evil, helps to account for the contradictory views of the serpent to be found in the Christian Bible as compared to Gnostic Christian and other writings (Kelly 2006). The serpent is the devil in the first source, while he is divine and healing in the second. Indeed, in some Gnostic writings, God is seen as the devil and the serpent as the true God. Adaptive studies of Eden provide reasons to support both views.

As for the Lord God, whom we meet long before he has made his covenant with Abraham and the Hebrew people, he is strikingly inconsistent in his dealings with humankind. While he makes a compassionate gesture in assisting Adam and Eve in dealing with their nakedness and thus with death and their existential death anxieties, he also does a great deal to render them especially vulnerable to death-related dangers and concerns. As noted, he first creates humans with what appears to be both divine wisdom and immortality, but in his second go around, he takes both of these gifts away from them. His uncertainties and ambivalence about allowing humans to possess sacred wisdom are further reflected in the manner in which he structures Eden. On the one hand, humans are crafted solely with common wisdom, but they are placed in a setting where the tree of divine wisdom stands in the center of the garden. God then forbids humans to eat from this luscious tree under penalty of death. If ever there was a set of mixed messages, there it is. Yahweh appears, then, to have some basic problems in dealing with death and death anxiety, and it seems to have greatly affected his creation of, and dealings with, humankind.

We might well wonder what kind of wisdom the Lord God possesses. Jung has seen Yahweh as nonreflective and without an unconscious mind, which is the locale of divine wisdom (Jung 1958; Edinger 1987). Yet even here God's uncertainties seem to prevail: He promises Adam and Eve death if they eat the forbidden fruit, but they do not die; instead they become acutely aware of death. He punishes the rebellious couple, expels them from Eden, and blocks their path to the tree of eternal life, yet he also clothes them so as to protect then in some way from the ravages of death and death anxiety that they are now fated to experience. Inconsistent in his dealings with death and in his offer of help to humans to cope with these issues seems to best describe the God of creation.

Finally, it is well to notice that while wisdom, sin, and death are at issue, neither evil nor morality are as yet manifestly in the picture. This too speaks for failed wisdom and unmastered death anxiety as the fundamentals from which evil and immorality emerge. None of the characters in Eden behave immorally, even though they do participate in sinning against God. There is a sense of guilt reflected in Adam's blaming Eve for their forbidden act, and in

Eve's trying to blame the serpent for what she did. To sin against God is in principle immoral, but sinning to gain divine wisdom does not appear to be a way of harming either God or other humans. In any case, moral issues arise immediately after the couple has left Eden and borne two sons, Cain and Abel. So let's turn now to this story so we can see what more it tells us about how the God of Genesis dealt with death and death anxiety, and the extent to which he did or did not eventually help humans to deal effectively with this ever-present threat, the anxieties it arouses, and the evil it can cause when these anxieties go unchecked and unresolved.

6

Cain and Abel

The first story after Adam and Eve are expelled from Eden touches on each of the three forms of death anxiety. The couple has two sons, Cain and Abel. When God accepts Abel's offering but not Cain's, Cain kills his brother. God discovers the crime and punishes Cain by making him a wanderer, yet he protects him by marking his forehead and swearing to avenge anyone who tries to punish him for his murderous act. In time, Cain and his offspring are the founders of humankind's first biblical city and civilization—indications of the creative and reparative side of death anxiety.

This is a tale of predator and prey. The Bible does not, however, describe any predatory death anxiety in Abel even though he is the victim of a murderer—he seems to go to his death without protest. For his part, Cain probably suffered from existential death anxiety when he realized that God would not accept his offering and thereby bless and protect him from harm. Indications are that this is an instance of unconscious death anxiety that was covered over by the evident anxieties evoked by being an unfavored sibling—that is, sibling rivalry issues as a mundane explanation of an act that is more deeply caused by existential death anxiety. This latter anxiety is the apparent source of the sinful violence that Cain then commits in a likely archetypal attempt to reassure himself that in his abandonment by God and his unprotected vulnerability to harm, rather than his being fated to become death's victim, he can be its cause. In addition, after committing the crime, Cain evidently suffers from intense predator death anxiety and conscious and deep unconscious guilt, which are manifested in his fear that he will be murdered for having murdered his brother—beneath the fear is the deep unconscious wish. All in all, this sequence of events appears to be a compelling example of how mundane wisdom is unable to offer sufficient insight to allay activated existential death anxieties and how these unmastered anxieties are, in turn, the source of evil acts.

In respect to God's role in these happenings, his seemingly arbitrary rejection of Cain's offering appears to be the source of Cain's existential death anxieties and the triggering event that leads to Cain's act of murder. God seems to be absent or to look away when Cain takes Abel into the field with the intention of murdering him. And after the crime, God reacts with mixed messages in that he both punishes and protects Cain, acting it would seem on the basis of his own predator death anxiety and deep unconscious guilt for having abetted Cain's murderous act. God also maintains an uncertain position in respect to how those who commit murder should be dealt with.

Through it all, God does little or nothing to reduce human violence or to allay the troublesome death anxieties experienced by Cain and possibly Abel. Instead, he acts in ways that seem to increase the levels of both uncalled-for aggression and death anxiety, and he also fails to offer clear moral guidelines in respect to wanton, evil acts of harm.

These patterns run like red threads through the Hebrew Testament. They reflect some of Yahweh's greatest weaknesses and suggest again that God himself was suffering from unresolved death anxieties that interfered with his effectiveness as a just overseer of human life. These observations also speak for unconsciously transmitted, basic flaws in Jewish morality and notable inadequacies in their adaptations to death-related incidents, responses that inevitably mirror the messages they have received from their God. Given that God should, in principle, be helping humans to adapt to their environments and cope with threats to their lives, we can only wonder how allowing for and supporting irrationally violent solutions to such threats can have positive effects. If such effects are not forthcoming, we must consider the thesis that the Hebrew God essentially has failed in his basic mission.

A CLOSER LOOK AT THE STORY

Adam and Eve have been banned from paradise and prevented from attaining eternal life. With that, life in a less than ideal world has begun, and the story of Cain and Abel gives us our first opportunity to observe humankind and God as they operate in this environment. We are told at the beginning of this story that the man knew his wife, Eve, who bore Cain with the help of the Lord, and she then bore Abel. Cain becomes a tiller of the ground and Abel a keeper of sheep. Each brings offerings to the Lord God, who has regard only for the offerings from Abel. Cain is angry; his countenance falls. We then read that the Lord God said to Cain, "Why are you angry; why has your countenance fallen? If you do well, will you not be accepted? And if you do not do well, sin is lurking at the door; its desire is for you, but you must master it." (Gen 4:6–7)

Cain invites Abel out to the field, rises up against him, and kills him.

Then the Lord said to Cain, "Where is your brother Abel?" He said, "I do not know; Am I my brother's keeper?" And the Lord said, "What have you done? Listen; your brother's blood is crying out to me from the ground." (Gen 4:9–10)

The Lord curses the ground so that it will no longer yield to Cain's strength and tells Cain that he will be a fugitive and wanderer on the earth. Cain finds the punishment unbearable and expects that anyone who meets him in the course of his travels will kill him to avenge the murder of his brother. But the Lord says,

"Not so! Whoever kills Cain will suffer a sevenfold vengeance." (Gen 4:15)

So the Lord puts a mark on Cain so no one will kill him. Cain then leaves the presence of the Lord and goes to Nod, east of Eden. He knows his wife, and she bears Enoch, after which Cain builds a city and names it after his son. The Bible goes on to name the descendants of Enoch, including the third generation, Lamech, who speaks of having killed a younger man for striking him, for which he expects seventy-seven fold vengeance. The section concludes with Adam knowing Eve again, and she bears a son to replace Abel, whom she names Seth.

What are the archetypal messages of this tale, the first story out of Eden? And what does it tell us about humankind and God?

In light of our orientation we may make immediate note of certain features of what happened. Strikingly, this story is not about the acquisition of knowledge or divine wisdom; if anything, it is about the failure to possess and invoke this kind of adaptive knowledge. Humankind evidently has not benefited manifestly from the acquisition by Adam and Eve of divine wisdom, which subsequently is granted only to a few selected biblical figures like Joseph, who is uniquely and wisely able to interpret Pharaoh's dreams.

As for the problems of death and death anxiety, they now loom large as humankind's basic, archetypal challenges. In this connection, the story explicitly introduces issues that touch on both the predatory death anxiety that is experienced by an intended victim of harm (however minimally it is developed here) and the predator death anxiety of a murderer who then experiences and yet objects to the need to be punished for his terrible deed.

As for God, he is asked to deal with human appeals for blessings, and when he acts with distinct prejudice, he is compelled to respond to an act of murder. In this regard, there are two arenas that touch on the issue of God's ethical fairness to humankind: First, the call for him to treat all supplicants as equals, and second, his responsibility to offer a clear and consistent set of guidelines for a moral and ethical life. In this regard, it is well to appreciate that the Lord God has, to this point in the Bible, pronounced but a single stricture and boundary, which served, as we know, to forbid humans to acquire divine knowledge. He has not defined the features of a moral life and has said nothing of murder—that is, until now—and has not commented on or forbidden other kinds of patently immoral and sinful offenses. Later on in Genesis, several implied moral strictures will appear—for example, against murder, as is seen here after the fact; evil (which is only vaguely defined), as indicated in this story and when God brings on the flood because of the predominance of human wickedness and evil acts; and adultery, as seen in the story of Abraham, Sarah, and King Abimelech. But on the whole, the God of Genesis does not present humans with an explicit set of moral guidelines. In addition, he responds in a mixed manner to the immoral acts with which he is confronted. We will have to wait until Exodus and Numbers for his first definitive statements on human morals.

Finally, we should pause to consider what are the first allusions to evil in the Bible. God does not explicitly accuse Adam, Eve, or the serpent of sinning against him. But when Cain becomes angry and his countenance falls after God rejects his offerings, God seems to foresee a turn to violence. In issuing his unheeded warning to Cain, God alludes to sin as if it were a living being who, if not resisted, will (unconsciously?) cause Cain to act in an evil manner. This, rather than the appearance of the serpent in Eden, may well be the first implied allusion in the Bible to Satan as an enemy of God and as the source of sin and evil.

THE VICISSITUDES OF WISDOM

In terms of knowledge and wisdom, there is a telling sequence in these early passages in the Bible:

First, divine ignorance sustains life in Eden.
Then acquiring divine wisdom brings with it an acute awareness of death and human mortality.
This acquisition also ends humankind's stay in Eden.

Neither Cain nor Abel, nor their parents, show any indication of consciously possessing and making use of divine wisdom in coping with
their death-related issues and death anxieties.

The story of Cain and Abel lends further support to the thesis that while
Adam and Eve became aware of death and their personal mortality, and while
this may have afforded them momentary flashes of conscious divine insight,
they did not develop a lasting conscious appreciation for this kind of knowledge, did not apply it to their lives, and did not teach it to their offspring. This
supports the conjecture God had secretly decided on a compromise in respect
to Adam and Eve's possession of divine wisdom, that he placed it in their
deep unconscious minds where they did not have direct access to its contents
and resources and thus could not make ready use of their hard-won wisdom.
Alternatively, if, rather than holding God accountable, we think of this outcome as psychological behaviors of Eve and Adam, we would say that the
couple—and Eve in particular—at first acted counter to the avoidance-of-
divine-knowledge archetype, only to quickly succumb to it.

Both versions of what happened have grains of truth to them. In either
case, it reflects another wisdom archetype in that gaining divine wisdom
evokes strong needs to return to divine ignorance in a never-ending psychical struggle—then and now. The archetype that entails a basic dread of
gaining and being consciously aware of death-related, deep unconscious
wisdom is far more powerful than the need to gain such knowledge, and this
dread persists to this very day. It appears, then, that for humans to cope successfully with death and death anxiety, the awareness of death needs to be
coupled with the acquisition of consciously usable divine wisdom. The
Lord God did not permit this to happen, and as a result, humans were faced
with death-related issues but lacked the effective conscious wisdom they
needed to cope with these issues—a most unfortunate and fateful outcome
that also persists to this very day.

Eve is reminiscent of the many patients I see, male and female, who begin
narrative therapy with me and thus engage in the pursuit of deep unconscious,
divine wisdom, only to flee therapy driven by an unconscious terror of the
grim insights that they begin to encode and trigger decode in response to
death-related triggering events that bring up their experience of past death-
related traumas. Even those who stay in treatment continuously alternate between encoding and accessing divine knowledge and shutting off this kind of
encoded imagery, a trend that they fortify by continuously turning away from
or avoiding the proper trigger decoding of their narrative themes.

The human preference to live life based on common or mundane knowledge and to eschew the use of divine wisdom has, however, interfered with

the religious and nonreligious pursuit of individual and collective peace on earth. This arises because of an archetypal fear of activating past death-related traumas and engaging in the brutal exploration of the nature, meanings, and sources of these incidents so as to neutralize their effects. This process evokes daunting experiences of helplessness in the face of life-threatening events, natural and human caused, and in response to the eventuality of personal demise; it also evokes rage against oneself and others for the harm involved. These insights help to clarify the compassionate and utilitarian aspects of God's opposition to the human acquisition of divine wisdom, as well as why, even though God seems to have begrudgingly provided this knowledge to humankind, he did so in a way that made it extremely difficult to access consciously.

There is, then, no indication that Cain or Abel had access to or made use of divine wisdom. In fact, their story is archetypal in respect to the consequences of failing to develop and turn to such knowledge in living one's life. Only divine wisdom about the existential and predatory death anxieties that he was experiencing could have enabled Cain to curtail his rage at his brother when God accepted Abel's offering but not his. The lack of divine wisdom also set the stage for this outcome because in the absence of such knowledge, humans inevitably compete for God's blessings and other kinds of reassurances against death. Thus, the failure to be blessed evokes unmanageable death anxieties and a turn to violence against and murder of others, especially those with whom we compete for blessings or who have already been blessed. Interreligious wars are based in part on these dynamics.

Both Cain and Abel sought God's blessings, and Abel was immediately favored, but Cain was not. While I will soon discuss God's contribution to the outcome of this story, this kind of inequality among humans is all but inevitable, be it parents with their children, teachers with their students, employers with their employees, or the like. Enacted in muted form, the murderous rage in Cain toward his favored sibling reflects the human archetypal response to these inequitable, rivalrous situations.

As for why murder eventuates, as I said, it seems reasonable to see the request for God's blessings as implying the wish for much more than productive harvests and ample offspring. At bottom, it expresses the archetypal wish for protection against harm and death. Thus, it is likely that existential death anxiety motivated Cain's murder of Abel—and that this is the basic underlying issue in all present-day rivalrous situations. In addition, once death anxiety has been activated, there is an immediate need for relief. Thus, God's promise to Cain of future blessings and his warning that impatience will render Cain vulnerable to sin are of no avail.

Implied here is the idea that Cain was, for reasons not mentioned in the Bible, suffering from existential death anxiety when he made his offering to God and that he had frantically turned to God for a blessing of long life that would have alleviated these anxieties. When God failed to bless him, Cain turned to violence and murdered his brother. He did so to get rid of his rival for God's favors—God did, after all, show an inclination for favoritism in blessing Abel but not Cain. But as I said, the act of murder also probably was an attempt by Cain to alleviate his existential death anxieties in that, as we have seen, the act of killing someone else creates the illusion or delusion that one is not vulnerable to death himself or herself—the killer is the cause of death rather than its victim. This may well be the unconscious motive for Cain's act—a hidden, unconscious motive that makes his murdering his brother seem on the surface to be quite irrational. This sense of illogic also seems to stem from the likelihood that Cain's murder of Abel was a displaced expression of rage against the Lord God, who seems to have irrationally favored one brother over the other and thereby to have preyed on and harmed Cain—archetypically, violence tends to beget greater violence.

This first story after Eden also supports the thesis that the combination of uncontrolled death anxiety and a lack of divine insight into these anxieties are the basic sources of sin and evil. Many of the subsequent events recorded in the Old Testament lend support to this archetypal connection. Examples include Jacob's sinful deception of his father so as to gain the birthrights—that is, protection against death—that are afforded to the firstborn son and the evil attempt by Joseph's brothers to murder him because he was the favored and protected child of their father, Jacob.

Basic to situations of violence is the experience of predatory death anxiety by the intended victim and predator death anxiety by the perpetrator. Predatory death anxiety tends to prompt the mobilization of the physical and psychological resources of the intended victim, and the effort is made to garner the strength and ability to call forth defensive and offensive efforts to destroy the threatening individual first. In Abel's situation, there is no sign of such efforts on his part, only a sense that he passively submitted to the unexpected act of his brother. This situation has its parallel in the later story of Abraham and his son Isaac, whose life Abraham plans to sacrifice to show his faith in God. Isaac too is largely passive as he aids his father in arranging for his own slaughter. However, as the climax builds, he does show signs of predatory death anxiety—he becomes alarmed when he realizes that there is no sacrificial animal in sight. None of this is evident in Abel.

On the other hand, Cain's predator death anxiety and unconscious guilt for having murdered his brother loom large in the aftermath of his murderous act. God punishes Cain in two ways that are reminiscent of his punishments of Adam:

> "When you till the ground, it will no longer yield to you its strength; you will be a fugitive and wanderer on the earth." (Gen 4:12)

Here too we may think of these punishments as coming from God on high or from Cain's own inner god and his deep unconscious system of morality and ethics, which will respond archetypically to the crime that he has committed. As I have indicated, the archetypal self-punishment for harm done to others—that is, for sins and misdeeds committed against others—is that of death, usually in the form of suicide or its equivalent in self-harmful decisions and behaviors. All of this is the result of the severity of the standards and demands of the deep unconscious system of morality and ethics, which unconsciously orchestrates terrible but real consequences for immoral acts, penalties whose actual sources go unrecognized by the conscious mind. Of note in the case of Cain is the fact that he, rather than God, pronounces his own death sentence, and for some reason, again unrecorded in the Bible, God elects to protect him and spare his life.

Cain pleads to God,

> "My punishment is greater than I can bear! Today you have driven me away from the soil, and I shall be hidden from your face; I shall be a fugitive and a wanderer on the earth, and anyone who meets me may kill me." (Gen 4:13–14)

God responds by saying,

> "Not so! Whoever kills Cain will suffer a sevenfold vengeance." And the Lord put a mark on Cain, so that no one who came upon him would kill him. (Gen 4:15)

The end of this story is generally understood to be the building of the first metropolis and the beginnings of civilization as recorded in the Bible. It is striking that these developments are preceded by, and in some sense are the result of, an apparent act of fratricide. This development reflects another death-related archetype, a proclivity to respond to predator death anxiety and deep unconscious guilt in part with constructive, creative forms of reparation and atonement. A similar expression of this archetype was seen many centuries later when the great city of Rome was founded, first, on the destruction or death of Troy, and second, on the basis of another murder of a brother by a brother—the killing of Remus by his twin brother Romulus.

It would seem that the best way to account for this sequence of events is that predators who are plagued by predator death anxiety and deep unconscious guilt not only enact unconsciously wrought punishments, but also may experience a deep unconscious need for atonement and forgiveness that prompts them to carry out unconsciously wrought deeds of reparation that are extremely salutary and life giving. Thus, unconscious guilt over harming others can wreak havoc with a human life because it evokes unconscious needs for punishment that translate into unconsciously orchestrated acts of self-harm. But as is true of death and death anxiety in all their guises, the destructive side of death has its counterpart in a reparative side—in seeking various forms of redemption. Even so, an individual needs to have extraordinary, God-given or natural gifts to respond to unconscious guilt in this manner, so we may well be seeing the hand of God or an unusual form of human ingenuity in the partly positive outcome of these otherwise gruesome tales. We can only hope that these reparative gestures will serve as a model for world leaders and individual humans today and for years to come.

The death-related archetype of the wish to murder those whom we envy also is with us to this very day. Competing religions, nonreligious belief systems, cultures, countries, and individuals who should be able to live side by side in peace all too often are unable to find the means to do so. Belief systems pertaining to God tend to be fiercely competitive rather than easily compatible with each other, so rivalries for God's blessings have had devastating consequences. The principle that the search for love and blessings is framed as a wish that excludes rivals does not augur well for the future of humankind. It is a principle that needs to be deeply appreciated, and its deeper, unconscious roots in existential death anxiety need to be understood so ways can be found to modify or lessen the effects of this harmful archetypal law of evil human need and behavior.

GOD'S ROLE IN THE STORY

The story of Cain and Abel is, then, a story about death and the activation of the three forms of death anxiety—existential, predator, and predatory. What role does God play either in evoking these anxieties or, most importantly, in helping Cain and Abel to deal with and minimize their occurrence and effects?

At first, God is part of the problem rather than part of its solution because he sets the stage for the murder of Abel by accepting his offering and blessing him, but refusing Cain's offering for no apparent reason. God does not appear to be either wise or omniscient in that he does not seem to understand the deeper effects of his favoritism, fails to foresee that his reassurances to Cain are falling on deaf ears, and does not anticipate that Cain will murder Abel. Strikingly, then, he appears to be operating on the basis of mundane rather than divine wisdom, and he is affected by all of the limitations and failings of common knowledge. In addition to creating a cause for homicide, he also fails to honor his blessing of Abel by protecting him from his brother. God thereby contributes to Abel's murder twice over. All in all, he seems to be both unreliable and untrustworthy; here too his own unresolved death anxieties may be playing a role in his behavior.

After the deed is done, God detects the murder of Abel, for which he holds Cain accountable, and he punishes him accordingly, but not to the extreme of having him executed or seeing to it that he dies as payment for his heinous crime. But then comes another of God's dramatic inconsistencies: When Cain appeals to God for protection against vengeance for his crime, God complies. He elects to bless a murderer! The implication is that God has not as yet developed a clear sense of morality—and despite the offer of the Ten Commandments to Moses, there are few signs that the Hebrew God, Yahweh, ever does so.

It would seem then that by and large, Yahweh is inclined to promote rather than minimize the human turn to violence, and he also is strikingly inconsistent in responding to violent deeds. Paradoxically, to this point in the Bible, the only human whose life he protects from death is that of a murderer. This cannot be the basis for a sound approach to helping humans deal constructively with death and death anxiety or for an effective, peace-loving kind of human morality. We seem to be coming up against further indications of God's own conflicts around issues pertaining to violence and death, and his inability to come up with a soundly adaptive, fully moral means of dealing with these inclinations. If we try to conceive of how God is trying to help humans to deal with death and death anxiety, and to survive in the world at large, all that can be said is that he favors violent solutions, accepts sinful, immoral acts, and advocates living by the sword. This does not sound like a recipe for peace on earth.

ANOTHER SURPRISING CONJECTURE

One question remains unanswered: Why did God choose to protect a murderer from harm and from a punishment that seems justified in light of the crime committed? This reaction, which runs counter to the deep unconscious archetype that insists on punishment for harming others, seems to be quite out of character for a deity. There is, of course, an evident motive for his decision in his awareness that he contributed to Abel's murder by unfairly favoring him over his brother and by not protecting Abel from the consequences of his partiality. In this light, God can be said to have punished Cain because he had sinned and acted in an evil and immoral manner, but protected him because of his own contribution to what happened.

There is, however, another less evident but possible reason for God's protecting Cain even though God held him partially accountable for Abel's death. My offer of this conjecture is based in part on Cain's reaction to God's query as to where his brother was, namely, his denial that he is his brother's keeper. Murderers do not, as a rule, deny their crime to God. In addition, I base my proposal on repeated clinical observations that speak for another extremely powerful deep unconscious, death-related archetype, one that is quite fateful for humankind: Universally, whenever someone close to us dies, no matter how little a role we have played in what happened, we unconsciously (and at times consciously as well) hold ourselves accountable for his or her death. From this it follows that God may have protected Cain from vengeance because he knew that Cain did not actually murder Abel.

This possibility is supported by Cain's initial denial of responsibility for his brother's disappearance even though he expects to be blamed and even executed for Abel's death. In addition, there is the way in which Cain responded creatively to the loss of his brother. Had Cain actually killed Abel, the archetypal reaction most likely would have been conscious and deep unconscious guilt and unconsciously orchestrated acts of self-punishment with little if anything in the way of reparation. In contrast, in cases of self-blame for a crime not committed, efforts at atonement and reparation are more likely to occur even though they may not lessen continued efforts at self-punishment. That said, it is entirely possible that Cain did not murder Abel, who died either of natural causes or at the hand of some other living being. Cain may have failed to protect his sibling, and this would account for both his innocence and his guilt, or he may have taken responsibility for the death of his brother even though he knew consciously, wishes to the contrary, that he had none.

This brings me to my next unexpected discovery. It too comes from Augustine's *Confessions* (1961) and another of his purported sins. In this case, the evil deed is a repetition of Cain's sin, which took shape as Augustine's holding himself accountable for the death from illness of a brotherly friend. Let's turn now to that story.

7

Augustine's Reliving of the Sin of Cain

It was soon after writing the first draft of my archetype-based discussion of Cain and Abel and offering the conjecture that Cain may not have murdered his brother that I discovered Wills's previously mentioned book on Augustine's sins (Wills 2003). As was the case with his repetition of Adam's sin, Augustine's writings on his reenactment of Cain's sin were accompanied by extensive narrative associations. In this case, they reveal a major, death-related triggering event for his so-called sin, and they also facilitate the formulation of the archetypal deep unconscious factors that contributed to his experience. As we shall see, his material fully supports the thesis that I had developed on the basis of trigger decoding dreams from my patients who appeared to be redreaming and reliving the sin of Cain, which Augustine believed he had acted out. But this is, of course, how archetypes operate within and on human beings—they are both eternal and endlessly repetitive, and both redreamt and reenacted.

Enactments are dreams lived out, and they are a reminder that deep unconscious experiences not only determine the encoded images in our dreams, but also strongly affect our emotional state and how we behave in interacting with others (Langs 1999). By and large, it is very difficult to ascertain the deep unconscious perceptions, meanings, and adaptive processing efforts that lie behind a seemingly irrational act when we examine the act on its own. To discover the deep unconscious meanings of our behaviors, we need to have narrative associations that arise in response to what happened or a contemporaneous dream replete with narrative associations to the dream's elements—a dream that has been dreamt in the context of the action under scrutiny.

In my work as an adaptive psychotherapist, I have again and again seen that patients both relive and redream the archetypal tales in the Bible. As I said earlier, I am not, however, implying that a particular biblical incident is reenacted in the manifest dream, although that may be the case in rare instances. But even in these situations, there is another, probably more threatening and more important story that is being encoded in the same imagery—encoding is an ever-present, God-given or evolved, natural, emotion-related, language-based, biological process. Patients generally do not, for example, simply dream of murdering a sibling whom a parent has favored over them in some manner. Instead, they react to a trigger of this kind with a dream that disguises the hurt and their upsetting view of it, and for that reason, narrative associations are needed to provide the imagery that encodes and reveals in disguise the underlying issues.

Important too is the finding that Bible-related dreams are triggered by current death-related incidents that are comparable to the death-related triggering events that have provoked the actions of the biblical character whose behavior is being archetypically reenacted and redreamt in the present. Much as the past and present go hand in hand, triggers and dreams also form units—similar triggers evoke similar dreams. Identifying an archetypal triggering event often is the key to understanding the deeper factors in a biblical incident.

The stories of the Bible are archetypal in the sense that they are dream-like narratives fraught with deep wisdom whose encoded meanings can be discerned through proper trigger-decoding methods. These efforts depend on recognizing the event to which the person is reacting deep unconsciously. In many cases, the triggers and meanings of triggers that we respond to deep unconsciously—that is, that do not register in awareness and of which we are unaware consciously—are different from and far more powerful than those we react to knowingly. It often is necessary, then, to allow the encoded themes in a dream (or enactment) to lead us to a trigger that has eluded our conscious awareness largely because the triggering event is death related and especially disturbing to our conscious minds. As you might expect, given the anxiety that these triggers evoke, they often are quite difficult to ascertain consciously.

Based on my study of death-related archetypes, I have suggested that there are two possible scenarios in connection with the death of Abel and Cain's role in it—and thus, two possible triggering events that are central to the tale and its meanings. In the first version, which I focused on in the previous chapter, Cain actually murders his brother in a rage over Abel's having received preferred treatment from God. God's rejection of Cain and his favoring Abel are the triggering events, and the story unfolds from there.

But in the second version, Cain does not murder Abel but takes responsibility for his death and, to some extent, accepts the punishments meted out by God for the sinful crime as if he had in fact done the deed. In this case, the triggering event is the death of Abel, and there may also be a prior trigger Cain suffered that made him vulnerable to accepting undeserved responsibility for his brother's death. Each of these versions of the story is archetypal, but each evokes somewhat different encoded narrative imagery, and each leads to a somewhat different interpretation of the incident — and to a distinctive view of God as well.

REDREAMING THE FIRST VERSION OF CAIN AND ABEL'S STORY

I have processed many disguised dreams from patients that point to each of the two proposed versions of the circumstances surrounding the death of Abel. In general, they are dreams triggered by incidents in which a patient has been the unsuccessful rival for the equivalent of God's blessings. The first version of the story is reflected in dreams that involve wishes to harm or murder a more favored rival, while the reliving of this interpretation of the story, which usually but not always falls short of physical violence, involves efforts that are made by the neglected person to psychologically harm or to otherwise cause pain and suffering for the more successful rival.

An example recently presented to me by a therapist who works adaptively involved a young male patient in his early twenties who dreamt of sticking pins in the back of a man with a dark complexion. In associating to the dream, the patient recalled having read of a voodoo doctor who stuck pins in a doll and caused the death of the man whom the doll represented. The request to do this came from a woman who was furious with the victim because he had left her for another woman.

One of the triggering events for the dream was the patient's overhearing a young female apartment-mate, to whom he was strongly attracted, having sex with her boyfriend. Evidently this was a disguised dream of the murder of a successful rival for the favor of a woman whom the patient coveted. But in addition to having had this dream, the patient had acted out his vengeful feelings against his rival by telling the woman in question about some illicit escapades in which his rival had recently engaged and by complaining to their landlord about his late-night visits to their apartment. While certainly not overt murder, the patient was making real efforts to get rid of his more successful competitor for the woman's affections.

There was however a second triggering event for this dream, one that affected the patient unconsciously far more than consciously. As often is the case with unconsciously registered triggers, it involved an intervention that the therapist had made around the ground rules of the patient's psychotherapy—patients' deep unconscious minds are extremely sensitive to this aspect of treatment. The trigger arose because this patient's psychotherapy was covered by an insurance carrier, and the therapist had recently been asked to complete a treatment report for the insurer. In the previous session, the therapist had gone over the report with the patient—it contained very little information, mainly the patient's diagnosis, which had already been transmitted to the insurer along with allusions to his need for further therapy. The patient's dream followed that discussion.

While this may seem to be a minor matter, it involves a departure from the ideal, archetypal framework of psychotherapy in that it violates the patient's uncompromising, deep unconscious need for total privacy and confidentiality. Despite the patient's conscious compliance, it therefore is deep unconsciously viewed by the patient as an evil, immoral act of violence directed at him by the therapist; it compromises the Eden-like conditions of the treatment experience and evokes predatory death anxiety in the patient. Indeed, the deep unconscious wisdom and moral systems are extremely sensitive to the least departure from the ideal conditions of treatment—and of life itself. In any case, in typical fashion, the patient experienced and reacted to his death anxieties quite unconsciously—it could be detected mainly in the association to the dream that involved the murder of the man who had abandoned the woman. In general, the deep unconscious experience of death anxiety is disguised in this manner—an allusion to a triggering event and the appearance in seemingly detached but actually closely linked imagery of a death-related theme.

An additional association to this patient's dream revealed its link to the trigger of the treatment report, which the patient knew about consciously without realizing the meanings he gave to it deep unconsciously. The association was to the patient's internist, who had a dark complexion, and it involved a situation in which the physician had spoken to the patient's mother on the telephone and had revealed that the patient was suffering from a sexually transmitted disease. The patient had felt betrayed by the internist and was infuriated with him; he felt that the doctor was more allied with his mother than with him. The patient was so enraged he could have killed both of them.

Consciously, the patient had fully supported his therapist's sending in the treatment report because he wanted to continue the therapy on that basis. Indeed, he had commented directly (consciously) that it was a routine form that would be processed mechanically and be of no consequence to him. But the dream and his associations show that deep unconsciously, he saw his therapist as betraying him by completing the report and sending it to the insurance company. And even though the report was sent with his best interests in mind, he still saw it as a sign that the therapist favored the insurer over him—and he wanted to murder the therapist for it.

Being defeated in a rivalrous situation is always experienced deep unconsciously as being murdered by the rejecting party and the rival. This is an example of a situation that seems consciously to be unrelated to death and death anxiety, which nonetheless deep unconsciously evokes predatory death anxiety, in response to which the defeated party reacts with predatory vengeance of his or her own. The universal archetype here is a familiar one: the unconscious wish of a defeated rival to murder a more successful contender. It is a variation on the death-related archetype that motivates those who, as victims of one kind or another, experience predatory death anxiety and respond by finding ways to prey on and destroy the perpetrator so they themselves may survive for another day—or longer.

THE SECOND VERSION OF THE STORY

In the second version of the Cain and Abel story, the rivalry between the brothers and God's favoring Abel are background triggering events that set the stage for a different, more immediate death-related triggering incident. The foreground trigger is, then, the death of Abel by some means other than direct harm caused by Cain. Even so, deep unconsciously—and to some extent, consciously—Cain accepts responsibility for his brother's death. This actually is but one subset of a broader death-related archetype in which, as humans, we deep unconsciously take responsibility whenever serious harm or death befalls a loved one, enemy, or rival even when we actually have played little or no role in what happened. This is an extremely common and troublesome archetype that causes much suffering in the person who takes responsibility for what he or she has not done—as we saw with Cain. The archetype also is difficult to identify and deal with because it operates deep unconsciously and eludes direct awareness. Trigger decoding is vital for the discernment of its active presence and telling effects.

The archetype of taking responsibility for harm done to someone with whom one is close evokes deep unconscious needs for punishment and thereby causes much personal suffering. The trigger for the relevant dreams tends to involve an acute trauma—an illness or death—suffered by someone in a person's everyday life. Because these events are death related and usually the source of conflict, they have meanings that are blocked from entering awareness, and they are instead registered and processed deep unconsciously.

Guilt-ridden dreams based on false assumptions of responsibility for harm that befalls someone else are not uncommon among psychotherapy patients.

In addition to triggers that stem from patients' lives outside of therapy, many dramatic instances of this archetype entail responses to something that their therapists have said or done. Most often the trigger involves direct or indirect indications that the therapist is or has been ill or injured. In a well-managed psychotherapy, this triggering experience-intervention takes shape as a therapist manifestly appearing to be ill or his or her suddenly canceling one or more sessions without explaining why. To maintain the ideal ground rules of psychotherapy, therapists should not tell their patients that they are ill or injured. Doing so is inappropriately self-revealing; it violates the ideal archetypal frame that calls for the therapist's relative anonymity without deliberate self-revelations. It is ill-advised and harmful to all concerned, and is experienced deep unconsciously by both patient and therapist as frame violating, immoral, and an appeal for succor from the patient.

To illustrate, I shall first describe a series of dreams reported to a male therapist by several different patients and then, after doing so, identify the triggering event that had evoked the imagery. This will give you an opportunity to identify the repetitive themes in these narratives and to speculate as to what could have happened to evoke them. Triggers evoke encoded themes, so encoded themes reflect their triggers.

One patient, a young man, dreamt that a man in a dark suit was running through a park. Notice that this manifest dream imagery is not overtly death related. Nevertheless, the encoded meanings of the dream will emerge through the patient's associations to its images and will pertain to the death-related trauma in question. Again, this is how we detect the presence of deep unconscious death anxiety.

The patient's first association to the dream was to a park he frequented as a child, a place that recalled many fond memories of playing games with his friends and father. The park also brought to mind a story he had read in the newspaper on the day of the dream; it was about a man in Jordan who was assassinated in a park. There was a horrible picture of the body on the front page of the newspaper. The story prompted the patient to remember something he hadn't recalled in years—an incident in the park of his childhood that had taken place when he was about fourteen years of age. He was riding his bike and he accidentally hit an elderly man who was walking along the path on which he was cycling. The man fell to the ground, and for a minute, the patient thought he was dead. Fortunately, it turned out that he was alive, but the man had fractured his wrist when he tried to break his fall after he was hit by the bike. There was a messy and upsetting lawsuit, and it took the patient years to get over his guilt over the accident—he felt terrible as he spoke about it now.

This *dream-associational network*, as it is called, is typical of the dreams that therapists hear after a particular class of triggering interventions—a term

I use in its broadest sense to include everything of note that a therapist says and does, including his or her appearance. Because of the nature of the triggering incident that had evoked this material, this supervisee-therapist was presented with dream after dream from patient after patient of people killing other people, maiming or harming them, or making them ill. The recollection of these events was accompanied by considerable guilt, some of it conscious and most of it deep unconscious and reflected in the dream images and patients' storied associations. It was quite evident that this therapist's patients were feeling guilty over their role in causing a death-related triggering event that the therapist had inadvertently imposed on them.

Dreams of, and associations related to, the 9/11 disaster also abounded, as did stories like the sinking of the *Titanic*, wartime carnage, the firebombing of Dresden, and more. Patients who had actually caused harm to others—for example, men and women whose children had birth defects or who had been involved in spontaneous miscarriages or elective abortions—had particularly gruesome nightmares of these earlier incidents and of horrendous disasters, planes exploding in midair, and mass killings. Other patients who had suffered the death of a sibling repetitively dreamt different versions of the loss, and with few exceptions, they were, in their associated stories, holding themselves responsible for what had happened.

What then did this therapist do to provoke these dreams? How are they connected with the story of Cain and Abel? And what are their deep unconscious, archetypal meanings?

The answers begin with the identification of the trigger for this dream material: These patients had endured an incident—an intervention created by their therapist—in which he unexpectedly was absent from his office for three weeks. The message he left on his answering machine was to the effect that he had a personal emergency and would be away from his office for at least three weeks—nothing more.

This message is, as noted, in keeping with a feature of the deep unconsciously sought, ideal, Eden-like frame that calls for the relative anonymity of the therapist, with no *deliberate* personal self-revelations. The therapist's adherence to this principle enabled his patients to work over and work through many of their own death-related issues, which were activated by this triggering incident, early-life traumas that had beleaguered them for many years of their lives. Had the therapist offered any particulars regarding his absence, deep unconsciously, his patients would have taken this as an appeal to them for help, and they would have worked over the therapist's need to violate the ideal framework of their therapy and his problems with death and death anxiety far more than, or instead of, dealing with their own issues in this regard.

When the therapist resumed hours, his patients had little to say directly about his absence. Consciously, they made up a variety of excuses for his sudden disappearance—for example, the thought that the therapist had taken an unanticipated vacation, had gone unexpectedly to a professional meeting, or had suffered an illness in, or the death of, a family member. Only when they noticed that their repetitive dreams were filled with stories about illness—for example, people who had cancer, heart attacks, and the like—did they consciously acknowledge having had the passing thought that the therapist might have been seriously ill. Even so, they quickly denied this possibility and dismissed the thought. It took additional repetitive dreams of people who died of various illnesses and injuries for these patients to more definitively acknowledge that they believed that while he was away from his office, the therapist had died, or that on his return, he was going to die quite soon.

While there is, of course, a fantasy element here, it is not based on patients' distortions of the situation with the therapist as caused by early childhood experiences. This is the definition of *transference*—distortions of the present based on confusing it with the past and its traumas and forbidden wishes (Freud 1905, 1923, 1940). Instead, these fantasies are attempts to fill in the gaps left by the information that the therapist had provided his patients regarding his absence from his office. Some of these fantasies or conjectures were made consciously; others, which usually were rather grim yet more on the mark than their conscious speculations, were reflected in his patients' encoded images. As such, they needed to be trigger decoded in light of his extended absence—a process that met with considerable resistance from his patients. These ideas are, then, conscious and deep unconscious assumptions and speculations based on an actual, contemporaneous traumatic event.

Totally unknown to his patients, the therapist had in fact been ill with a mild heart attack. The point for us, however, is that these patients tended to consciously dismiss and deny this very likely possibility, but reported a long array of death-related images and themes that reflected their deep unconscious conviction first, that the therapist had indeed been seriously ill, and second, that they themselves had caused it. This is how deep unconscious death anxiety is expressed and worked over without awareness intervening.

CONNECTIONS TO THE STORY OF CAIN AND ABEL

Let's turn now to the question of how this triggering event and this dream-related material tie into the story of God, Cain, and Abel. In light of the trigger—the therapist's absence and the evident likelihood that he had been seriously ill or had died—it can be proposed that the therapist had taken on, or had been assigned by his patients, the role of Abel, the murdered brother. In responding to this trigger, each of his patients unconsciously took on the role of Cain, his attacker and supposed killer. In keeping with the second version of the story, each of them was taking blame and suffering from deep unconscious guilt for their therapist's absence and imagined death or illness, and for the death that they believed was pending now that he had returned. Each was being accused by his or her own inner god and subsystem of morality and ethics of having criminally and sinfully killed him. For some of these patients, their motives involved envy of his favored position as their therapist. For others it was the seemingly predatory qualities of the pursuit of their guilt-ridden unconscious secrets, which they wished to keep concealed from both the therapist and themselves. And even more importantly, for all of them it was the predatory aspect of the therapist's sudden desertion of his patients. Whatever the death-related reason, all of these patients were unconsciously convinced that they were responsible for what they believed was their therapist's pending demise.

The therapist's absence had, then, triggered dream equivalents of Abel's murder by Cain. But the murder hadn't taken place. Instead, the therapist had fallen ill on his own. Even if he had been dying, which was not the case, the illness he had was one for which his patients had no responsibility. In his absence, however, they had deep unconsciously accused themselves of causing his disappearance and death, much as God accused Cain of causing the death of Abel. Indeed, whenever there is an untoward trigger that could speak for illness or injury in a therapist, patients' deep unconscious beliefs center around the therapist's pending death—the deep unconscious system perceives life in terms of the worst possible extremes. But to say it again, here is the rub: While all of this therapist's patients accused themselves of his murder and all of them accepted full blame, none of them had actually made him ill or set him on the path to death.

Archetypically, this means that when the Lord said to Cain, "Where is your brother Abel?" and Cain answered, "I do not know; am I my brother's keeper?" Cain was not lying but telling the truth. Abel was dead, but Cain was not the responsible party. Nevertheless, once accused by the Lord God of the murder of Abel, Cain accepted blame for what had happened. And he may have done so because of his deep unconscious guilt over having caused Abel other kinds of harm, having wished Abel ill or dead, having failed to defend Abel when he was faced with some kind of threat, or having harmed or killed other people in the course of his life. Who among us has not caused harm to others and experienced predator death anxiety and deep unconscious guilt because of it? All of the patients involved in this incident had been party to, and had to some extent caused, physical or psychological

harm to others—incidents that caused them to unconsciously blame themselves for the disastrous fates of others whom they had not harmed.

Summing up, archetypically, deep unconscious guilt over actually harming others begets deep unconscious guilt for the suffering of others for which
one has no responsibility. These patients' archetypal dreams suggest that
such was the case with the death of Abel—Cain irrationally accepted blame
for something he had not done. This means that on some level God knew the
truth of the matter. And it provides a crucial reason for his protecting Cain
from further—in this scenario, unjustified—punishment and harm.

The wider implications of this version of the story of Cain and Abel need
to be stressed. Conscious and deep unconscious guilt prompt humans to act
in ways that are self-destructive as well as harmful to others. Conscious guilt
often leads to efforts at expiation, but unconscious guilt is guilt without
awareness—a blind need to cause harm to oneself and others so as to be punished for unconsciously experienced misdeeds. This is another unconscious
source of the seemingly irrational violence we see in the world today—and it
may well play a role in the questionable acts of violence initiated by terror-
ists and world leaders in particular. If we are going to master this source of
harm, pain, and grief for so many people living in the world today, we need
to fully grasp the deep unconscious situation and master these unjustified
sources of deep unconscious guilt. This mastery also will aid us in our quest
for a viable and effective set of religious doctrines for believers and facilitate
our search for a rational basis for a sound and healing human spirituality for
nonbelievers as well.

AUGUSTINE'S REENACTMENT

It is here that the story of Augustine's second sin comes into play. Augustine
places this incident in the context of Cain's sin of the murder of his brother
Abel—a tale whose meanings Augustine accepts at face value. Indeed, the
story of Cain is one of his associations to the triggering event with which his
own sinful act is connected. This event is the death of a close male friend with
whom Augustine experienced some rivalry when Augustine was about
twenty-one years of age.

Oddly enough, many years later, toward the end of his life, Augustine re-
considered this sin and decided that his view of it was an empty rant and non-
sense; centuries later, Nietzsche also found it ridiculous. These assessments
reflect the kind of failure of understanding and turn to denial that come from
the conscious examination of the Bible and of death-related triggers. It also
arises from being unable to appreciate the deep unconscious meanings and

implications of these triggers and one's own encoded deep unconscious reactions to them. Within this realm, that which the conscious mind ridicules is usually viewed with grim regard by its deep unconscious counterpart.

This is the story as told by Augustine in his *Confessions* (Augustine 1961; Wills 2003):

After spending several years in Carthage and glorying in its intellectual richness, Augustine had been, as we heard in the story of the theft of the pears, obligated to return home to Thagaste. At the time of the incident he describes here, he had a son who was four years old; he was living with his mistress and his parents; and he felt sorely deprived of the kind of intellectual stimulation that was so dear to him. The situation was saved by the presence of a bright, younger male friend with whom Augustine had bonded. But the friend soon fell seriously ill, and his Christian family had had him baptized as he lay in bed in a coma. The friend recovered and clung to his restored faith, a development that Augustine, who had not been baptized, roundly objected to. He tried to change his friend's mind, but his efforts were rejected. Soon after this happened, the friend died in the comfort of the sacraments — as Augustine put it.

Augustine reacted strongly, and in his own eyes, sinfully, to his friend's death, which was the triggering event to which he was reacting both consciously and deep unconsciously. His writings on the subject, which we may again take as his associations to the incident, are once more quite revealing. Augustine felt that he and his friend shared a single soul and that the friend lived on in himself; seeing to it that the friend survived in this way prevented Augustine from committing suicide, which he seriously considered doing. Augustine also experienced a dread that he too would soon die. He saw death everywhere and had a sense that death would now devour the whole human race. He described himself as luxuriating in his misery over his friend's death and as insisting on not giving up his grief. He also felt a sense of rage at his friend's abandonment. Augustine accused himself of the sin of raging against his friend for dying in peace and redemption, and for his friend's finding favor with God in a way that he himself had not been able to do — a clear replica of the Cain and Abel situation.

Augustine asked himself, citing Psalm 41:6, "Why, in your anguish, are you whirling me about?" For Augustine, the psalm echoed God's words to Cain after he rejected his sacrifice: "Why, in your anguish, is your face contorted?"

Augustine believed that Cain sinned twice: once in his anguish over his brother's good fortune, and then in the murder of his brother. Similarly, Augustine saw himself as sinning twice against his friend: once in his anguish over the friend's baptism and his making peace with God, and then in his anguish after the friend had died — an anguish that was quite debilitating.

Augustine soon fled Thagaste for Carthage, much as Cain fled his parents' home after his crime—both of them turned to wanderings.

For us, the essential point of this tale is that Augustine reacted and treated himself as if he had actually murdered his friend, even though such was not the case. The main deep unconscious motive appears to have been Augustine's envy of his friend's turn to God and the sense that God had accepted his friend's offerings, while Augustine had not as yet made his own peace with God. His deep unconscious guilt also seems to have stemmed from his rage against the friend's desertion while he was alive and then completing the abandonment by dying.

This archetypal constellation suggests another reason for Cain's murder of Abel. In being accepted by God when his bother was rejected by him, Abel, with God, had inadvertently created a breach between the two brothers—a breach that Cain must have deeply resented. This suggestion shows how the study of latter-day lives in which the Bible is being archetypically relived and redreamt can help to shed fresh light on the biblical tales themselves—as long as the event is accompanied, as it is here, by narrative associations that lend themselves to trigger decoding.

In his own way, Augustine unconsciously experienced predator death anxiety and deep unconscious guilt in the belief that he had killed his friend. He suffered accordingly with feelings of sinfulness and with self-recriminations. He unconsciously expected to be punished for his murderous sin, which accounts for his expectation that he too would soon die and for his thoughts of suicide. In addition, the death of a friend with whom he was closely identified probably aroused Augustine's own existential death anxieties. These anxieties also may have contributed to a dread of his own demise, and they also account for his denial of the friend's death through the belief that his friend's soul lived on in himself. Augustine nearly died as he went through these tortured days, showing how gravely this kind of archetypal guilt can affect a person.

Finally, there is the evident *survivor guilt* that Augustine almost certainly experienced, and this too is the source of needs to even the score through the suicide or death of the guilt-ridden, surviving party. This kind of guilt intensifies the need for self-harm evoked by the deep unconscious belief that the survivor has murdered the person who died.

Augustine's later conviction that this entire matter was an empty illusion and rant treats his experience as a falsehood and seems to be an attempt to deny the seriousness of his straits at the time—essentially it appears to be an existentially related denial of death. To belie this denial, his image of death devouring the whole human race seems to express the ultimate existential fantasy—that personal death is the eradication of all humankind, and psychologically speaking from a personal vantage point, the end of life on earth.

Honing in on the relevance of this material for the present discussion, there are, then, clear indications that Augustine held himself responsible for his friend's death. He had tried to kill the friend's faith and raged against the calm that the friend had found in his closeness to God, something that Augustine had not as yet accomplished. But the crucial evidence for Augustine's unconscious picture of himself as his "brother's" murderer is found in his self-punitive emotional breakdown after the friend died, and even more so, in his suicidal thoughts and impulses. The latter are a sure sign of deep unconscious guilt over an act of murder, another expression of the archetypal talion principle that states, If you take a life, you must give your life as payment.

Augustine did not, of course, murder his friend, yet he accepted punishment from God above and from his own inner god as if he had actually carried out the deadly deed. His reliving the story of Cain and Abel in such detail, and his associations to this traumatic triggering event, fully support the second version of the biblical story. I refer to the one in which Cain did not murder his brother, but accepted God's punishment because of his unconscious guilt over his envy of, and rage against, his sibling—or because of other sources of deep unconscious guilt.

Because the Bible omits so much of each story it tells, we can only wonder in light of present-day, archetypal dreams whether Cain had been involved in a death-related trauma before his encounter with God and his brother—and if that trauma was the source of his dire need to have his offerings accepted by God. The same question applies to Augustine's tale of his sinning in connection with the death of his friend. Prior death-related traumas were present in all of the patients who redreamed this biblical story in response to their therapist's absence from his office. It was from them that the clues to this unusual second meaning of this story in Genesis first emerged. Once again Freud's psychotherapeutic subuniverse, suitably modified with adaptive ground rules and therapeutic principles, gave this therapist and me a chance to observe a most compelling and affecting archetype and to unveil a set of likely hidden meanings and lessons for today that can be gleaned from the all too concise tales of the scripture. The archetypal past is alive in the present much as the present illuminates the archetypal past, and it does so in ways that allow the past to further illuminate the present. With this in mind, I turn now to a broader look at Yahweh as his interactions with humankind unfold in the Hebrew Bible.

8

The Failure to Master Death Anxiety: Yahweh

In the period after Cain and Abel, there is an odd passing example of predator death anxiety, and it is strangely configured.

> Lamech said to his wives: "Adah and Zillah, hear my voice; you wives of Lamech listen to what I say: I have killed a man for wounding me, a young man for striking me. If Cain is avenged sevenfold, truly Lamech seventy-sevenfold." (Gen 4:23–24)

Cain slew Abel without provocation or valid cause, while Lamech killed a man in self-defense, yet he expects to be punished far more than Cain was punished. Clearly, morality is awry, and predator death anxiety and its ever-present companion, deep unconscious, and at times conscious, guilt arise even when there is just cause to harm another human being. The need for punishment for a murder that is nonetheless justified is another variant of the predator death anxiety archetype. It tells us that regardless of cause or grounds on which it is based, humans experience deep unconscious guilt and a need for punishment whenever they are a cause of someone's death. Even so, God is nowhere to be seen in this brief interlude in the listing of the descendants of Adam. As we move forward in the Hebrew Testament, then, we continue to find a lack of clear moral principles and guidelines.

In this chapter I shall take on the unwieldy task of trying to characterize how Yahweh dealt with death and the three forms of death anxiety as the Old Testament unfolds. This is no easy task because we soon come upon Yahweh's selection of the Jews for special favors and an extended history of his relationship with a series of Jewish leaders and prophets—a history that covers many different individuals and many diverse situations and events. Unlike the New Testament, which is centered on a relatively short span of time and on one individual, the story of the Lord God, Yahweh, and the Jews is extended and complex. To bring some order to this chaos, I shall focus mainly on the remainder of Genesis and some material related to Exodus and Job. Continuing to concentrate on the early history of Yahweh should enable us to identify basic, repetitive patterns and finally answer the questions that I have been raising: How did the Lord God personally deal with death and its encumbrances? What did he do and not do to help humans come to terms with their own issues with death? And to what extent did he establish a clear and uplifting moral code for humankind to live by?

THE PROGRESSION OF GENESIS

After the listing of the lineage of Adam has been completed for the moment, the next incident we come to is manifestly death related, and this time God plays a very active role in what happens. First there is mention that daughters were born to the people inhabiting the earth and that the sons of the Lord God took them as wives. There follows an uncertain passage about the wives bearing children to the sons of God and an allusion to giants in the earth who became warriors of old and renown. It is not clear who these characters are, but one interpretation is that the giants were the offspring of this mating. The men who left heaven are thought to have been fallen angels who had sinned by deserting God and abandoning his assignment to them as watchers of humankind. In any case, trouble soon enters the picture:

> The Lord saw that the wickedness of humankind was great in the earth, and that every inclination of the thoughts of their hearts was only evil continually. And the Lord God was sorry that he had made humankind on the earth and it grieved him to his heart. So the Lord God said: "I will blot out from the earth the human beings I have created—people together with animals and creeping things and birds of the air, for I am sorry that I have made them." (Gen 6:5–7)

Life on earth is about to be destroyed, but at the eleventh hour Noah finds favor in the eyes of the Lord, and the Lord tells him his plan. He then instructs Noah as to how to build an ark and makes a covenant with him, advising him to enter the ark with his sons, their wives, and his own wife, along with two of every living thing, male and female, to keep them alive.

Faced with the pervasive evilness of humankind, then, God is ambivalent, deciding one minute to destroy all living flesh and the next minute saving two or more of each species. In addition, his punishment seems to be extreme and unnecessarily violent, as well as unfair in that all living beings, the guilty as

well as the innocent, are to be done away with. This radical outburst of destructive violence—this predatory rage—will soon be repeated when God
deals with the evil people of Sodom and Gomorrah. These incidents do not
speak well for God's temper and predatory inclinations, nor does it offer humans a reasonable moral compass or a fair sense of justice.

After the flood, when Noah makes burnt offerings to God, the Lord God
repents and recants:

> The Lord said in his heart, "I will never again curse the ground because of hu-
> mankind, for the inclination of the human heart is evil from youth; nor will I
> ever again destroy every living creature as I have done. As long as the earth en-
> dures, seedtime and harvest, cold and heat, summer and winter, day and night,
> shall not cease." (Gen 8:21–22)

Next, God makes a covenant with Noah that includes the talion principle
of shedding blood for blood that has been shed, a principle that advocates violence for violence, which God invokes because he made humankind in his
own image. God's advocacy of retaliatory violence when threatened, entrapped, or endangered is one of several red threads that run through Genesis
and also is prominent in Exodus. As we know all too well today, this kind of
violence leads to horrendous vicious circles in which assault from one side
leads to a counterassault on the other side in repetitive sequences that are virtually without end. This approach of doing harm to those who harm us does
not mark a strong moral path for humankind, nor does it provide ways of
dealing with predatory and existential death anxiety that can eventually lead
to lasting peace. The Hebrew God seems to advocate surviving through the
use of unbridled aggression and domination over others.

In terms of death anxiety, then, God acts as a predator, and living beings
of all kinds are his victims—those who are innocent as well as those who
are evil. There are, however, indications that before creating the flood, God
suffered from predator death anxiety and deep unconscious guilt because of
the wanton destructiveness he planned to carry out. This may be why he accepts Noah's offerings and saves a viable pair of all living creatures so the
earth can be fully repopulated—a striking sign of regret and repentance. In
addition, he promises to never again destroy all living creatures even when
humans act in evil ways. Even so, given the devastation that he created with
the flood, it would be difficult for humans to take God at his word. As a result, their dread of harm from Yahweh and their predatory death anxiety
would likely go unabated. Evoking the fear of punishment and death in humans seems to be another way that Yahweh tried to keep human violence
and evil in check. This too is a dubious approach to gaining peace on earth,
individually or collectively.

The devastation caused by God must have evoked strong residuals of existential and predatory death anxiety in Noah and his family. This archetypal sense of vulnerability would, to some extent, be a repetition of the death anxiety that was experienced by Adam and Eve after they ate from the tree of divine knowledge. The link between gaining divine wisdom or God's blessings and suffering from mass destruction is striking. Adam and Eve's sense of defenselessness against the inevitability of death seems to have been the basic meaning of their newly configured awareness of their nakedness. Strikingly, the theme of nakedness also comes up with Noah after the flood.

Noah, who, like Adam, was a man of the soil, plants a vineyard. He then drinks some wine, gets drunk, and lies in his tent naked. His youngest son, Ham, sees the nakedness, tells his brothers Shem and Japheth about it, and they cover their father so they will not see his nakedness. When Noah awakens and realizes what his youngest son has done, he curses Ham's son, Canaan, marking him to be the lowest of slaves to his brothers and to Shem and Japheth.

This puzzling interlude makes sense in light of the equation of nakedness with vulnerability to death. Adam, the first man, experienced existential death anxiety after surviving God's promise—or curse—that he would die if he ate the forbidden fruit. It may well be that Noah, the second Adam, experienced a comparable sense of death anxiety after he survived God's curse of humankind as expressed in its near-annihilation through the flood. For Noah, the likely aftermath of this experience also would be a sense of vulnerability to death, and as in the story of the emperor's new clothes where no one but an innocent child acknowledges the emperor's nakedness, Noah's sons do not want to see that their father is naked—that is, that he too is subject to the existential rule that death follows life. Evidently, Noah also wishes to deny his vulnerability—after all, he just saved the lineages of living beings from annihilation by God—and for this reason he curses Ham's son and punishes him for bringing up the matter. As God later says, the sins of the father shall fall upon the sons for generations to come.

For his part, God is again showing signs of unresolved death anxiety, possibly because he is fearful that an evil world will deny his existence and in a sense destroy him. He also is unable to establish and sustain a clear moral line of thinking: He destroys living beings indiscriminantly because some of them are evil; behavior of this kind can only increase human feelings of existential and predatory death anxiety without offering a means of gaining relief from the suffering they cause. Indeed, paradoxically, his vengefulness is likely to increase rather than diminish humankind's bent for evil acts designed unconsciously and at great cost to alleviate these anxieties.

We are left with a picture of Yahweh as a merciless, vengeful predator who seems to be at a loss as to how to deal with evil and sinfulness. He seems, then, resigned to concede humankind to Satan, and by implication, after the flood, he is no longer inclined to punish humans for their evil deeds. His resignation may have arisen from his realization that his response to evil has been irrationally harsh and that this kind of uncontrolled, punitive violence is without redeeming features. This prompts him to promise to never again resort to such devastation.

All in all, then, at this juncture we seem to be seeing God acting as a predator but then suffering from guilt-ridden predator death anxiety and thus trying to redeem himself and to make amends. Still, his shifting back and forth in his attitudes toward life and death and in his approach to morality must be taken as further evidence that he himself has not come to terms with death and its attendant issues.

THE TURN TO ABRAHAM

After the flood and the events linked with the tower of Babel, God takes a sharp turn away from his broad commitment to humankind in general and becomes quite selective. He chooses Abraham, with whom he makes a covenant and on whom he promises to bestow his blessings; make of him a great nation; protect him, his family, and followers against enemies; and bless those who bless Abraham. For this to happen, Abraham must make a new beginning and create a new life by leaving his adopted homeland. He then must go through a series of ordeals that include struggling for years with the barrenness of his wife, Sarah; being witness to God's destruction of Sodom and Gomorrah (an act that Abraham tries unsuccessfully to dissuade God from carrying out); banishing his firstborn son, Ishmael, and his mother, Hagar, who was Sarah's servant, into the desert, thereby sending them to their all but certain death (they are saved by one of God's angels); and responding to God's command that he sacrifice his son, Isaac, finally given to him by Sarah, which he is about to do in all faith when God arranges an eleventh-hour reprieve. In surviving these trials and tribulations, Abraham becomes the founding father of both the Israelites and Arabs, and ultimately the Jews, Christians, and Muslims.

By selecting the lineage destined to become the twelve tribes of Israel for his covenant and favored people, Yahweh has opened a proverbial can of worms. His decision is in a sense a repetition of his interaction with Cain and Abel where he favored the younger brother over the older. Despite the disastrous outcome of that interlude and God's possible regrets over the role he played in it, we now find him doing something similar on a much larger scale. This kind of partiality is experienced by outsiders as predatory and can only promote violence against his favored people. It fans the flames of warfare and, as happened with Abel, creates the serious risk that God might fail the Israelites at their time of need and thus see great harm befall them. In addition, those who are favored will believe that they are unique and special in the eyes of God—which they are—a feeling that will cause them to develop a sense of entitlement that is likely to lead to many uncalled-for claims against others and acts of aggression that can only interfere with the quest for peace.

Lastly, this kind of inequality in God's approach to humankind will be perceived by both the favored and unfavored parties as inequitable and immoral, if not in some sense evil. God has therefore made a fateful choice that can only increase the death anxieties of those who are preferred and provide them with false reassurance against their existential death anxieties. His position is certain to intensify hostilities between the Israelites and neighboring tribes, all the more so because God has willed some of their precious land of Canaan to Abraham and his descendants. Worse still, future Jews are likely to delude themselves into believing that they are invincible, while their newfound, God-made enemies will be out to prove otherwise—and in many cases they will in fact be quite successful in doing so. None of this bodes well for God, religion, or human morality, nor does it seem to enhance the possibilities of individual and collective survival in the face of death-related dangers. God's master plan is likely to activate a full range of unresolved death anxieties in both those whom God prefers and those whom he rejects.

There is a great deal more to document about God's interplay with Abraham and his descendants. Because issues of knowledge acquisition have, by and large, fallen by the wayside, I shall focus on the tales that illuminate two central themes: death and its anxieties, and morality and ethics. I shall select illustrative moments from the unfolding flow of biblical events in Genesis that move from Abraham's call from God to his near-sacrifice of Isaac, to the devious means by which Isaac's son Jacob steals the birthrights from his older twin brother Esau, to Jacob's twelve sons, who established the twelve tribes of Israel—sons who so envy their more favored brother, Joseph, that they try to murder him. I also shall consider aspects of the story of Exodus in which both Moses and God tend to act, often in consort, in violent and otherwise inexplicably cruel ways. And finally, I shall take a brief look at the story of Job, whom God treated in a most brutal manner in order to win a bet with Satan. At first blush, then, none of this seems to bode well for Yahweh's relationship with humankind.

PREDATORY DEATH ANXIETY

The fear of being destroyed by either natural disasters or other living beings, especially other humans, inherently stems from existential death anxiety—from the fact that biologically, except for moments of severe emotional disturbance, human beings want to live on for as long as possible. The experience of predatory death anxiety tends to bring about a mobilization of physical and psychological resources in an effort to defend oneself against the threatening predator and possibly destroy it or otherwise master the danger involved. Since the earth became overpopulated with living organisms, virtually every living entity has been faced with a predatory threat that endangers its life. This has led to countless predator-prey arms races in which enhanced means of predation are pitted against enhanced means of defense and retaliatory attack, with the survival of one of the combatants at stake.

In light of the archetypal qualities of predator-prey interactions, the Bible is strikingly mute about the subjective experiences of both predators and their prey, and it has little to say about the motives of those who prey on others. In addition, victims of predation who are personally known to their attackers, like Abel and Isaac, tend to be relatively nonreactive and quite submissive to their fates; they show few signs, if any, of protest or efforts at self-protection. God too tends to be silent at these moments of evident injustice or to sanction the predatory act—be it murder or theft. Predatory violence and harm are commonplace in these sacred writings, and they are carried out by fathers, mothers, siblings, sons, daughters and, as we have seen, God himself. The victims range from enemy tribes to other family members. The Hebrew Testament is to a great extent a story of predatory violence and exploitation.

Predatory death anxiety plays an early and frequent role in the story of Abraham, the father of both the Israelites (through his son Isaac, borne by his wife, Sarah) and Islam (through his son Ishmael, borne by Sarah's servant, Hagar). After God has chosen to favor him with bountiful but as yet undelivered blessings, Abraham goes to Canaan and quite soon is faced with a severe famine. Beset with a measure of existential death anxiety and feeling predated by nature—or God—he and his clan take refuge in Egypt, where they expect to find food and other supplies. Fearful that the Pharaoh will want to make Sarah his concubine and that he therefore will murder Abraham if he is told that Sarah is his wife, Abraham deals with his predatory death anxiety by lying to the Pharaoh and telling him that Sarah is his sister (she is in fact his half sister).

Early on, then, God's chosen leader experiences predatory and existential death anxiety, and they motivate him to lie and sin as a way of trying to survive the threat. Whatever natural inclinations humans have toward having an interpersonally cooperative moral life are trumped by the need to act immorally when death anxiety is activated—and this holds true for each of the three forms of death anxiety. With existential and predatory death anxiety the sinning is in the service of trying to survive a threat to one's life, while with predator death anxiety, where the person has harmed others, the sinning is a means of inviting others to punish the predatory sinner. And the Bible is showing us that the default position—the natural archetype and basic inclination among humans—leans toward cheating and sinning rather than a more honest approach to endangerment.

Notice too that God does not intervene to ensure the safety of Abraham, nor does he provide him with a candid, moral means of surviving the situation with the Pharaoh. The Pharaoh takes Sarah into his house, and because of her beauty, he rewards Abraham with slaves and animals. But then the Lord God afflicts the Pharaoh and his house with great plagues, so the Pharaoh realizes that Sarah is Abraham's wife and in response, simply sends him on his way. Neither God nor the Pharaoh punishes Abraham for his deceit. Where, we might wonder, are sound standards for human morality in all of this?

God does, however, intervene in a most unexpected way when Abraham is faced with a similar threat to his life while staying in Gerar, where his host is King Abimelech. Here too, fearing for his life, Abraham tells the king that Sarah is his sister, and so the king takes Sarah as his bedmate. We then learn this:

> But God came to Abimelech in a dream by night, and said to him, "You are about to die because of the woman whom you have taken; for she is a married woman." (Gen 20:3)

This is the first dream in the Bible. In it God visits someone who is not affiliated with Abraham, his chosen one. And without prior warning, God announces that adultery is a sin punishable by death. This pronouncement is in striking contrast to how God stood by silently when, after the destruction of Sodom and Gomorrah and the death of Lot's wife because she defied God's warning to not look back at the devastation, Lot's daughters committed incest with him because they were afraid that there were no men left on earth and they wanted to have offspring. Moral contradictions seem to abound here.

As for what happens with King Abimelech, even though he has not yet approached Sarah, he fears God as a predator and existentially is afraid for his life. So he protests his innocence by pointing out to God that both Sarah and Abraham claimed that they were siblings. The king insists that he has acted in the integrity of his heart, and God acknowledges that this is so, adding that it was he, God, who had kept the king from sinning against him. God directs the king to return Sarah to Abraham, and Abimelech does so in anger and fear because God has told him that Abraham is a prophet who will pray for him. At this point, Abraham explains that Sarah is in fact his half sister, in that they share the same father but not their mothers. Once more the story ends with Abraham being richly rewarded for his guile. His survival is assured, but mainly through deceit, and morality again goes wanting.

There are other significant interludes in the story of Abraham in which predatory death anxiety looms large. For one, God seems to be predatory with both Abraham and Sarah by promising Abraham that he will be father to a great nation yet keeping Sarah barren. Sarah laughs when in her old age God promises her that she will soon bear Abraham a child, but there is little else in the way of direct responses to this frustrating and hurtful situation. The couple seems to be experiencing existential death anxiety because they lack descendants, but this too is a situation for which God must be held accountable since it is God's angel who eventually announces the advent of Sarah's pregnancy.

Lot, who is Abraham's nephew, is kidnapped by a band of marauders, and Abraham mobilizes his followers and rescues him. A more telling tale of predation occurs when God becomes enraged at the evil doings in Sodom and Gomorrah. The cities are in land occupied by Lot, but God informs Abraham of his intentions to destroy everyone living in the two cities. Abraham pleads with God, arguing that if there are righteous men in these cities, God should spare them rather than killing the innocent along with the guilty. God says that if ten righteous men are found in the city, he will spare it. But the next thing we know, angels arrive to warn Lot of the pending holocaust, and God soon destroys both metropolises. Lot and his family are spared for the sake of Abraham but are told to not look back at the burning cities. When Lot's wife does so, she is turned into a pillar of salt. Suffering from what appears to have been predator death anxiety and unconscious guilt, God evidently did not want his impulsive, predatory handiwork to be seen and remembered by any human being. Lot and his two daughters hide from the devastation in a cave, and his daughters, fearful that there are no more living men who can enable them to produce descendants, get their father drunk and on consecutive nights, each daughter sleeps with him and conceives a son. The first son becomes the ancestor of the Moabites, and the second that of the Ammonites.

PREDATORY INCIDENTS

Two major death-related, predatory incidents follow in the story of Abraham. The first occurs after Sarah at long last has given birth to a son, who is named Isaac. Observing Isaac at play with Ishmael, the son of Hagar, and concerned with Isaac's birthrights, Sarah asks Abraham to expel Ishmael and Hagar from their campsite. Because it is likely that they will not survive being cast into the wilderness, Abraham is upset by this request. However, God intervenes and supports Sarah's position, so Hagar and Ishmael are given supplies and sent out from the camp. Eventually, the pair run out of their provisions and are on the verge of dying, but God hears the voice of the boy and sends an angel to save them and to promise that he will make a great nation of Ishmael.

Hagar cannot bear the sight of Ishmael dying, and this is one of the few times in Genesis that we hear of an individual reacting with emotion to experiences of existential and predatory death anxiety. Sarah, Abraham, and God behave as predators. God again reverses his position—expelling the twosome and exposing them to near-certain death and then saving their lives. But there are hints that he never intended for Ishmael to die because he repeatedly promises him that he will make him into a great nation. Nevertheless, God's predatory tendency to favor one brother over another surfaces again—while he blesses both half brothers, he will make his covenant only with Isaac.

As for the predator death anxiety and deep unconscious guilt and need for punishment that we would expect in response to these predatory acts, once more there are no manifest indications of repentance in any of the three offenders—Sarah, Abraham, or God. Yet the presence of deep unconscious guilt may have been a factor in the sequelae to this incident—God's request that Abraham sacrifice his son Isaac, and the death of Sarah in childbirth. Both of these events involve the loss of a child, which could well be a talion punishment for nearly causing the death of Ishmael. Indeed, God's asking for the sacrifice of Isaac has long been one of the more profound unexplained mysteries of the Hebrew Bible, and predator death anxiety and the need for punishment in both God and Abraham might well be a key unconscious factor in this incident.

God speaks to Abraham:

> "Take your son, your only son [*sic*] Isaac, whom you love, and go to the land of Moriah, and offer him there as a burnt offering on one of the mountains that I shall show you." (Gen 22:2)

Acting in the manner of cruel, senseless predators, both God and Abraham conspire to ruthlessly murder Isaac. Yahweh's demand that Abraham show his faith in him by sacrificing his son intermixes violence and faith in ways that seem to be quite unjustified. Furthermore, after God spares Isaac, he rewards Abraham not only with legions of descendants, but also with the power to defeat his enemies—that is with support for war instead of offering a basis for lasting peace in the world. Meanwhile, there is no sign of anxiety or hesitation in Abraham as he moves forward with the planned sacrifice of his son, no indication of predator death anxiety or guilt. In this instance we observe blessings and survival based on poorly rationalized intended violence.

As for God, when it comes to death and its encumbrances, a repetitive pattern begins to surface—a Yahweh archetype, if you will. It appears to be based on a striking amount of unresolved death anxiety and emerges in a variety of ways as an indiscriminate use of violence to punish evildoers and those who disobey his commands, a preference for advocating violent ways for humans to express their faith in him and for interacting with others, an absence of remorse or guilt for his own predatory acts, his failure to atone when violence is expressed, and little or nothing in the way of the predator death anxiety or guilt that would help to restrain his impulses to harm others. These archetypal inclinations infuse our view of Yahweh to this very day, but they also characterize an archetype that applies to us as humans as well. The result is a world filled with uncalled-for violence against others for which neither humans nor God, including Jesus of Nazareth, who did his best to have it otherwise, has found a solution. Indeed, all of this gives new meaning to God's crafting us in his image with, it would seem, an in-built inclination toward violence without remorse.

All three forms of death anxiety play a role in this first drama of Yahweh's interaction with his chosen people. Existential and predatory death anxieties are reflected in the threat to Isaac's life, while predator death anxiety is inherent in Abraham's intention to sacrifice his son. The sole expression of death anxiety seen in Isaac emerges as he and his father move alone to the site at which the sacrifice is to be made. Abraham has placed the wood for the fire onto his son, and he himself is carrying the torch and knife:

> Isaac said to his father Abraham, "Father!" And he said, "Here I am, my son." He said: "The fire and the wood are here, but where is the lamb for a burnt offering?" Abraham said, "God himself will provide the lamb for a burnt offering, my son." (Gen 22:7–8)

There are several other death-related archetypes in the Hebrew Testament that appear repeatedly in its dramatic stories. One such archetype involves a threat to the life of a favored son at the behest of God or without God's objecting to the evil deed as it is being carried out by someone on earth. This archetype can be found when Cain slays Abel and when Isaac's younger son, Jacob, steals the life-saving birthrights due to his elder twin brother, Esau—after which God actually blesses Jacob. We see the archetype again with the attempt to murder Joseph, Jacob's favorite son, by his less favored brothers, and yet again, in the abandonment of the newborn Moses by his parents carried out to save his life even as it threatens to end it. In a variation on this archetype, there also is God's failed attempt to murder Moses after he has honored and called on him to rescue his people, the Jews, from Egyptian bondage.

In these situations, Yahweh's predatory inclinations are quite prominent. And the list of such acts does not stop there. To these injustices we must add the ruthlessness of God in protecting and aiding the Jews to escape from bondage in Egypt as seen in the ten plagues that God visits upon the Egyptians, his wanton murder of Egyptian firstborn sons, and the drowning of Pharaoh's troops when they pursue the fleeing Jews. There also is God's punishment by death of thousands of the followers of Moses when they engage in idolatry and rebel against Moses because they are suffering from extreme hardships in the desert into which they have fled. The last example of this kind that I shall cite here is the story of Job, on whom God wreaks havoc with the death of his family and a series of other catastrophes in order to win a bet with the devil that despite all, Job would not lose faith in him, the "good Lord."

Examples of this kind in the Old Testament can be multiplied a hundredfold. How then are we to understand the Hebrew God, Yahweh, in light of his dealings with issues pertaining to death and the conscious and deep unconscious anxieties it evokes? His behavior lends itself to several conjectures. For one, there continue to be strong signs that God himself suffers from unresolved versions of all three forms of death anxiety. Existential death anxiety is reflected in his fierce opposition, often backed with violence against offenders, to the worship of other gods and to any indication of a loss in faith in his existence and power. There is an element of predatory death anxiety reflected in these reactions, in that he evidently views the loss of faith as an annihilatory attack. This idea is in keeping with God's violent responses to disbelievers. Archetypically, those who feel threatened with annihilation generally try to strike at their enemies before they themselves are destroyed. Signs of predator death anxiety—of guilt, need for punishment, and possibly wishes to atone—also appear on rare occasions, but on the whole, God appears to suffer his death anxieties silently and perhaps unconsciously, alone in his solitude.

A God who cannot make peace with death and his own death anxieties cannot offer an effective means through which humans can gain peace of their own with these issues. The result is a world full of the unbridled use of violence, with a stress on the search for power and a turning to God for support in attacking personal enemies as well as other clans, tribes, ethnic groups, and nations. There is an overuse of extreme violence to punish others for transgressions that seem to deserve far less—as seen, for example, with Jacob's sons, who responded to the rape of their sister Dinah by a prince of a neighboring tribe by deceiving and then slaughtering all of the male members of the offending group.

Finally, the pervasive signs of death anxiety in Yahweh bring up yet another facet of the idea that God initially created humankind in his image. It would appear that this implies that he passed on his death anxieties to us along with whatever else he gave us. Yahweh may well be partly or fully responsible for our own pervasive problems with death and death anxiety by arranging for us to suffer as he does with these problems (biologically, this speaks for a genetic heritage of vulnerability to death and death anxiety) and by not doing much to help us solve them. His lack of a moral compass also aggravates the situation; here too we see a likely link between the failure to resolve personal death anxieties and the tendency to behave in immoral ways. All in all, God has made these issues more difficult than they would otherwise be for us to deal with—faith in Yahweh does not seem to bring peace to us personally or collectively.

SOME FURTHER ILLUSTRATIONS

The archetypes that pervade the Hebrew Testament seem to be well established and amply demonstrated, so I shall comment briefly on a few additional highlights. By and large, they support the contention that Yahweh failed his chosen people in his responsibilities to help them to deal with the fundamental forms of death anxiety with which they inevitably suffered, and, as I said, at no point did he offer them a clear, consistent, and strong set of moral guidelines.

Jacob

Abraham's son Isaac was the weakest of the patriarchs; this probably was due to the lasting effects of his near-murder. He did, however, become the father of twins with his wife and cousin, Rebekah. Esau was the elder and Jacob the younger of the pair. With the help of his mother, Jacob steals the birthrights of his elder sibling. As for the *unconscious* motives for the theft, existential death anxiety seems to have played a role because possession of these rights would imply that he has God's blessings and his assurances of a healthy, productive, long life.

The sinful, immoral, predatory dishonesty involved in Jacob's act and the boundary violations and disregard for fair play and ground rules that are involved are quite evident here. Despite this, after Jacob leaves camp in fear of his brother's vengeance, he dreams of a ladder to heaven and hears God's voice blessing him and his descendants, thereby confirming his stolen birthrights. In the years that follow, Jacob lives with his uncle Laban, who twice tricks him into servitude before Jacob marries the sister with whom he has fallen in love.

Years later, in the course of Jacob's journey home to be reunited with Esau, he is again blessed by God's angels. It is only then at long last that there is an implied punishment from God for his ill deed. Jacob spends the entire night before the brothers are to meet caught up in a dream-like experience in which he is wrestling with a stranger, only to awaken in the morning to realize that his opponent was Yahweh and that he had permanently damaged Jacob's hip joint, leaving him with a noticeable limp. But even so, near the end of the struggle, Jacob gets Yahweh in his grip and refuses to let him go unless Yahweh blesses him once more, which he does by giving Jacob the name of Israel and pronouncing him the father of the twelve future tribes of that name. This blessing is repeated by God after Jacob resettles in Canaan, and this is the last appearance of God in Genesis. We might assume that he was tired of waffling, discouraged by how humans had behaved and how his relationship with them had gone, and in need of a long, long rest.

As for Jacob's story, the key point is that once more predation is blessed and only minimally and belatedly punished—then blessed again. Here too it is all but impossible to extract a sound moral code for humankind because the same evil act is both condemned and affirmed several times over.

Joseph

Existential death anxiety exerts a favorable and creative influence on Joseph after he is nearly murdered by his brothers, who turn against him because he boldly flaunted a pair of dreams in which he lords over his siblings. Joseph is rescued from certain death, and he ends up in Egypt, where, after several misadventures and a betrayal, he is able, with God's implicit help, to foresee and forestall the consequences of a pending famine by correctly interpreting the dreams of the Pharaoh, who is holding him prisoner. In the midst of his triumph, his predatory bothers come to Egypt, and Joseph saves their lives and forgives them their evil, sinful ways without a word of recrimination.

Exodus

Exodus deserves mention here for many death-related reasons. God chooses a self-exiled murderer, Moses, to rescue the Jews from enslavement by a Pharaoh. But then, during the journey back to Egypt, God attempts to murder Moses for unstated reasons. Later in the story, God brings ten plagues down on the Egyptians, including the slaying of their first-born children, and then destroys the Pharaoh's army when they pursue the escaping Jews. Still later, when some of the Jews complain about conditions in the desert and lean toward idolatry, Moses, with the help of God, arranges for the priests to murder some twenty thousand of their own. After favoring Moses for years, in the end God punishes him for unspecified crimes by not allowing him to enter the promised land to which they finally journey.

Both God and Moses are unforgivingly punitive, allowing little or no room for reform, repentance, or atonement for sins committed. They are predatory of the Egyptians to a catastrophic degree and quite demanding of blind faith in their followers. They show no sign of remorse for their acts of violence and nothing in the way of predator death anxiety or guilt—in a blaming way, this may be why God prevented Moses from entering the promised land. By and large, however, there are few if any restraints on the punitive behaviors of both God and Moses, and in the absence of predator death anxiety, they appear to have no reason to reform their senselessly violent ways.

All in all, being Yahweh's favorite people is either a mixed blessing or no blessing at all. Yahweh's insecurities and death anxieties evidently render him overly threatened by rebellion and fearful of losing his grip on his chosen people to the point where they would render him nonexistent—that is, they would no longer recognize and worship him. As the history of the Jews unfolds, both they and humankind seem to be in dire need of a far more secure, stable God, one that would adopt and sustain a far more certain moral position and offer workable, peace-creating moral standards. Nevertheless, it took centuries of suffering on all sides before Jesus of Nazareth answered this call.

Job

Yahweh's predation of humans is seen in yet another guise in the story of Job, a biblical story that Jung (1958) has explored in great detail. God makes a bet with the devil that his devout follower, Job, will sustain his faith in him in the face of the most horrendous setbacks. Despite Job's suffering through one ordeal after another, including the loss of his family and worldly possessions, Job does sustain his faith in Yahweh and eventually is rewarded for doing so. Nevertheless, in consorting with Satan, Yahweh himself becomes satanic and loses his moral center and sense of fairness, including his balance of rewards and punishments—a message that has not been lost on humankind.

BOUNDARIES AND GROUND RULES

There is a critical set of God-given or natural archetypes that pertain to the crucial necessity for humans to establish and maintain adequate and sound ground rules and interpersonal and physical boundaries, and to modify these boundaries in a controlled manner only at necessary and appropriate moments. Such boundaries help to establish and sustain a person's identity and offer him or her security, safety, and comfort. They also are the basis for, and are themselves capable of, healing emotional and bodily wounds. There is then for all situations and relationships a set of ideal boundaries and ground rules that are universally sought by the deep unconscious mind of all humans; they make up the archetypal framework of life and living (Langs 1998b, 2004c).

Boundary violations are experienced deep unconsciously as assaultive and as inappropriately seductive, damaging, and harmful. Even so, paradoxically and for reasons related to unresolved forms of death anxiety, there is a human archetype that expresses a deep unconscious need to violate boundaries and ground rules in order to avoid or flee secured frames in which boundaries and rules are well established. By and large, these conflicting archetypes, which speak for securing frames on the one hand and violating them on the other, are such that the conscious mind adopts a mixed position in this regard: It seeks and appreciates in limited fashion the archetype that favors secured frames and sensible ground rules, but is more strongly inclined to express and seek the archetype that prefers boundary violations, especially when death anxieties are activated. The net result is a strong conscious system preference for modified frames. In contrast, the deep unconscious mind, as reflected in the encoded narratives that are activated by boundary-related issues, takes a very different position on frame issues. Consistently and unswervingly it advocates the use of secured frames and the invocation of the archetypal set of ground rules that accompany such frames.

In the Bible, issues pertaining to ground rules and boundaries are raised as soon as the Lord God creates Adam and provides him with a secured, bounded setting in the form of Eden. God immediately establishes the ground rule that Adam—and Eve—should not eat the fruit of the tree of divine wisdom. As a result, if they do so it will violate a boundary that the Lord God has set for them. Their decision to disobey this ground rule sets the drama of human life in motion. This frame-related boundary violation is marked as a sin against the Lord God and thus is viewed as an immoral act—and for some students of the Bible, it is also seen as an evil deed. This too touches on an archetype in that all frame violations are universally perceived deep unconsciously as immoral and sinful acts, even as adhering to the ideal frame is viewed deep unconsciously as moral and good—a finding that is well documented in the psychotherapy situation.

As I have discussed, the study of archetypes indicates that the triggering events and deep unconscious motives that drive humans to modify ground rules and boundaries always involve an unresolved form of and issue with death anxiety. In Eve's case I presented evidence that she had suffered a spontaneous miscarriage. On the whole, humans experience a powerful, unconsciously driven urge to defy archetypal ground rules and boundaries when faced with one or more forms of death anxiety—predatory, predator, or existential. In addition, because harming others is almost always frame violating, predator death anxiety tends to arise in the context of a frame or boundary violation directed against others.

With events that trigger predatory death anxiety, departures from the ideal frame are invoked because of the need to ruthlessly defeat the attacking enemy in any manner possible. As a result, the restraints inherent in rules of conduct and interpersonal and physical boundaries are discarded and ignored. On the other hand, in situations that evoke existential death anxiety, the aim in modifying ground rules and boundaries is to escape the constraints and entrapment that they impose on the person involved. The unconscious intention is to assure oneself that he or she is an exception to the ultimate entrapment in human life as expressed in the existential rule that it is followed by death. In everyday life and in psychotherapy, triggers that involve firm commitments and evoke entrapping, existential death anxieties tend to cause people to destroy or flee situations and relationships in which they nevertheless often are deep unconsciously experiencing quite safe, secured, healing, and supportive frames.

Boundary violations—for example, the invasion of territories that belong to others, harming others or seizing their possessions, and invasive intrusions into their lives—are quite common in the Old Testament. They tend to be supported by Yahweh and seldom are treated as immoral or sinful and thus rarely are the cause for punishment. Their predatory aspects tend to be ignored, and the guilt that we would expect them to evoke seldom materializes. These attitudes are an essential factor in Yahweh's failure to provide the Jews with clear moral guidelines.

After the Lord God's pronouncement of his first ground rule, little more is explicitly offered in the ways of boundaries and rules until we come to Exodus, Leviticus, and Numbers. There, God lays down a series of commandments and rules that are essential for a moral life, and yet they suffer from some glaring omissions and often seem to be extremely harsh.

The Ten Commandments are the most well known of these ground rules. After offering four commandments that speak to having faith in God, there are rules to honor thy parents; not commit murder, adultery, or theft; not lie; and not covet thy neighbor's wife or house (property). Missing from this list of forbidden acts are certain forms of incest, an archetypal ground rule that does not find explicit expression in the Hebrew Bible. While sibling incest is forbidden in both Deuteronomy and Leviticus, father-daughter and mother-son incest are not explicitly condemned. In this connection, we may recall that Abraham was married to his half sister, and alliances between blood relatives are common in the stories in Genesis. God did not condemn Lot's daughters for having incest with their father, nor did he curse their offspring. In addition, I have cited many instances in which God allowed or encouraged behaviors that violated the very commandments that he handed down to Moses on Mount Sinai.

On the side of severity, while in the desert and as Moses went up Mount Sinai to receive these commandments, his followers made a golden calf and turned to idolatry. Moses then had his priests murder some three thousand of these idolaters, and God set a plague upon the others. Soon after, God incites Moses to attack and destroy the Midianites, including all of the men, male children, and women who were not virgins. We also find in Leviticus the proposal that the death penalty be meted out to those who curse their parents, turn to homosexuality, engage in bestiality, and violate the Sabbath—to name a few of its extreme restrictions. The punitive violence reflected here has little or nothing to do with sound archetypal ground rules, but instead speaks for a kind of dictatorial rule that can only foment rebellion and warfare among nations and individuals.

Both peace among humans and a viable set of moral guidelines depend on God and humans respecting clear and fair physical and psychological boundaries and adhering to the archetypal ground rules that ensure justice and peace for all. Despite some noble efforts in these directions, Yahweh does not offer such guidelines to humankind and instead seems to have promoted their neglect and violation, in part through messages to prophets like Moses and partly through the example of his own behavior.

SUMMING UP

All in all, God in Genesis and Exodus shows many signs of existential death anxiety, a fear of being rendered nonexistent. He is strongly inclined to be predatory of humans, yet he rarely shows signs of the predator death anxiety that could serve to restrain his inclinations toward violence against both Jews and non-Jews. Thus Yahweh is seldom regretful or guilt ridden after he destroys seemingly innocent human lives or when he overdoes his punishments of those who go against his wishes, complain to him, or are sinful. Even his pledge after the flood to refrain from the wholesale murder of humans, which is a notable exception to his failure to react to his own unjust and harmful activities, is violated in his reaction to the people of Sodom and Gomorrah. God also is ready to support violence and carnage when it will advance his personal agenda or the cause of his favored Jews and enhance their belief in and worship of him. This position was certain to arouse the anger and violence of non-Jewish tribes and to delude the Jews into believing that they are invincible vis-à-vis their enemies—a belief that eventually came to grief when they suffered a string of conquests by other tribes and nations.

In addition, Yahweh repeatedly waffles when it comes to moral issues and guidelines, making it all but impossible for the Jews to establish sound and fair moral precepts through which they could live in peace with themselves and other nations. On the whole, Yahweh seems to have given humans license for personal corruption and sinning, and to have increased rather than diminished the warfare and exchanges of violence among nations. Peace and harmony on any level could not and did not materialize under these conditions, and in fact, in the years before the coming of Jesus Christ, there was no extended period during which such conditions prevailed.

As for Yahweh's responsibility to help humans cope with the three forms of death anxiety from which they suffer, indications are that none of these disruptive anxieties, as experienced consciously and more importantly, deep unconsciously, were alleviated through God's activities in the Old Testament. Instead, it would seem that these anxieties were intensified rather than diminished by the choices God made. Despite Yahweh's handing down the Ten Commandments to Moses and his offering other formal rules of moral conduct, God repeatedly permitted the Jews to violate these tenets in time of need. In addition, Yahweh offered no clear means for human repentance and atonement after sinning and no pathway to salvation in the face of inevitable human failings—there is no afterlife or path to redemption in the Hebrew Testament. Psychologically, there simply was no appreciation of the importance of death in human life nor of the death anxieties it causes. Indeed, there are few if any psychological insights in the Hebrew Testament and no real effort to understand human nature—even though its dramatic actions are fraught with psychological implications and meaning.

Judaism takes shape as asking the Jews to have faith in a God who actually cannot be counted on to advocate for peace, reward the good, or punish the bad. Neither individual nor collective peace is served in this way. And to make matters worse, when the Jews entered the period of recorded history, we find that they were repeatedly conquered and persecuted by hostile tribes and nations. Over those many years they fell to, and were enslaved by, the Assyrians, Babylonians, Greeks, and Romans, who were most ruthless of all.

This was the situation in Palestine and the lot of the Jews when Jesus of Nazareth was born. Whatever the nature of his birth, he came into the world at a time when the Jews were filled with despair and losing faith in their God—a time when they sorely needed a new savior of some kind. The God of the Old Testament had failed them in countless ways and had not brought them relief from their archetypal death anxieties. Something drastic had to happen to change the lot of the Jews and to bring peace to humankind in general. It was Jesus Christ who intuitively offered the Jews and the world at large the means of achieving that much-needed relief.

9

Resolving Death Anxiety: Jesus Christ

There is perhaps no more complex and enigmatic figure in the history of Western religion than Jesus of Nazareth. There are two basic views of Jesus to contend with: the *historical Jesus*, who lived in Palestine for some thirty odd years during the first century AD, and the *Jesus of faith*, who, abetted by the proselytizing of Paul of Tarsus and the synoptic gospels, many believe to have been the Son of God or God incarnate. In this light, Jesus is God anew or reformed, a descendant of the Yahweh of the Hebrew scriptures (Edinger 1987; Miles 2001).

Jesus is, then, a new version of God with his own morals and ethics, and a particular set of solutions to death and death anxiety, a transformation in the character of God or the coming of a new God. In either case, the coming of Christ represents, as Miles (2001) put it, the second chapter in the history of God. In this context, as we go over his life and teachings, and evaluate his successes and failures in providing for humankind's most basic needs, it will be well for us to ask if we are, at present, once again at a crisis point in the history of God. If so, strange as it may sound, we or God may be in need of finding a way to begin to move toward a third chapter in his history—his third incarnation, if you will. More on that later.

My plan is to explore the story of Jesus mainly in terms of how he is viewed by and what he offers to those who fully believe that he was and is God incarnate. The key question I shall ask in this context is this: Given that Jesus is at one with God for much of the Western world today, what does he offer to those who believe in his holiness in the way of dealing with death and death anxiety, and to what extent does he provide them with sound moral guidelines? That said, to fully appreciate the psychological and emotional

125

impact of Jesus as God or the Son of God, I shall first comment on the historical Jesus, after which I shall turn to the Jesus of faith.

THE HISTORICAL JESUS

As I have tried to show, death is everywhere for everyone—there are no exceptions. To be convinced of this archetypal truth, all one needs to know is how to recognize its presence, be it manifestly in our awareness as is the case with acute traumas, or deep unconsciously and encoded in our narrative messages in response to traumatic incidents whose death-related effects are neither self-evident nor conscious. Possibly taking form as a significant but unmentioned trauma, death may well have been at the very center of humankind's first interactions with God in the Garden of Eden. Death also set the tone for life outside of Eden, beginning with the tale of Cain and Abel, and it runs like a red thread throughout the Hebrew Testament and colors almost all of humankind's negotiations with Yahweh. As we shall soon see, death is omnipresent in the story of Jesus Christ as well.

As a perspective on the power of the deep unconscious, invisible hand of death in writing the story of great religious figures, we may recall that while he is perhaps best understood as a quasi-religious figure, the Buddha, who was born in 623 BCE, lost his mother soon after she gave birth to him. His father then tried to protect him from contact with suffering and death, but in time, it happened nonetheless. When his first child, a son, was born, the Buddha embarked on his life journey in search of tranquillity and happiness, and he eventually found success through a moral, peace-seeking, ascetic way of life that had religious overtones even though it did not require a belief in God (Armstrong 2001). At that time in history—to this day, timing and newly expressed human needs, many of them death related, play a notable role in the history of religious thinking—humankind was in need of a new spirituality because it was entering the axial age in which individuality and individual needs were becoming far more prominent than those of the group (Armstrong 2001, 2005)—a critical transition from mass-centered to person-centered need systems.

Muhammad's father died six months before he was born in 610 AD, and his mother died when he was six years old. Here too death and lingering forms of death anxiety evidently set the stage for his later calling as a prophet who was recruited by Gabriel—the same angel of God who revealed to Mary that she had been chosen to bear the Christ child—to establish the religion of Islam. Muhammad is considered to be a descendant of Ishmael, and his role as the prophet to whom the Qur'an was divinely revealed was established at another time of great need because the Muslim community was sorely lacking in its own religious revelations and leadership (Armstrong 1992).

As for the historical Jesus of Nazareth, he was an infant whose biological father was absent and unknown to him—some historians lean toward the possibility that his father was an itinerant Roman soldier (Chilton 2000). In the deep unconscious mind, such a father is experienced as having abandoned his infant son to die and thus as a man who has attempted to murder his own child. A version of this murderous archetype is to be found in the story of Abraham and Isaac, which involves a father's intention to kill his son, who is saved by a last-minute reprieve from God's angel. This archetype of parental violence also is the fundamental trauma and driving force behind the myth of Oedipus—and in the personal life of Freud as well (see chapter 11).

To fully understand the life of the historical Christ, we need to appreciate that there is a basic archetypal response in children who are the victims of parental violence and abandonment. Characteristically, it entails the sometimes conscious, and more often deep unconscious, effort, carried out directly as well as indirectly, to cause harm to and destroy the offending parents. Most often this is done through real but symbolic means, much of it with self-harmful qualities. It is a kind of cutting off one's nose to spite one's face, that is, harming oneself as a way of harming one's extremely damaging parent. More rarely, the victim's predatory death anxiety and reactive, vengeful violence to this horrendous, sinful act of predation takes the form of a direct physical attack against the assaultive parents. That said, there are rare individuals who, for deep unconscious reasons, behave in ways that run contrary to this archetype—both Christ and Freud evidently followed this path.

Historically, then, at the very beginning of his life on earth, the historical Jesus experienced a severe dose of predatory death anxiety and a threat to his very existence. As a child without a father, he also suffered as an outcast—a *mamzer* (Chilton 2000)—which had further predatory qualities. In addition, according to some historians, the baby Jesus was faced with an external threat to his life: Having been warned that a pretender to the king of the Jews was about to be born, Herod, the Roman ruler of Palestine, issued an order that his troops murder all newborn Jewish males. Jesus spent much of his life being pursued by the Romans for this and other contentious reasons as he grew into adulthood (Chilton 2000). He managed to stay one step ahead of his predatory pursuers—including an early trip as a newborn to the safety of Egypt—until the fateful day on which he stepped into the temple and made himself known to them—and all of Palestine—as a rebel and renegade.

This historical information, however controversial it may be, has several important ramifications. For one, it shows the extent to which death and death anxiety, especially its predatory and existential forms, played a role in the development and the unfolding life of Jesus. Yet common knowledge indicates that Jesus was not a man of anger and belligerence, but instead a man of peace at all costs. This means that by and large, he did not adhere to the archetype that presses for revenge on his offending parents, although as an adult, he did reject his family and family values when he returned to his home town to preach as a rabbi. Christ showed, then, what Freudians would call a strong "reaction formation" in response to these early life events— essentially a turning into the opposite, transforming vengeance into peaceful loving. Even so, Jesus's last provocations of and challenges to his fellow Jews and the Romans may have had their roots in his early death-related traumas, and historically, his evident need to give up his life may have unconsciously been directed at his parents—in particular, his mother, Mary, who was witness to his crucifixion.

Deep unconsciously, there are, then, all but universal, death-related archetypes, and rarely expressed counterarchetypes, that drive and direct human behavior based on deep unconscious experiences with death and death anxiety. The vengeful archetype that is aroused in victims of predation is most clearly represented in the myth of Oedipus, who murders the father who maimed and tried to murder him, and causes his mother, who was party to the original crimes, to commit suicide. Oedipus lived out the archetype that Jesus turned against.

THE JESUS OF FAITH

In approaching the Jesus of faith—a subject recently explored productively and in some detail by Wills (2006a, 2006b)—I shall focus on his dealings with death and death anxiety and his moral teachings. As I indicated, in the main, I shall be asking how the belief in Jesus Christ as the Son of God or as God incarnate enables humans to cope effectively with these archetypal issues. In this connection I shall also explore the extent to which Jesus showed signs of being in possession of divine wisdom, and I shall deal with the question of the nature of this wisdom as well.

Jesus's story essentially begins with his baptism by his cousin, John the Baptist, an event cheered on and blessed by God himself. There immediately follows a forty-day trial of survival in the desert without food during which Jesus is challenged and tempted three times by Satan. Asked to prove that he is the Son of God, Satan first asks Jesus to turn stone into bread, but Jesus finesses this dare by replying,

"Scripture tells us, bread alone does not give man his life." (Lk 4:4)

Next, Satan shows Jesus all the realms of the world in a single glance. If Jesus will but bow to him, Satan proposes to transfer their power and glory, which he himself possesses, to Jesus. This time Jesus's response is

"Scripture tells us, to the Lord alone will you bow, and him only serve." (Lk 4:8)

Finally, Satan takes Jesus to the temple in Jerusalem, places him on the pinnacle, and chides him by saying that if Jesus is God's son, he should throw himself down from the pinnacle since the scripture tells us that God will send his angels to see to it that no harm comes from the fall. Jesus's response to this death-related threat is

"Scripture tells us: You will not experiment upon the Lord, your God." (Lk 4:12–13)

Jesus's forty days of temptation and deprivation in the desert echoes the forty years spent by Moses and the Jews in the desert before they reached the promised land. Existential death anxiety and issues of survival are prominent here, but there also is a strong predatory challenge: In Exodus, it is made by nature—the conditions in the desert—while for Jesus, it is posed by both nature and Satan. Life-threatening challenges of this kind are a crucial part of the stories that embody the hero archetype from Gilgamesh on down. Both the Buddha and Muhammad went through such ordeals, as did Oedipus when he was challenged by the riddle of the Sphinx, who put his life at risk as he journeyed toward Thebes.

The archetypal parallel between Satan and the Sphinx is striking. Both Oedipus and Christ show a strong capacity to deal with these life-threatening challenges using divine wisdom of a kind that is lacking in the common man. It seems likely that their very early experiences with abandonment and death played a role in their acquisition of this unique wisdom.

Crucially, however, Oedipus's answer to the riddle of the Sphinx is knowledge based and reflects divine insight into the nature of man and the human condition—wisdom that he may have garnered firsthand through his brush with death. His is, then, a form of *divine psychological wisdom*. In contrast, Christ's knowledge is *divine wisdom of faith* and is based on an abiding belief in God. Even though Satan's temptations and Christ's ability to finesse them have extensive psychological meanings, Christ does use psychological insights to deal with and defeat Satan—his wisdom is numinous and religiously spiritual. This difference in the knowledge base is, as I shall soon try to show, of great import in understanding the Christian religion and its successes and failures.

THE PARABLES

Another feature of Jesus's responses to Satan is that they are indirect, mysterious, and enigmatic, with a strong aura of profundity. They appear to be fore-
runners of the parables that Jesus makes use of extensively in his sermons and
meetings with his disciples. These stories are narrative and, as discovered in
studies undertaken from the adaptive vantage point, they therefore have the
potential to carry deep or divine insights that cannot be conveyed in a
straightforward, nonstoried manner. Jesus evidently intuitively understood
that parables carry unconsciously expressed, encoded meanings that reflect
and encode divine wisdom. But he also appreciated—and this is often overlooked today—that only a few of his most gifted followers had the ability to
grasp the deeper meanings of these tales. Even as his surface messages were
for all of humankind, his encoded messages were not for the common man.
This is, by the way, another archetypal feature of divine communications including those that are exceptional in a spiritual way.

Jesus's use of parables and his comments on these extraordinary vehicles
of communication are perhaps best illustrated in the parable of the sower
whose seeds could grow only in a fertile field.

On that day Jesus went out of the house, and was sitting by the sea. And great
multitudes gathered to Him, so that He got into a boat and sat down, and the
whole multitude was standing on the beach. And He spoke many things to them
in parables, saying,

"Behold, the sower went out to sow; and as he sowed, some [seeds] fell beside the road, and the birds came and ate them up. And others fell upon the rocky
places, where they did not have much soil; and immediately they sprang up, because they had no depth of soil. But when the sun had risen, they were scorched;
and because they had no root, they withered away. And others fell among the
thorns, and the thorns came up and choked them out. And others fell on the good
soil, and yielded a crop, some a hundredfold, some sixty, and some thirty.

"He who has ears, let him hear."

And the disciples came and said to Him, "Why do You speak to them in parables?" And He answered and said to them, "To you it has been granted to know
the mysteries of the kingdom of heaven, but to them it has not been granted. For
whoever has, to him shall [more] be given, and he shall have an abundance; but
whoever does not have, even what he has shall be taken away from him. Therefore I speak to them in parables; because while seeing they do not see, and while
hearing they do not hear, nor do they understand. And in their case the prophecy
of Isaiah is being fulfilled, which says, 'You will keep on hearing, but will not
understand; and you will keep on seeing, but will not perceive. For the heart of
this people has become dull, and with their ears they scarcely hear, and they

have closed their eyes lest they should see with their eyes, and hear with their ears, and understand with their heart and return, and I should heal them.'

"And the one on whom seed was sown among the thorns, this is the man who hears the word, and the worry of the world, and the deceitfulness of riches chokes the word, and it becomes unfruitful.

"And the one on whom seed was sown on the good soil, this is the man who hears the word and understands it; who indeed bears fruit, and brings forth, some a hundredfold, some sixty, and some thirty."

All these things Jesus spoke to the multitudes in parables, and He did not speak to them without a parable, so that what was spoken through the prophet might be fulfilled, saying, "I will open My mouth in parables; I will utter things hidden since the foundation of the world." (Mt 13:1–50)

In many instances, Jesus first tells and then translates or in a limited way decodes the hidden meanings that he has disguised and embedded in his parables. His offerings are, however, broad, general translations, and they are not adaptation oriented—triggers are seldom if ever addressed or used as decoding keys. Nevertheless, with great consistency, their hidden, divine messages deal with the rewards of being a believer in God such as residing some day in the heaven in which he sits on his throne—they are then words of wisdom from a God on high. There also is a strong moral message in many of the parables; consistently, they manifestly teach that one is rewarded for being good, kind to others, disinterested in gaining worldly possessions, and the like.

All in all, then, the parables are mixed communicative vehicles: They are packed with directly conveyed, conscious, mundane wisdom for all to hear and understand, but they also are fraught with deep unconscious, encoded, divine wisdom that is open to only a select few. However, on both levels they are offered in the service of enhancing one's faith and belief in God and in the service of establishing guidelines for righteous behavior. These morality tales are not concerned with insights into the psychology of human nature except for indicating how certain kinds of malignant and self-serving needs and inclinations tend to interfere with both morality and faith, and how those who do good and lead model lives will be rewarded with an eternal afterlife in heaven.

In this connection, we may recall that adaptive studies of human communication indicate that divine, deep unconscious wisdom finds expression solely through encoded narratives (Langs 2004c). This means that stories like parables are a distinctive way of expressing oneself; they are to be distinguished from explanations and other kinds of intellectualizations that are unidimensional and carry a single, straightforward meaning along with an evident set of extractable implications. Implications are very different from

disguised or encoded meanings in that implications are extracted from manifest messages in light of their broad contexts—for example, his cough implies
that he is ill. In contrast, an encoded meaning is disguised in a story, and it
must be decoded in light of the *triggering event* that has evoked it—for example, his story about the angry teacher encodes his *unconscious perception*
that his father wants to murder him for failing history.

Narratives carry two messages in a single tale. One message is manifestly
or directly stated, while the second message is encoded or disguised in those
same contents. As for divine wisdom, it is never conveyed through an intel-
lectualization because no matter how clever they may be, these communications are conscious system–based and capable of conveying only mundane
knowledge. On the other hand, numinous wisdom is expressed through the
encoded meanings of dreams and other storied communications that are reflections of deep unconscious reactions to triggering events. It cannot be said
often enough that this kind of wisdom is adaptive and expressed unconsciously, that is, without our conscious awareness that we are experiencing
and communicating such god-like insights that must be trigger decoded to reveal their extraordinary richness. Nevertheless, Christ seems to have been
aware that he was expressing a form of divine insight and to have had some
sense of the more palpable hidden or implied meanings of his parables,
which, all things considered, seem to communicate knowledge that is partly
mundane and partly divine.

Divine wisdom is unconsciously expressed and encoded. It is activated,
adaptive wisdom that is a reflection of our efforts to cope with some of the
most emotionally painful dangers and death-related threats that befall us
and to do so without conscious awareness of the meanings and processes involved. It is archetypal wisdom that is pertinent to a current adaptive challenge, rich in perspectives that are missed consciously, and fraught with
god-like, numinous, universally invoked solutions for dealing with traumatic events. It is of a different order from conscious system-mundane wisdom, and far superior to it as well. In its religious sense, it marks out the
pathways to humankind's transcendental God and speaks for our inner god
of wisdom and morality as well.

Because divine wisdom is based on the uncompromised recognition of the
most base and harmful intentions and behaviors of ourselves and others, and
because this wisdom also is connected with painful realizations pertaining to
our human vulnerabilities and mortality, the conscious mind, by holy or
evolved design, has little or no interest in gaining access to this kind of
knowledge. When offered the opportunity to do so, the conscious mind tends
to be opposed to and to resist decoding narratives in light of their evocative
triggers, and more basically, it is disinclined to acknowledge that deep un-

conscious experiences and wisdom actually exist. Most thinkers either ignore this realm or try to reduce its divine wisdom to mundane insights. This is one of the reasons that mainstream psychoanalysts have failed to make use of trigger decoding and have been unable to develop a body of divine, death-related wisdom applicable to emotional life and its neuroses. Psychoanalysts are, in general, phobic about death and death-related traumas, and they sustain their avoidance of death with a variety of highly intellectualized, conscious system, denial-based defenses. Essentially, they write about and work with patients focused on any subject as long as it is not death-related. This is also the case with most religious writers as well.

Coming back to Jesus, one of the differences between him and Yahweh is that the Hebrew God spoke to humans in a direct, straightforward manner, while Jesus often spoke using narratives. On the other hand, if Yahweh dictated the Pentateuch to Moses, he was as great a narrator as Jesus. In any case, neither Yahweh nor Jesus did much more than tell stories; they did not engage in any kind of deep interpreting or trigger decoding.

The offer of encoded, divine wisdom in interacting with humans is the first feature that distinguishes Jesus from the Hebrew God. Still, we should keep in mind that the divine wisdom that Jesus propounds centers on the benefits of faith in his teachings and not on self-knowledge or on the understanding of human psychology, especially as it pertains to death and death anxiety. Instead, Jesus shines a beacon light on the road to salvation in which love, compassion, and sacrifice are set as moral guidelines and a path is forged along which devotees can or will in the future follow Jesus to heaven. Even the Gnostic gospels, which present Christ as advocating divine self-knowledge, are developed around the idea that knowing oneself is a means of salvation (Pagels 1989; Barnstone and Meyer 2003). They do not, however, show how such knowledge is to be garnered or how it pertains to the psychological forces within the human mind.

PREDATORY DEATH ANXIETY

Jesus approached death and death anxiety in ways that are radically different from those of Yahweh. There are strong indications that the God of the New Testament was a changed divine being who had made peace with his issues with death and death anxiety. On this basis, he was able to offer humans the means by which they could solve their own conflicts surrounding death and make peace with their experiences of conscious and deep unconscious death anxiety. Importantly, the solutions he had to offer depended solely on a person's believing in the divinity of Jesus, God's son or God incarnate, and therefore essentially was available to anyone who saw the light, Jewish or otherwise. This potential for universal applicability was buttressed by the fact that Jesus preached to and performed miracles for Jews and non-Jews alike; in contrast to Yahweh, Jesus very much practiced what he preached.

Most astounding, however, is the discovery that through his parables, preachings, miracles, moral guidelines, and behavior Jesus actually offered remarkably solid solutions to each of the three very different forms of death anxiety. Where Yahweh had completely failed to bring relief from this disruptive scourge, Jesus seems to have completely succeeded—in principle, if not in all practicality.

As I have said, *predatory death anxiety* arises when another living being or a natural event threatens to harm or destroy us. For his part, Yahweh did a great deal to increase rather than diminish predatory death anxiety in the Jews as well as their enemies. He did so in countless ways such as advocating war, resorting to violence against innocent victims when it served his purposes, punishing those who offended him in the least manner, not punishing many individuals who harmed or murdered others without good cause, and not offering clear moral guidelines that spoke against the use of violence against others.

Christ dealt with this form of death anxiety in a very different way. He intuitively addressed the problem of human violence on the level of its most basic and manifest sources, such as being inclined to be territorial, fearing the loss of resources, being mistrustful of strangers, being greedy and overvaluing worldly possessions, reacting aggressively to being attacked by others, becoming angry at oneself and others in response to one's own state of illness or injury, suffering from poverty or deprivation, being prejudiced against others who have different opinions from oneself, entering politics and generally contentious political debates, invoking politically motivated claims against others, promoting highly conflicted political or religious causes, and the like.

In regard to each of these controversial issues, Christ preached avoidance, self-control, and renunciation. He sermonized against responding to predators with the use of provocative and retaliatory violence and favored nonviolent, passive resistance to all manner of threats. He advocated the acceptance of one's enemies in lieu of vicious counterreactions, and he especially honored the ill and downtrodden. He promised them heavenly salvation as a way of uplifting them so they would not be unduly aggressive against those who had more than they had. In addition to teaching and preaching these principles, Christ lived by these credos and was thus an exemplar of nonviolence and living with others in peace, respect, kindness, and harmony.

Jesus's sermon on the mount begins

Blessed are the poor in spirit: for theirs is the kingdom of heaven. (Mt 5:3)

Jesus goes on to bless those who mourn; the meek, who shall inherit the earth; those who hunger and thirst after righteousness, for they shall be filled; the merciful, who shall obtain mercy; the pure in heart, who shall see God; the peacemakers, who shall be called the children of God; those who are persecuted for righteousness' sake, for theirs is the kingdom of heaven; and those who are reviled, persecuted, and spoken against falsely as evil for his—Jesus's—sake. Christ then advises his followers and disciples,

Rejoice, and be exceedingly glad: for great is your reward in heaven. (Mt 5:12)

There is as well the admonition to turn the other cheek when struck and to not support those who exploit, seek power, and strive for wealth:

Little ones, it is very hard to enter God's reign. It is easier for a camel to get through a needle's eye than for a rich man to enter into God's reign. (Mk 10:23–25)

Christ expands on this theme through the parable of the rich man whose accumulated wealth goes for naught, and he offers direct advice to those of means to not worry about food or clothing, to sell their goods and give to the poor, and to invest in the rewards of heaven, where the heart is. He then says that humans cannot serve both God and greed, while arrogance, wealth, and power are enemies of the spirit.

Jesus also lived his life and offered guidance in ways that were very likely to reduce human predatory inclinations. He did so through his belief that all humans are equal and that contentious religious hierarchies should be eliminated. Christ actually mingled with and helped all manner of people, many of whom were rejected and shunned by others. The long list of those whom he succored include Jews, non-Jews, the much-maligned Samaritans, women, prostitutes, and others in similar straits, and tax collectors and Roman officials. Jesus deeply understood that prejudice, bias, hierarchical ordering, and the like breed violence and predation. His opposition to such attitudes and practices offered an implicit set of moral guidelines that could promote peaceful coexistence regardless of race, color, creed, and religious beliefs. Nothing of the kind previously had been offered by Yahweh.

Christ also spoke out directly against the use of violence, and he lived his own life accordingly. A sampling of his words shows the extent to which his moral guidelines were explicitly geared toward reducing predatory death anxiety in both offending parties and their victims:

I say to all you who can hear me: Love your foes, help those who hate you, praise those who curse you, pray for those who abuse you. To one who punches your cheek, offer the other cheek. (Lk 6:27–38)

This sermon goes on in this vein for a while and concludes with a promise to those who heed his advice that they will be the children of the Highest One, who also favors ingrates and scoundrels. As a lover of peace, Jesus also orders Peter to not use his sword when Roman soldiers come to take Jesus to prison. He also advocates the use of nonviolence in the political arena, although he suggests that it is best and most moral to avoid politics entirely lest it lead one to violent confrontations. Thus,

Caesar's matters leave to Caesar. (Mk 12:17)

Jesus does make one allusion to coming to earth with sword in hand, but this image clearly is meant metaphorically rather than implying a turn to violence under any circumstance. "Live the peaceful, righteous, moral life and you will enter heaven's reign," was Christ's ultimate message. It was by this means that humans were to be spared being preyed on and could live their lives without—or with a minimal amount of—predatory death anxiety. All in all, it can be said that if humans could clearly grasp and consistently heed Christ's teaching vis-à-vis predatory death anxiety, this dread as it pertains to provocations by other humans could be all but eradicated, leaving us with only natural disasters to worry about. The implied hope was that if humans came to love their fellow humans, God would spare us these material dangers as well.

PREDATOR DEATH ANXIETY

The second form of human death anxiety for which Jesus offered a remarkable and compelling form of relief is *predator death anxiety*—the conscious but even more powerful deep unconscious experience of the need for punishment for harm done to others—harm that almost always is quite real, but also may be imagined. There is, as I said, a strong and abiding archetype that lies deep within the human psyche—that is, in the deep unconscious system of morality and ethics—that insists that an offender be punished by death for having damaged others physically or psychologically. This brutal deep unconscious archetype is reflected in the psychotherapy situation through displaced allusions to suicide by guilt-ridden patients. Such images appear at some point in sessions in which their deep unconscious guilt is triggered by a death-related incident and is being worked over and processed outside of awareness. Because they emerge in other contexts, these suicide images seem to be disconnected from the sources of their guilt, but they are strongly linked deep unconsciously.

In terms of human morality, uncalled-for damage to others is viewed as a sin against humankind, God in heaven, and our inner God—and Christ dealt with it as such. This amoral need to harm others is, as I said, driven by anxieties caused by a death-related trauma, and the activated death anxieties may take any of its three forms. When existential death anxiety is aroused, for example, it tends to motivate violence against others as a magical unconscious attempt by the perpetrator to create the illusion of immortality— that is, the belief that if the victim dies, the perpetrator will live forever. On the other hand, the arousal of predatory death anxiety tends to motivate an overreaction to threat that often leads to unjustified violence against innocent victims as a way of asserting one's power and wished-for invulnerability to assault from others. Finally, the relentless guilt and need for punishment that is inherent in predator death anxiety unconsciously causes a person to act with undue violence against others as a way of goading them to carry out the punishment that those who do harm to others deep unconsciously believe is, and want as, their due.

As we saw, the Old Testament has little to offer when it comes to predator death anxiety. Yahweh does not seem to have been aware that this kind of anxiety plagues humankind. From the first moment when Eve and Adam defy his wishes and sin against him, the Lord God is insensitive to their guilt for having done so. While he does punish them for their transgression by expelling them from Eden and in other ways, he also protects them by clothing them despite their having sinned against him.

On the other hand, after actually murdering his brother (one version of this tale), Cain is one of the rare individuals in the Hebrew Testament who overtly suffers from predator death anxiety and the expectation of punishment through execution—a just outcome from the point of view of the deep unconscious system of morality and ethics. But even so, God protects Cain against this likelihood by marking his forehead and swearing vengeance against anyone who harms him.

All in all, guilt is rarely mentioned in this part of the Bible, and Yahweh tends to either ignore the problem of guilt over harming others or to take an ambivalent and uncertain position in that regard. We are left with the impression that the Hebrew God is inclined to protect abusers and murderers, which certainly is untenable morally and socially, and of little help in enabling humans to cope with predator death anxiety and their guilty needs for self-punishment.

In contrast to all of this, Jesus offers a truly remarkable and incisive solution to the problem of deep unconscious guilt and the personal need for punishment for sinful crimes committed. He appears to have intuitively recognized the fact that deep unconscious guilt is one of the most fundamental and

devastating plagues of humankind. And most importantly, his way of reliev-
ing us of this archetypal burden is reflected only to a small extent in his
preachings; instead, it is dramatically and incisively conveyed in the actual
path he chooses for his life.

It is almost impossible to overestimate the importance of God's decision to
incarnate as a human being, to come to earth to live a life of passion and pain,
to do far more than sermonize and tell deeply meaningful parables. Yahweh
becomes increasingly distant from humankind as the Old Testament unfolds.
But the Christian God is wrought real and of human flesh as Jesus Christ as
he walks among his fellow Jews and countless others. He not only preaches
peaceful coexistence and high morals, he lives and practices these values in
his everyday life. Teaching through living example is far more influential
than teaching through words alone.

Jesus alive on earth as both a man and God, or Son of God, has many missions. He endeavors to bring belief and faith in himself and God for all of humankind, excluding none; he tries mightily to bring peace to a war-weary
world and populace; he strives to offer humankind a new moral code of deep
benefit to both oneself and others; he shows the world the power of faith to
heal the ill and to bring the dead back to life; and to the extent that he is able,
he tries to correct the inequities and evils of both religion and the secular
world. None of this can be said of Yahweh.

That said, there are two critical missions that fall to Jesus's lot that Yahweh
did not even think of carrying out, two gifts to humankind that stand out far
more than the others. Each involves bringing relief to humans vis-à-vis their
most terrible forms of death anxiety—predator and existential. Far more than
predatory death anxiety, they are our most awful afflictions and undoing.
Kept within reasonable limits, predatory death anxiety has a positive and
adaptive side to it in that it stimulates potential victims of aggression to mo-
bilize their resources against the predatory threat. Thus, when responses are
kept within reasonable limits, the experience of predatory death anxiety tends
to enhance adaptation to danger situations. The human tendency to overreact
to the threat of harm is what makes this form of anxiety so self-defeating and
harmful to oneself and others.

By and large, however, predator death anxiety, which is linked to deep unconscious guilt and needs for punishment, contributes far more to the undoing of human lives than to serving as a source of creativity or peace. I say this
despite the conjecture that predator death anxiety and deep unconscious guilt
may serve adaptively to reduce the human inclination to act violently against
others—and as we saw with Cain, this constellation also may lead to creative
acts of atonement. Even so, by and large, these constructive mechanisms are

quite rare, and the unneeded destructiveness caused by deep unconscious guilt dominates the world today.

In this context, we may think of Christ's approach to the problems of sin and guilt—that is, to predator death anxiety—as an attempt to improve on the solutions evolved by nature, or alternatively, as an effort to solve the problems of life, death, and human morality left unresolved by Yahweh. Much the same can be said of Jesus's approach to the problem of existential death anxiety that I shall discuss in the next section of this chapter.

What then was Christ's cure for this grave form of death anxiety that arises when humans harm other humans and other kinds of living beings, or destroy properties or natural resources?

The answer is not explicitly stated in the Bible but comes as a widely accepted and logical interpretation of the events of the passion—the last twelve hours of Christ's life. The belief is that the crucifixion of Christ was orchestrated by God and that it fulfilled the ultimate reason for Christ's mission on earth, namely, so he could die as an accused sinner and criminal in order to expiate and have God forgive the sins and crimes of humankind, past, present, and future. Only a divine pact between God and his Son could accomplish this for all humankind, and the Christian God in his mercy arranged for it to be so.

Paul put it succinctly:

Christ died for our sins. (1 Cor 15:3)

That is, Christ's divine mission was to pay God the ultimate price for sinning against others so that mortal humans would need only to believe in Christ and pledge allegiance to him in devout faith to have their own sins forgiven by God as well. Both Paul (Wills 2006b) and Saint Anselm (Wills 2006a) argued persuasively that this was the case, adding that even Judas, who betrayed Christ to the Romans, was playing a role assigned to him by God. This point is made despite Judas's suicide, which appears to be the result of his own predator death anxiety—his deep unconscious guilt and need for punishment—for the part he played in Jesus's crucifixion.

Another way of describing the divine archetypal implications of Christ's execution is the belief that before he went to heaven, he descended into hell and brought forgiveness to all those who had sinned and had been condemned to spend eternity with Satan. Indeed, Christ's death on the cross—the healing crucifix—is itself a divine act, a healing of the wounds of sinners and a way of paying the requisite price of death for all those who deep unconsciously deserve and seek death as punishment for their sinful crimes against others. The magnificence of Christ's gift to humankind in taking care of and resolving their predator death anxieties is both numinescent and awe inspiring; it is a facet of the belief in the Christian God that has an almost irresistible appeal.

Christ gave his life, then, to save others, sinners who, beginning with Adam (and Eve), acted against God's will and precepts. Adam and Eve's defiance of God was considered by Augustine and many others as the original (the fundamental or archetypal) sin that has been passed down from one generation to the next and for which all future humans would have to pay. This idea pays homage to the realization that to be human is to be a sinner, that life and death are such that sinning is inevitable, and that Christ died to redeem all of humankind in light of this burden. Christ's death on the cross, which he accepted almost, though not entirely, without protest as his human side cried out to God, broke this chain of transmitted sins and universal sinning. Given that the roots of the sin were divine, its resolution also had to be divine: No mere mortal could do what God's son, Jesus Christ, could do—and did.

The compassion for human suffering and the need to bring relief from these travails, so lacking in Yahweh, are evident in the Christian God and help to explain the wide appeal of the basic tenets of Christianity to this very day. Indeed, the relief from the burdens of sinning that was afforded to believers in Jesus Christ drew many men and women to his faith.

By no means, however, is this the end of the story. I shall soon raise the vital question as to whether Jesus's ingenious, faith-based solution to predator death anxiety has in fact solved the problem of human violence and predation. But before I turn to this troublesome subject, let's look at how Jesus offered relief to humankind for the third and most daunting of the types of death anxiety—its existential form.

EXISTENTIAL DEATH ANXIETY

Ever since Eve bit into the forbidden fruit and acquired divine knowledge of death, we, as humans, have been aware of its inevitability for each and every one of us. Death is our ever-present enemy, and *existential death anxiety* is our ever-present, albeit usually deep unconscious, source of emotional suffering. Death is an antagonist against which we valiantly fight at times of emotional and physical crisis in the hope of loosening its stranglehold on us so we may survive for another day or longer. Nevertheless, we also are keenly aware that we can defeat death for only so long (or short) a period of time, and that eventually and inevitably we will be defeated in this battle, which some commentators view as being carried out against Satan

(Kelly 2006). This realization is at the heart of human helplessness and despair, and despite many different efforts to create the illusion or delusion that it can be otherwise—that is, that we can live forever—the ultimate secular truth, the existential ground rule and most basic archetype of life, is that without exception, it ends in death.

Human responses to existential death anxiety tend to be basically maladaptive and only rarely constructive and salutary. As a result, they cause a great deal of harm to oneself and others. This arises mainly because humans deal with the inevitability of personal demise by invoking a wide variety of denial mechanisms, not only in thought but also in behavior. Many of these behavioral responses are damaging to both oneself and others—denial, which usually is involved unconsciously without conscious recognition of its use or purpose, tends to be a very costly mechanism for all concerned. The missteps and loss of insight caused by obliterating reality are a major source of violence against oneself and others. Denial also causes humans to engage in many harmful death-defying and death-denying acts such as killing others; ignoring life-threatening bodily symptoms; engaging in violent acts of conquest; seeking undue power, property, and wealth at great cost to others and oneself; engaging in destructive rituals and sacrifices as a way of dismissing the threat of dying; and much more. Most of these unwitting efforts to deny death have immoral, sinful qualities to them, and inevitably, they fail to bring lasting peace to those who invoke them. Instead, they provoke predatory death anxiety in their victims and predator death anxiety in the perpetrators of harm, thereby leading to enmity, violence, and war.

In the main, the Hebrew Bible simply accepts death as a natural end to life and blandly alludes to the death and burial of many of the prominent figures whose stories it tells. Death is accepted as such with little fanfare or consolation. There is a vague sense that God may well sit in heaven and that good souls may join him there, but even though some of the prophets ascend to heaven for a brief period of time, there is no explicit allusion to an afterlife as such. Death is death, may the dead rest in peace. This does little to assuage the human fear of nonbeing, and it allows existential death anxiety to flourish unchecked and unabated.

The Christian God offers a remarkable solution to existential death anxiety, which Christ simply enacts and lives out at the end of his mortal life on earth: He dies and is resurrected, that is, he returns to life to show his followers and others that although he had died in the flesh, he lives on in spirit and in some sense in body as well.

This touches on the second basic mission of Christ's incarnation: the palpable offer to humankind of the opportunity to live on after death and to sit beside God in the kingdom of heaven for all eternity. Christ promises that on the day of reckoning, judgment day, those who are deemed good and moral will be raised from the dead and brought to heaven, while those who are deemed bad, sinful, and immoral will be sent to the fires of hell for all eternity.

The prelude to Jesus's resurrection takes place when Christ brings back to life the dead child of a Roman official and the body of Lazurus, who has been dead for several days. These doings indicate that death can be undone and defeated, however temporarily, and it sets the stage for the resurrection. Enacted with both a non-Jew and a Jew—that is, without prejudice—these miracles created a strong belief in Jesus as the Son of God and attracted many followers to Christianity. Even so, it was trumped by Christ's reappearance after his crucifixion, a materialization witnessed by many of his followers, to their utter amazement and spiritual transformation.

Paul, who, according to some biographers (e.g., Wilson 1997), saw the resurrected Jesus many times after his conversion and who preached and promoted a universal belief in Christ and Christianity, described the essence of the resurrection in this way:

> My main concern was to pass on to you what was passed on to me, that Christ died for our sins, in accord with the sacred writings, that he was buried, that he arose on the third day, in accord with the sacred writings, that he appeared to Kephas, then to the twelve. After that, he appeared at the same time to more than five hundred of our brothers, many of whom are still with us, though some have died. After that, he appeared to James, then to all the emissaries. Last of all, he appeared to me, as by a late birth. (1 Cor 15:3–8)

The risen body of Jesus was both spiritual and corporal in that he allowed himself to be touched by Thomas—a most convincing experience. Jesus also shared meals with wayfarers, fishermen, and others, events that were foreshadowed by the last supper and followed through down the ages in the Eucharist, in which the faithful share in the body and blood of Christ. Also relevant is the heavenly banquet promised by Christ for his followers, who he said will feast in God's reign. At the last supper, Jesus also vowed that he would keep to his pledge to not drink from the vine until he drinks new wine in God's reign.

Jesus's stay on earth ends with his ascension, said to have occurred after he was last seen by Paul. He is now in heaven, at one with the Father and Holy Spirit. Jesus promises to send a Paraclete to spread the good news of life in Christ, and this announces the Pentecost, the moment when his followers go out to do exactly that. Jesus is resurrected in his followers, and his life is lived by all who have faith in him, a life that will end, as did Jesus's life, in a resurrection and an eternal stay in heaven beside the trinity-in-one of the Father, the Son, and the Holy Spirit. Here too, Jesus not only preached and promised, but also lived out that promise before the world at large.

SOME FINAL PERSPECTIVES

Believe in Jesus and be assured that you will not die—existential death anxiety is disposed of. This incredible solution to the most daunting form of death anxiety, made available to all of humankind by Jesus and then Paul and others, has greatly facilitated the spread of Christianity and related religions throughout the world. In this connection, it is noteworthy that Paul, who was born Saul of Tarsus and who was a Jew said to have been devoted to weeding out Christian doubters of Judaism, has an interesting story of his own. Some historians believe that he was present in some official capacity at the crucifixion of Jesus (Wilson 1997). Many, although not all, historians also believe that it was on the road to Damascus, where he intended to bring Christians "to justice," that he experienced the presence of Jesus and was struck blind, only to be soon healed according to Jesus's instructions (Wilson 1997; but see also Wills 2006b). These events transformed Paul into a devout believer who devoted his life to the establishment of Christian churches and to the telling of the divine story of Christ.

It is in keeping with our understanding of death anxiety to conjecture that if he was indeed present at Christ's execution, deep unconsciously Paul would hold himself accountable for what happened to Jesus—an expression of the archetype that moves us to hold ourselves responsible for the death of others who are important to us in our lives. Paul would have, then, experienced deep unconscious guilt and a strong need for punishment, but rather than commit suicide, as did Judas, he became blind and then, once sighted again, atoned for his sin by bringing Christ's teachings to the world at large. In this sense, he would be among the rare humans who found a way to atone for his sins in a creative manner. Still, there are signs of residual unresolved guilt in the way in which, late in his life, he may well have arranged for his execution by the Romans (Wilson 1997; see however Wills 2006b).

Along different lines, it is well to appreciate that the solutions to death anxiety offered by Jesus are among the most basic and richest rewards he provides for those who believe in his divinity. These cures for death anxiety have played a role in the spread of Christianity throughout the world, much of it through the martyrdom of early believers. Many Christians allowed themselves to be sacrificed for sustaining their belief in Christ in defiance of Roman law for at least three death-related reasons. First, because they identified with Jesus, who had allowed himself to be sacrificed on the cross, and they felt blessed accordingly; second, because Jesus's passively resistant solution to predatory death anxiety prompted them to die without protest when persecuted and prosecuted; and third and perhaps most importantly, their belief in the resurrection assured them that being martyred was a sure way to spend eternity in heaven—a belief that has spurred martyrs of all kinds to this very day, many of them senselessly violent and destructive toward others.

Summing up, Christ's presentation of three seemingly ideal solutions to each of the forms of death anxiety had—and still has—much to offer humankind in its quest for individual and collective peace and contentment. Yet the least glance at the world today shows that for most of humankind, these goals have not been achieved in any lasting way. Why this is so is the subject of the next chapter.

10

The Failure of Religious Beliefs

I have explored in some detail how Yahweh and Christ dealt with death anxiety and the extent to which they did or did not present humans with effective ways of coping with these issues. We have seen that Yahweh showed indications that he suffered from notable unresolved death anxieties and that he offered his followers little in the way of relief from any of the forms of death anxiety with which, inevitably, they would be obliged to cope. Indications are that by and large Yahweh adopted positions that aggravated and increased rather than alleviated these archetypal anxieties. And while there are many different factors that have contributed to the history of the Jewish people, their story does seem to bear out their continuous problems with death and death anxiety and the inability of their faith and religious beliefs to bring them peace on earth. Yahweh has not been especially good to or for the Jews.

Jesus on the other hand seemed to find ways to bring humans relief from each of the three forms of death anxiety. And in each case, the solution appeared to be ideal: Keep the peace in order to eliminate predatory death anxiety; accept Jesus's crucifixion as punishment for your own misdeeds and to gain relief from your own predator death anxieties; and believe in the resurrection of Jesus, and as a devout and moral believer, expect to be resurrected as he was, and anticipate living your life for all eternity in God's kingdom of heaven.

There can be no doubt that adhering to this creed and set of beliefs has through the centuries brought peace, joy, productivity, happiness, and love to many individuals and a measure of peaceful coexistence among nations. But it is equally certain that many of those faithful to Jesus have not only failed to find peace and fulfillment, but also found cause to act violently, often in

145

blatantly unjustified ways, both individually and collectively. The Christian religion and its various incarnations have been the basis for many a crusade, holocaust, and war (Harris 2004; Dawkins 2006; Hitchens 2007).

Without attempting a detailed appraisal of the effects of Judaism and Christianity on the history of humankind, it seems fair to say that looking at the state of the world today, we would have expected more from Yahweh and even more from Christ. Poverty, oppression of minorities, internecine warfare, ethnic cleansing, religious wars, international conflicts, undue individual suffering, pervasive, blind quests for power and immortality, dishonesty, exploitation of others, and downright sinfulness seem to hold sway. Satan tells Christ that God decided to dwell in heaven and willed Satan the world below; it would seem that throughout recorded history, granted the presence of saints, holy men and women, and the like, Satan nevertheless has been the dominant force in human behavior—and death and unresolved death anxiety his most powerful weapon (Kelly 2006).

Characterizing this state of affairs in terms of the focus in this book, it appears that Christ's solutions to death anxiety have failed to bring peace to the world ever since they were set in place by his disciples and Paul and became part of the widely accepted Christian faith. In the absence of a dramatic change in religious beliefs or in the ways God manifests himself, it seems clear that the past and present predict the future. This means that we sorely need to search for ways to change the workings of God—we (and he) need to begin the third chapter in his history. The story that began with Yahweh and moved on to Christ now needs another version of the Lord God and the morality and faith that he teaches and asks of us. Nothing less seems likely to change the world for the better.

As a first step toward this goal, given that Yahweh's provocativeness and ineptitude need little comment, I shall offer some insights into the probable reasons why Christ failed to bring peace to humankind. If we can identify the sources of his lack of success, they should point us toward the attributes needed for a God who can have more salutary effects on humankind and identify the hallmarks of a deeper and more satisfying moral life and religious experience. Along the way these insights can serve as a basis for a sound and workable secular spirituality as well.

THE MISSING ELEMENTS IN CHRIST'S TEACHINGS

The inability of Christ's model life on earth and his teachings to calm the world has at least four basic sources: a failure to appreciate the fundamental problems inherent in human nature; a related failure to recognize the pervasive impact of the three forms of death anxiety on human thinking and behavior; the advent of inexplicable natural catastrophes that harm seemingly innocent people and the related failure of God to answer the prayers of seemingly deserving souls in need of help; and gaps and limitations in Christ's teachings.

In this context, it is well to appreciate the scope of the problems God and religion face in their mission to bring individual and collective peace and love to humankind. To show how daunting the challenge is, the field of psychoanalysis, which ultimately seeks to achieve comparable goals, has done far less than religion to bring them to fruition. But even if psychoanalysis had begun to deal with the relevant underlying issues, the fact is, as I know full well as a practicing adaptive psychoanalyst, that every insight-oriented effort to bring truly divine, adaptive insight to a beleaguered individual meets at some point with unfathomable obstacles that are difficult, or at times impossible, to resolve. This is powerful testimony to the overwhelming struggle that is inherent in having a solidly grounded, deeply satisfying human life and to being able to live comfortably in harmony with others.

Where Freud spoke of teaching, parenting, and psychoanalysis as impossible professions, I would put at the top of this list living life itself, largely because it is haunted by death and the trio of anxieties it causes us. This is all the more reason to identify and acknowledge the basic flaws in religion. The failure to do so has been yet another major obstacle to change and to enabling us to have more fulfilling lives. Psychoanalysis has been of no help in this regard because it has been unable to turn inward to discover its own drastic shortcomings—impressionistic sciences that lack measurable data have enormous problems in doing so. We need to find the flaws in both disciplines—here I shall concentrate on religion and shall consider psychoanalysis in the next chapter—so we can offer believers and nonbelievers a more reliable and serviceable God or belief system to help them to better negotiate and survive the stormy seas of life.

Human Nature

There are many aspects of human nature and its psychology that challenge and often defeat religious faith, features that Christ either underestimated or failed to recognize and address. Many of these dysfunctional attributes are difficult to modify through any means, but some of these attributes have not been examined in any detail so we do not yet know the extent to which we can change these particularly disadvantageous aspects of our nature. For example, Christ preached high moral standards, nonprovocation, love and sacrifice for others, and peaceful coexistence. He offered as rewards for adhering to these creeds both the forgiveness of one's sins and eternal life. But in so doing, he did not take into account the many natural human inclinations that must be overcome to achieve these goals. These features are in-built—be they wrought by God or nature—and culturally programmed, and they tend to entail the very characteristics that Christ spoke against. They need to be recognized, their influence, much of it operating unconsciously, appreciated, and then dealt with and resolved or constructively modified in a definitive manner. Ignoring them has impaired the positive effects of religious thinking and faith in God throughout the ages.

A sampling of these troublesome aspects of human nature includes

Intense needs for safety and for having one's own secured space, and to be assured of adequate care and nurturance. These archetypal needs evoke a tendency to react violently against those who threaten or interfere with their satisfaction.

The natural inclination to seek a variety of self-serving, personal satisfactions in ways that often do not respect the rights and needs of others.

A strong tendency to react irrationally, violently, and immorally when threatened, challenged, or endangered by others or when in dire straits.

The need for revenge, regardless of cost, against those who have harmed us.

The tendency to turn to immoral ways of achieving frustrated goals and satisfactions.

The in-built tendency to be unaware of the death-related meanings of many traumatic incidents and to experience death anxiety unconsciously rather than consciously, and to thereby fail to appreciate the often relentless pressures they create to act in harmful, sinful ways against oneself and others.

The inclination to react violently when threatened or made anxious for any reason, and in particular, when religious beliefs are challenged by nonbelievers or by those who believe in other versions of God.

In substance, then, Christ underestimated the enormity of human insecurities and greed when it comes to surviving, and he also failed to appreciate the extent to which we turn to violence when we are endangered or threatened by others or by natural disasters over which we have no control. He also did not appreciate the extent to which, for countless reasons, humans turn to immoral and sinful ways of achieving their goals, especially when they are suffering from deprivation and deep unconscious death anxiety.

Direct preaching, the use of profoundly meaningful parables, the offer of a sound moral code, exemplary living according to this code, and the promise of relief from sin and death—as strong as this package is, it does not get beneath the surface of human life and delve into conscious system psychology or more importantly, the emotionally powerful realm of deep unconscious experience and adaptation. As a result, it does not provide a well-grounded basis for resolving the fatefully problematic design problems of the human mind and their adverse consequences. There is a clear need in religion for a supplementary psychology of human behavior that must, to be of help to all humans, provide access to divine wisdom as it illuminates the deep unconscious sources of these persistent, nefarious human traits—and that points to their salutary modification.

Death and Death Anxiety

While religious doctrines do of course deal with death, they have little to say about death anxiety, especially its unconsciously experienced manifestations. Short of a blatant death-related trauma, the conscious mind seldom thinks about death and has little if any appreciation that death anxiety has many subtle and unconscious manifestations and effects on both thinking and behavior. Looked at from the psychological viewpoint and placing issues of validity aside, the belief in the resurrection of Christ is one among countless ways that humans deny the finality of death. Denial is the archetypal human antidote against death and the existential death anxiety it evokes in us. And while denial may, through the blindness it creates, bring a measure of comfort to the denier, this relief is very costly because of the loss of vitally important knowledge it entails. In addition, the need to sustain the denial of personal mortality causes much harm to self and others; at best, any respite it offers is fragile and temporary. This means that faith in the resurrection is easily shaken and that religion needs a more effective and insightful way of dealing with humankind's existential death anxieties.

All in all, then, religions need to find ways to deal more comprehensively and effectively with death and the three forms of death anxiety it evokes. These anxieties, which tend to operate unconsciously, are the basic cause of the sinful traits and immoral needs and acts that undermine the salutary effects of religious beliefs. But in seeking to illuminate and change this state of affairs, religious leaders cannot rely on the conscious mind, because it is the seat of mundane wisdom, which is infested with denial-based mechanisms. As a result, it is unlikely to help us to arrive at the divinely wise solutions needed to deal more effectively with death and death anxieties, be it through religious or secular means. Strange as it may sound, we need, then, to turn to our inner god—to our own divinely gifted deep unconscious wisdom systems—in order to buttress and set right those religious beliefs in respect to a transcendental God that have interfered with our gaining personal inner peace and peace for all humankind.

Natural Disasters and Unanswered Prayers

Destructive natural events on both a massive scale and in individual lives are among the most daunting challenges for the religious belief in a loving and just God. Humankind has, from its earliest origins, experienced a wide range of natural disasters such as droughts and famines, hurricanes, tsunamis, earthquakes, and the like in which countless seemingly innocent or good and moral people are killed. On an individual level, there are countless fatal illnesses and injuries, many of them quite unexpected, that befall those whom we love, young and old. There also are innocent victims of murder and lesser but significant kinds of harm, and the randomness of being born into poverty and other kinds of personally damaging family and living conditions. In addition, there are countless situations in which seemingly reverent individuals have prayed for blessings and healing for themselves and those whom they love, only to find that their prayers go unanswered.

These kinds of incidents occur without letup, and they pose a serious challenge for religious believers. Christ had little to say about such happenings, and Christianity has done little to illuminate their meanings and how they can best be dealt with. Lacking too are insightful explanations for what appear to be irrational and unjustified acts of God against seemingly good souls and those who appear to be entirely innocent such as newborn babies and infants. Here, too, deeper insight into death and death anxiety is needed to provide well-grounded succor for those who suffer from these kinds of seemingly unjust God-given catastrophes. Unanswered prayers often touch on the search for miracles, and this too is a relatively unexplored area in need of clarification.

Religious Doctrines

I have proposed that Christ offered humankind significant avenues of relief from the three forms of death anxiety; it is time to account for their failures by asking what it was that he overlooked in his religious offerings and what were the flaws in his teachings. I have already made suggestions along these lines, so I will try now to pull them together into a comprehensive summary of how and why Christ inadvertently failed many his followers—and why they failed him.

One of the main problems lies with Christ's overriding focus, to the near-exclusion of all else, on moral guidelines and, most critically, on reasons why people far and wide should have faith in God and, by implication, in his teachings and in him as the Son of God or God incarnate. In essence, Christ's wisdom is a divine wisdom of faith and belief, of blind trust; it does not, however, also embrace a divine wisdom of human nature.

Christ's wisdom is divine in the religious sense of the word, but not in its secular sense. His teachings are conscious system teachings, and remarkable as they are, they are not based on trigger decoding or deep unconscious insights into human nature and its intricate psychology. His offerings appear to be the ultimate archetypes of religious beliefs, so it must be stressed that the relief that he offers from the three forms of death anxiety are all faith based. But for faith to hold strong and to not be shaken by discordant human needs and unexpected traumas, it must be supplemented with an understanding of the death-related archetypes that drive human behavior toward both inner peace and harmony with others on the one hand, and on the other, toward disharmony and conflict.

Given that there are mundane and divine forms of wisdom, we must expand our grasp of the sacred form in particular, because of the new insights and adaptive resources, many of them pertaining to death and death anxiety, that it alone can give us. There also are other kinds of wisdom that need to be identified and fathomed, such as a wisdom of faith and a wisdom of understanding, a wisdom of belief and a wisdom of insight into human psychology, and thus, spiritual wisdom and secular psychological wisdom.

In chapter 9, I illustrated the two kinds of wisdom by comparing Christ's answers to the threats posed by Satan with Oedipus's answer to the threat posed by the Sphinx. Both spiritual and secular knowledge come in mundane and divine forms, and both Christ and Oedipus appear to have had the ability to recruit the divine versions of their respective wisdom bases. There is, however, a sense of mystery as to the exact nature of the divine deep insights that each drew on, an uncertainty that we have seen before, for example in the story of Adam and Eve. Oedipus's knowledge appears to touch on the course of human life, and Christ's knowledge on the love of God and the moral way, and each of them uses these divine insights to cope effectively with a death-related threat. Still, for religion to effectively bring peace to humankind it must use and offer both kinds of divine wisdom—the spiritual wisdom of the parables and the knowledge wisdom of our inner god as encoded in our dreams and other stories.

Christ's religious wisdom can readily hold sway in good times, but it can be badly shaken when things do not go well. When faith seems manifestly rewarded, it is reinforced, but life seldom goes smoothly, and trauma is in such abundance that it repeatedly challenges faith. Divine psychological wisdom is a much-needed supplement that can enable believers to withstand the pressures that threaten to undermine their faith in God at times of crisis, be it Yahweh or Jesus Christ. This wisdom also must be called forth when individuals, common citizens as well as political and religious leaders, believe that they have reason to react belligerently when offended or hurt. This is the case because only deep unconscious divine wisdom can provide the necessary restraints and perspectives on the unconsciously experienced, death-related triggering events that move humans to act with irrational and unjustified violence against each other. Without such insights, these impulses tend to go unchecked, especially when they are unconsciously driven and uncalled for by prevailing circumstances. This brings us back to religion's need to delve deeply into death and death anxiety because divine psychological wisdom revolves around the experience of death-related traumas and their insightful mastery.

Let it be said, then, that the loving wisdom of faith must be supplemented by the loving wisdom of the psychology of death.

In addition to the crucifixion and resurrection, there are scattered allusions to death in the New Testament, the most dramatic involving Christ's bringing the dead back to life. And while there is the promise of eternal life, there are no allusions to death anxiety and no effort to alleviate its effects on our conscious, let alone deep unconscious, levels of experience. Even the Gnostic Gospels, which view gaining self-knowledge as identical with gaining knowledge of God, provide only the broadest and vaguest outlines of how to acquire this seemingly divine psychological wisdom (Pagels 1989; Barnstone and Meyer 2003). These writings have little or nothing to say about the specific nature of this wisdom and how it can bring peace to the faithful.

> If one does not [understand] how the fire came to be, he will burn in it, because he does not know his roots. (Pagels 1989, p. 126)

> If you bring forth what is within you, what you bring forth will save you. If you do not bring forth what is within you, what you do not bring forth will destroy you. (Pagels 1989, p. 126)

> Jesus said: "Let him who seeks continue seeking until he finds. When he finds, he will become troubled. When he becomes troubled, he will be astonished, and he will rule over all things." (Pagels 1989, p. 127)

> For God sent the son into the world . . . that the world might be saved through him. He who believes in him is not condemned; he who does not believe is con-

demned already, because he has not believed in the nature of the only Son of God. (Pagels 1989, p. 124)

At bottom, Christ's teachings and all the related religious beliefs created by his followers are based on conscious perceptions, thinking, and coping strategies—they are the output, and reflect the inclinations, of the conscious mind. But as I have tried to show, the conscious mind is beset with denial and ignorance, and it has a strong bias against dealing in depth with the death-related issues that are at the heart of emotional life. The conscious mind is inclined to develop answers to religious problems that are influenced and misguided by strong defensive, denial-based needs. As a result, the conscious mind is inclined to make imprudent and ill-advised decisions and to develop personally biased and often unhelpful decisions and opinions. Its religious biases also leave much to be desired.

These tendencies are reinforced by the fact that while the conscious mind and our conscious choices and actions are not influenced to any significant extent by deep unconscious wisdom (its link to death and death-related traumas rendering it anathema to conscious awareness), they are strongly affected by predatory death anxiety and unconscious needs for self-punishment as instantiated by the deep unconscious system of morality and ethics. These needs unwittingly skew conscious thinking and actions, religiously based as well as secular, in misguided and self-defeating directions.

This set of factors also explains why conscious morals cannot be relied on and why they are easily compromised. Conscious minds tend to turn to immoral acts when they are in need of punishment or death-related denial. As a result, conscious morality is inherently corruptible and often selfishly self-serving and harmful to oneself and others, tendencies that are buttressed by the conscious mind's frequent use of denial—in these cases, by the denial that one is behaving immorally, sinfully, and badly. On the other hand, deep unconscious morals exist as ideal, archetypal values that are unswervingly constructive, fair, and pristine, and that always are in the service of our best interests with full consideration of the interest of others. This is, of course, a major reason why we need to access and make use of deep unconscious, divine wisdom and morality to reshape and buttress religious standards—and secular morality as well.

It appears then that Christ—and Yahweh—failed us in part because at bottom their religious beliefs and moral standards were the products of unreliable conscious minds and essentially mundane wisdom that reached out to the easily threatened and compromised conscious minds of their followers. As I have said, without deep unconscious, divine wisdom, we do not handle the most vital aspects of life very well—it is the missing ingredient in religious thinking.

That said, the question arises as to how religion was—and is—to acquire the divine psychological insights it needs to bring peace to the world, individually and collectively. The answer is plain to see: These insights should have come from psychoanalysis, the in-depth study of human psychology and emotional life. It is quite clear, however, that, beginning with Freud, psychoanalysts did not answer this call. We therefore must disassemble psychoanalysis, identify its flaws and failings—and their sources—so we may understand why psychoanalysts failed to answer this implicit and imperative call. Only then can we begin to develop the correctives that will enable analysts to join with religion and secular efforts to produce a viable, sound spirituality. With this in mind, I turn now to a brief study of how and why psychoanalysts did not answer the unspoken call to play their part in the history of God and religion—and how we can help them to change course so they can do so.

Why Psychoanalysis Failed Religion

Despite efforts on both sides to separate and create enmity between religion and psychoanalysis (Freud 1927) and the occasional but marginal efforts to bring psychoanalytic thinking to religious ideas (Rizzuto 1979; Meissner 1984; Grotstein 1997a, 1997b; Waugaman 2000; Akhtar and Parens 2001; Ostow 2007), it is unmistakable that the two disciplines are or should be united in common cause: the devoted effort to bring peace and harmony to humankind. From the perspective of this book this means that both are—or should be—basically committed to helping humans to find solutions to and effective ways of coping with the fundamental issues raised by death and death anxiety. With this as their central commitment, other shared goals can then be identified and pursued.

In addition to looking at the extent to which psychoanalysis has fulfilled this mission—and more to the point, why it has failed to the remarkable extent that it has—there are several additional reasons for detouring into this thorny realm. For one, this book is a psychoanalytic study of religion and its wisdom, an undertaking that takes us into the realm that Jung called *archetypal psychohistory* (Edinger 1996). It seems important, then, to understand why psychoanalysts have had so little to say about and found so few ways to understand religious needs and beliefs and to aid religion in its development. In addition, we need to be clear about the features of the adaptive psychoanalytic approach on which this book is founded that makes this alliance not only feasible, but an absolute necessity.

Sigmund Freud, the founder of psychoanalysis, is largely responsible for the contentious qualities of the relationship between psychoanalysis and religion (Freud 1927). I therefore will try to offer new insights into why he took the antagonistic position that he did. Related to this subject is Freud's choice of the foundation myth of human emotional life (Freud 1917, 1924, 1925, 1940). He selected the Oedipus myth rather than the story of Adam and Eve in Eden, as I have done here, or of Jesus Christ, as Jung preferred (Edinger 1987)—an issue explored recently by Grotstein (1997a, 1997b). The role of death and death anxiety in Freud's thinking will come under scrutiny, and more broadly, I shall take a look at how psychoanalysis in general has dealt with these issues, especially as they pertain to its fractured ties to religion.

There are, in principle, two basic ways in which psychoanalysis and religion can and should be aligned: first, in the aforementioned pursuit of providing humankind with effective ways of gaining relief from the plagues of death anxiety, and second, by engaging in mutually beneficial interdisciplinary efforts to share ideas, insights, and adaptive strategies—that is, by striving to discover what religion can bring to psychoanalysis and what psychoanalysis can bring to religion.

Finally, the chapter includes a fresh description of the adaptive approach and presents its claim as the second chapter in the history of psychoanalysis. I shall also begin to indicate how this version of psychoanalysis can help to lay the foundation for a third chapter in the history of God.

TWO VERSIONS OF PSYCHOANALYSIS

Much as there have been two versions of God—Yahweh (distant) and Christ (interactive)—there are now two versions of psychoanalysis. They are essentially mind-focused or inner mental-Freudian (and its offshoots) with secondarily interactive features on the one hand, and on the other, basically adaptive and interactive-Langsian. Just as this book is an interpretation of religion based on the new psychoanalysis, I shall interpret the history of psychoanalysis and the story of Freud's work on the same basis. Given that the adaptive approach is a new way of understanding the nature and operations of the emotion-processing mind and of viewing the emotion-related world, the story that I am about to present will be very different from that made from the classical Freudian vantage point.

The Freudian Viewpoint

In essence, the Freudian view of emotional adaptation focuses on our inner needs and wishes as the source of both human creativity and human emotional suffering (Freud 1923). All of the versions of Freudian psychoanalysis—

Jungian, self-psychological or narcissistic, object relations or relational, inter-subjective, and the like—see disruptive inner mental needs and the mental experience of relationships and interactions as the basis for emotional ills—they are all mind-centered approaches. Most importantly, they are grounded in a way of listening to and formulating the meanings of human communications—essentially, what patients say and do in their therapy sessions—in a manner that is focused on these inner needs and wishes. These strivings are thought to be reflected in the direct and implied meanings of what is being said and done without consideration of an adaptation-evoking triggering event. A patient says he's angry at his father or his therapist, and at first glance, that is exactly what he means. Beyond that, there also is the idea that there is a superficial unconscious mental process at work that enables the patient to say that he's angry with his father when he's really—that is, unconsciously—angry at his therapist, or contrariwise, to say that he's angry at his therapist when he really is angry with his father. This displacement is referred to as *transference*, in that the patient is transferring his anger at his father onto the undeserving, innocent therapist. Notice that it's the patient's inner anger that is at issue here—there's little or no thought of what the therapist may have said or done to evoke the patient's displaced anger, although some latter-day analysts might give this question some superficial consideration.

In sum, then, mainstream psychoanalysts listen superficially, attend to manifest messages in isolation, disconnected from the triggering events that have evoked them, and propose that the unconscious meanings of these messages lie with implications of which the patient is unaware. The psychology involved is focused on troublesome inner needs that adversely affect the patient's emotional life. Even when interactions with the therapist are recognized as being in play, what matters is how the patient interprets these experiences. As for these symptom-causing inner proclivities, Freud saw them as incestuous wishes for the parent of the opposite sex and aggressive wishes against the rivalrous parent of the same sex. Latter-day analysts have focused on other aspects of inner needs to account for emotional dysfunctions.

Given that he is the founder of the field, I shall focus on Freud's thinking alone. Suffice it to say that the critical point for psychoanalysis vis-à-vis religion is that, no matter how defined, a psychology of inner wishes and needs has a restricted (nonadaptive) vision of how human beings function mentally and emotionally. From this vantage point an analyst has no choice but to conclude that the belief in God is little more than another inner wish, one that reflects the human longing for an omnipotent and omniscient caretaker—and in the case of Christianity, the wish to not die. For classical Freudians, that was and is the end of the story—their theory leads them to dismiss religion in a way that is demeaning for all believers.

That said, it is noteworthy that granted their limited and biased view of religion, as quasi scientists, mainstream psychoanalysts nonetheless could and should have asked why some 90 or so percent of humans entertain such wishes and show a broad need for a belief in God. Crucially, Freud did not take this step, and later in this chapter I will offer some new conjectures as to why he failed to do so.

The Adaptive Viewpoint

Adaptive psychoanalysis arose when it was discovered that something critical was missing in how analysts listened to and understood their patients. The missing element turned out to be the trigger or stimulus that had evoked the patient's responses—that is, his or her communications and behaviors. It became clear that the things patients were talking about were not determined primarily or solely by their inner wishes and needs; they were first and foremost a response to a disturbing communication or incident, efforts to cope with or adapt to traumatic events and their meanings. Inner needs were playing a role, but only by being activated by the event and shaping how, within the constraints of universal proclivities, a given patient reacted to a particular trauma. The new focus was on emotional adaptation, and it was in keeping with the evolutionary biology of living beings for whom, humans included, adaptation to environmental challenges has been and is the primary task. Put simply, to understand the operations of the human mind, both the stimulus and response have to be known, especially those stimuli that are experienced and processed outside of awareness—that is, deep unconsciously (Langs 2004c, 2005a, 2005b, 2006).

In psychotherapy sessions, it was only when the triggering event was identified that the response could be properly studied. These emotionally charged reactions occur on both the conscious and deep unconscious levels of experience and are conveyed through direct and encoded communications. Quite surprisingly, it turned out that for patients in psychotherapy or psychoanalysis, the triggers to which they were most sensitive came from their therapists—that is, they were constituted as their therapists' interventions. More rarely, the trigger proved to be a significant death-related trauma in the life of the patient. And in respect to listening to what patients said in response to these traumatic incidents, it emerged that they occasionally responded directly and consciously with manifest comments, but more often than not they automatically obliterated any conscious awareness of these anxiety-provoking inputs and said nothing directly about them. This arose because these patients were dealing with very damaging and consciously unbearable interventions in both word and deed, which accounts for why patients reacted to them with unconscious perceptions and deep unconscious adaptive processing efforts that were then encoded in their dreams and stories.

To illustrate: A therapist whom I supervised forgot a scheduled session with a young woman who was an inpatient at the hospital where he was a psychiatric resident. In the following session he apologized for his lapse, and the patient responded by telling him that it was all right, she knew how busy he is — he can add a session or two to make up for it. She then told a story about how her boyfriend had promised to come to the hospital to see her during visiting hours the previous night, but forgot to show up. She was furious with him and knew she should stop seeing him. He hates her because she won't sleep with him and he's trying to drive her crazy; he'd like to see her dead.

There's a lot to understand here from the adaptive viewpoint. There is the patient's conscious forgiveness of the therapist, which suggests that the conscious mind is denial prone — the therapist has been provocative and has earned her anger. The denial is buttressed with the wish to see the therapist more often. The patient's story comes next. It is manifestly and consciously about her boyfriend's lapse — a consciously addressed, traumatic triggering event — and her reaction is sensible and understandable as such. But we also know that there is another traumatic triggering event as well, namely, the therapist's lapse. The allusion to the boyfriend's abandonment is called a *bridging theme* because it connects the manifest story about the boyfriend with the encoded story about the therapist. It thereby serves to convincingly indicate that the surface story is indeed encoding an unconscious reaction to the therapist's absence. By recognizing that the story about the boyfriend reveals the patient's deep unconscious perceptions of and reactions to the therapist's lapse, we discover that her deep unconscious response to the therapist's error is very different from her conscious response.

On the deep unconscious level, the patient is furious with the therapist (compare that with her conscious forgiveness) and is telling herself to leave treatment (compare that with her conscious request for more sessions). She also understands deep unconsciously, but not consciously, that the therapist is angry with her because she has not been cooperating with him in the therapy. This last thought is expressed in disguise through the theme of the boyfriend's anger at the patient for not sleeping with him. In addition, the patient's thought that her boyfriend would like to see her dead seems to reflect her deep unconscious experience that the therapist's lapse was a way of treating her as if she did not exist. The deep unconscious mind expresses itself candidly, using very powerful, emotionally charged, raw images — and these undiluted experiences exert a powerful unconscious influence on our behaviors.

The vignette shows that *the emotion-processing mind* is a two-system, adaptive entity with a *conscious system or mind* that is linked to awareness and a *deep unconscious system or mind* that operates entirely without our conscious awareness. The main difference between the two systems is that the deep unconscious mental system perceives many of the most disturbing, death-related meanings of our most intense traumas, meanings that the conscious mind obliterates because they are intolerable to behold directly. But in addition, conscious adaptive processing is, as I said, denial prone, inclined to be self-defeating, relatively unwise if not downright ignorant about what matters most in life, and morally corruptible. It also is a highly individualized system whose perceptions and responses to incidents tend to vary from one person to the next.

In contrast, deep unconscious adaptive processing is profoundly knowledgeable and wise beyond anything that the conscious mind can muster. Its adaptive processing efforts are always carried out in our best interests and with a moral attitude that is considerate of the needs of others and in principle, grounded in sound ideals. The system operates on the basis of archetypes and broadly shared viewpoints that are timeless — it is the seat of what Jung called the *universal unconscious mind* (Jung 1968, 1972). The deep unconscious mind also is extremely death sensitive, and it processes the death-related implications of traumatic incidents in ways that arrive at highly adaptive responses that are unavailable to the conscious mind, responses that are, as noted, encoded in our dreams and stories.

The views and adaptive solutions of the deep unconscious mind almost always are diametrically opposite to those of the conscious mind. Thus, you arrive at one set of insights — limited, individualized, self-harmful, and often erroneous or false — with conscious guidance, and quite another set of insights — expansive, archetypal, valid, and constructive — using deep unconscious guidance. Similarly, you arrive at one set of insights about the Bible and psychoanalysis using the conscious mind, and in many respects, a very different set using the deep unconscious wisdom of your inner god. This means that adaptation-oriented trigger decoding of narrative communications is the sine qua non for accessing the divine wisdom that can best guide us in our studies and understanding of religion and psychoanalysis — and human life in general.

The bottom line is that because the adaptive approach is centered on how we cope with emotionally charged traumatic incidents and thus on death-related traumas, it bridges over to and joins forces with religion in seeking ways to understand the nature of these traumas and finding the best possible means of coping with them using divine cognitive insights in one case and divine religious insights in the other. An alliance with religion that cannot be forged in any truly meaningful manner from the inner-need vantage point of the first psychoanalysis is inevitable and productive on the basis of its second version.

THEORY AS CONFESSION

Armed with the newly won insights into the adaptive approach, I turn now to the life of Sigmund Freud. Given that he has had almost as much influence on the history of humankind as Yahweh and Christ, it behooves us to understand in some depth and in light of the key triggering events in his life how Freud dealt with — or failed to deal with — death and its attendant anxieties in both his psychoanalytic thinking and personal life. This understanding should provide us with some fresh insights into his position in respect to religion — and to the human mind in general. In this connection, I shall offer the conjecture that Freud's psychoanalytic formulations and attitudes toward religion were strongly influenced unconsciously by a significant death-related trauma of which he may not have been fully aware consciously.

In the prologue to this book, I suggested that Maugham's "Appointment in Samara" sums up the story of my choice of profession; much the same could be said for Freud. But there is another way to describe the death-related influences that affected his life and psychoanalytic thinking. It was penned by the philosopher Friedrich Nietzsche, who wrote,

> Gradually it has become clear to me what every great philosophy so far has been: namely, the personal confession of its author and a kind of involuntary and unconscious memoir. (2003, p. 37)

My own biography was written by fate as empowered by death anxiety for reasons that I eventually became aware of to some extent. Freud's biography was, I believe, driven by similar forces, but I have been unable to determine if he consciously knew what was driving his choices. My sense is that by and large, he was not aware of these forces, yet the intriguing question remains: Did Freud know his own secret?

Classical Conjectures

To begin with the classical picture as it pertains to Freud's disbelief in God and religion — a subject of many books and articles (see for example, Anzieu 1986; Krull 1986; Vitz 1988; Rizzuto 1998), his position is accounted for largely in terms of his disillusionment with his father, who was a devoutly religious, somewhat rebellious, Jew. Freud vividly remembered an incident that he learned about when he was about ten or twelve years of age, one in which his father had been humiliated by a street ruffian for being a Jew. He also lost respect for his father because he never earned a decent living and was only barely able to support his family. In addition, it appears that it was his father's failures in business that made it necessary for him to move his family from Freiburg to Vienna, a move that frightened and infuriated the four-year-old Freud.

As for Freud's latter-day avoidance of death and death anxiety, this heritage has persisted among mainstream psychoanalysts to the present time, and as a result, they have not recognized the resultant lacuna in psychoanalytic thinking as such or subjected it to exploration. There are, however, a handful of nonmainstream psychotherapists who have, with some superficial success, explored the subject of death and death anxiety in terms of the conscious, manifest issues that they raise (Piven 2004). Most of these writers are followers of Ernest Becker, who wrote *Denial of Death* (1973).

Freud denied that the concept of death exists in "the unconscious" and claimed that only castration anxiety dwells there (Freud 1923). He also proposed that we do not fear death, but deeply wish to die—an expression of what he believed to be a *death instinct* (Freud 1930). Strikingly, these pronouncements came from a hypochondriacal man who predicted the year of his death three times—and got it wrong each time (Schur 1972). A handful of psychoanalysts have suggested that the death of Freud's brother Julius when Freud was eighteen months old, which Freud saw as the fulfillment of his death wishes against his rival, may have played a role in his avoidance of death-related issues (Gay 1988).

Based on research that has not as yet been brought to bear on Freud's issues with death or religion, Krull (1986), using standard, conscious system psychoanalytic methods, has garnered suggestive indirect evidence that by age ten—and possibly much earlier—Freud was convinced that his mother, Amalie, had had an affair with her stepson, Philipp. Freud's father, Jakob, was twice as old as Amalie, his third wife, and he traveled a great deal; Philipp was in his early twenties, Amalie's age. There are debatable indications that when he was three years old, Freud interrupted them while they were having intercourse. An early memory of his mother being missing and of Philipp looking for her in a cupboard was self-interpreted by Freud later on as reflecting the fantasy that Philipp had somehow given his mother a baby—his sister Anna. Another of Freud's dreams, which led to sexual associations, has also been linked to his mother having a sexual liaison with Philipp. Krull suggests that the first Oedipal figure in Freud's family was Philipp and that when Jakob abruptly sent Philipp and his brother to England just before the rest of the family moved to Vienna, Freud developed the fantasy that he was the new rival to his devalued father. Most of Freud's biographers have not picked up these speculations. Gay (1988), for example, glosses over this material and makes it sound like a small child's passing fantasy.

Adaptive Conjectures

In turning to Freud's story as seen through the eyes of adaptive psychoanalysis, it is well to be reminded that the relationship between theory and observation is a tricky one at best. Theory is the result of observation, and a new theory emerges from observations that do not support the existing theory but previously had been overlooked or had been unavailable until new instrumentation made it possible for them to be seen. Theory guides—both expands and restricts—observation until someone is able to see something new and significant that contradicts or cannot be explained by the existing theory and calls for revisions in present thinking. However, in a field in which quantitative data are sparse or nonexistent, the recognition of theory-challenging data is extremely difficult. In addition, mainstream practitioners tend to resist these shifts in observation and theory, whatever the field of endeavor (Kuhn 1962). When new observations and theory bring those who work in a particular field face to face with death and death anxiety, we can expect that the resistances against accepting the new way of thinking will be fierce.

That said, the push to reexamine key aspects of the life and work of Freud arose as a coincidental result of my decision to write a book on love and death in psychotherapy (Langs 2006). My clinical observations, many of them not previously made by others, led to the thesis that love is the puppet and death the puppeteer—that is, that death has dethroned love as the basic issue in emotional life. This prompted me to take a fresh look at the Oedipus myth to see if, despite Freud's emphasis on the incest issue, death and death anxiety play a significant role in that tale—and if so, whether the time had come to see this story in a fresh light.

THE OEDIPUS MYTH REVISITED

The adaptive view of this story was developed in two stages. In the first, the myth was reexamined to determine if sex (as per Freud) or death (as per the adaptive approach) appears to be the central issue, while in the second stage, the story was examined in light of several timeless, universal, death-related archetypes that I had discovered in my clinical work.

The story essentially is as follows (D. Taylor 1986):

Laius, who has a dark past, becomes King of Thebes and marries Jocasta. An oracle warns Laius not to have a son because the son will kill him, so he avoids having intercourse with Jocasta until one day, flushed with wine, he succumbs. When a baby boy is born, Laius pierces the child's ankles with brooches and gives him to a herdsman, who is directed to expose the child to wild beasts on Mount Cithaeron. Instead, in an act of mercy, the herdsman gives the boy to a shepherd, who then gives him to Polybus, the childless, married king of Corinth, who brings him up as his own, naming him Oedipus (swollen foot) because of his deformity.

When Oedipus turns eighteen, a friend taunts him, claiming that he is a bastard. Oedipus goes to the oracle at Delphi to confirm his parentage, but is told instead that he will kill his father and sleep with his mother. This prompts Oedipus to leave Corinth and journey toward Thebes. On his way, he meets Laius and others in his party on a narrow road where three roads meet. Laius's herald, Polyphontes, orders Oedipus to make way for their entourage, and when Oedipus fails to obey, he kills one of Oedipus's horses. In a rage, Oedipus kills Polyphontes and Laius and then continues on his journey toward Thebes.

Thebes is being terrorized by a monster, Sphinx, with the body of a lioness, the head of a woman, and the wings of a bird. She poses a riddle to those who, like Oedipus, come her way, and she devours anyone who cannot solve it. The riddle asks, "Which animal has one voice, but becomes four-footed then two footed then three-footed?" Oedipus correctly solves the riddle—the answer is "man." The Sphinx responds by committing suicide, and Oedipus is rewarded for destroying their nemesis by being made king of Thebes and being wedded to Jocasta, the queen. In time, he gives her four children, two girls and two boys.

Sometime later, Thebes succumbs to a murderous plague that is seen as God's punishment for some grievous sin. Oedipus sends his brother-in-law, Creon, to the oracle at Delphi to have him ask God the nature of the sin that is causing the plague, and the oracle informs him that it is being caused by the unpunished murder of Laius. Oedipus places a terrible curse on the unknown killer and turns to the blind prophet, Teiresias, for help. The prophet tells Oedipus that he is Laius's killer and hints at other crimes as well. Oedipus sees this as a plot by Creon to dethrone him and rejects what he has been told. Jocasta supports his denial, pointing out that several robbers rather than a single man had murdered Laius. Oedipus is not fully reassured, so he seeks a witness to the crime. Meanwhile, a messenger appears to tell him that Polybus is dead and goes on to inform Oedipus that Polybus was not his father, that he had been given to Polybus by a shepherd from Thebes.

Jocasta now realizes that Oedipus is her son and calls for the Theban shepherd to whom her baby had been given. He reveals what he had actually done with the baby, at which point Oedipus also understands who he is. He rushes off to find Jocasta, who has disappeared, and discovers that she has hanged herself. He then takes the shoulder pins from her dress and blinds himself. Creon becomes king of Thebes and orders Oedipus into the house to await his fate. Oedipus asks to be sent to Mount Cithaeron and left to die as the gods originally intended, but he is not granted his wish. He dies a natural death some time later.

This is a powerful tale with allusions to a great deal of violence and a single, extended incestuous relationship. For the Greeks at the time that this myth was told through the play *Oedipus the King* by Sophocles (D. Taylor 1986), the family was the center of life, and the worst conceivable crime was to kill one's father, while the second worst crime was to sleep with one's mother. Oedipus thus is portrayed as enacting the two worst of all human crimes.

The Initial Adaptive Reformulation

The first phase of the adaptive critique of Freud's thinking about this myth was built around two realizations. The first is that acts of violence, self-inflicted and directed against others, outnumber the act of incest by a ratio of eight to one. This violence includes Oedipus's father's maiming his son and his attempt to murder him, the killing of Oedipus's horse by Polyphontes, Oedipus's murder of Laius and his herald, the suicides of the Sphinx and Jocasta, and the self-blinding by Oedipus. The dominance of violence in this tale and its presence at the beginning and end of the story challenge Freud's belief that the core issue is Oedipus's act of incest with his mother. It is far more parsimonious to theorize that this is primarily a tale of violence and death, with prominent themes of murder, suicide, and physical and psychological harm. The incest, while a source of conflict and guilt, is thereby relegated to a secondary role in the story. By extension, this assessment supports the thesis that archetypically, sexual conflicts take a backseat to death-related issues in human emotional life in general—and in all probability, the Bible as well.

It is striking too that from Oedipus's vantage point, his story expresses efforts to cope with all three forms of death anxiety: He is the victim of three major predatory acts, instances in which he would be expected to have experienced *predatory death anxiety*. First, there is his maiming and the attempt to murder him as an infant. He is, of course, unable to combat this threat, but the shepherd to whom he was given is equal to the task, and he saves the infant's life.

The second act of predation against Oedipus occurs when his father's herald murders Oedipus's horse, by implication thereby threatening Oedipus's life. In this case, Oedipus responds by murdering the herald, and in a seeming overreaction that is characteristic of human responses to such threats—and Yahweh is so inclined too—he also murders his father. These are archetypal responses to activated predatory death anxiety, and they take the typical form of mobilizing one's psychological and physical resources. Indeed, to some extent, Oedipus's act of vengeance was sanctioned by the Greek culture of his time.

The third predatory threat arises when the Sphinx threatens to devour Oedipus if he does not solve her riddle. In this case he turns to his mental prowess to successfully defend against this threat, thereby causing her death instead of his. In so doing, he was able to call upon the kind of divine wisdom that is usually possessed by oracles, wisdom that not only is death related, but also calls forth a solution to predatory death anxiety that is not available to the conscious mind and common man.

As for *predator death anxiety* and the deep unconscious need for punishment, Oedipus experiences this form of death anxiety and inner guilt when he discovers that he has slept with his mother and murdered his father. Rather than fulfilling the archetypal response in its extreme through an act of suicide, he blinds himself, but he does, however, wish to be sent to die on Mount Cithaeron where his father (and mother) had sent him to perish as an infant. This seems to indicate that the need for the ultimate punishment was present in Oedipus but went unfulfilled, while it was left to Jocasta, for reasons of both incest and participation in the attempted murder of her son, to carry out this sentence to the fullest.

Oedipus deals with his *existential death anxiety* in rather unusual ways. His solution to the riddle of the Sphinx implies a recognition that life ends in death, but rather than deny this fact—the basic archetypal response— Oedipus has made it part of his essential knowledge base and uses it to survive. This is a prime example of how death-related traumas like those that Oedipus suffered as an infant can be the source of divine wisdom, which, in turn, can be recruited adaptively in the service of survival when later life-threatening events occur.

All in all, then, the Oedipus myth is a powerful tale of death and death anxiety in which forbidden sexuality plays a secondary role.

The Problem of Knowledge Acquisition

Another set of adaptive insights into this myth involves the recognition that, as we saw in the story of Adam and Eve in Eden, Oedipus's problems with death and death anxiety are linked to the other core problem for humankind that has gone relatively unexplored by classical psychoanalysts, that of knowledge acquisition. This quest takes two forms in the myth: The first involves answering the question "Who are Oedipus's biological parents?" And the second entails solving the riddle of the Sphinx.

Both questions are answered through divine wisdom, and both involve death and death anxiety: Oedipus's biological parents had abandoned him to die, and the Sphinx threatened to devour him. Much as I have theorized that Eve sought divine wisdom because of an unmentioned death-related trauma—a miscarriage—Oedipus is driven to acquire divine wisdom in response to two explicit threats to his life.

The exciting action for Oedipus's adventures is his being told that the king and queen of Corinth are not his biological parents. Oedipus's fundamental death-related quest is, then, devoted to discovering the identity of his biological parents. This echoes the story of the historical Christ, who also did not know who his father was. All three forms of death anxiety accrue to the absence of such knowledge: *existential*, in that were it not for the father, the child would not exist; *predatory*, because the abandoning father is experienced as having left the child to die; and *predator*, because the deep unconscious wish in the abandoned child is for vengeance in kind—essentially, to murder the offending parent.

All in all, the Oedipus myth describes the unconsciously orchestrated enactment of the archetype of vengeance through murder that is sought by those who have been abandoned or harmed by parental figures early—and even later—in life. This harm may take any number of forms, such as abandonment through divorce or desertion; a significant illness or the death of a parent; the child's being born with a congenital defect; and similar traumas. These triggering events are universally experienced deep unconsciously by the child-victim as parental attempts at murder. The response in the victim is to retaliate against the offending parents by murdering them symbolically, or more rarely, in actual deed—efforts that are, as a rule, very costly to the vengeful child-victim and to those who are his or her targets for revenge.

WHY FREUD CHOSE THE OEDIPUS MYTH

It is time now to ask and try to answer some key questions. Why did Freud choose this myth above all others as the foundation myth of human emotional life? Why did he stress the incestuous component of the myth when it so clearly is, first and foremost, a myth centered on death and death anxiety and knowledge acquisition as it pertains to one's origins? Why in substance did Freud focus on fantasy and wish rather than reality and death? And what do the answers to these questions tell us about why he rejected God and religion and had a major blind spot in connection with death-related events and unconscious forms of death anxiety?

The basic answer to these questions revolves around the conjecture that Freud suffered a very early death-related accident of fate over which he had no control, but which nonetheless had profound and probably largely unconscious effects on him throughout his life. It involves a piece of divine knowledge that was, I believe, the most powerful determinant, however unconsciously mediated, of his personal life and professional thinking, including the theory of psychoanalysis that he forged in the course of his career. The sense is that fate shaped Freud, much as Freud shaped psychoanalysis, and psychoanalysis shaped the world's view of who and what we are emotionally and psychologically—including our ways of dealing with death and death anxiety and our view of our religious beliefs.

In a few words, there is, I believe, overwhelming trigger-decoded evidence that Sigmund Freud never knew who his biological father was—that is, whether he was Jakob, his mother's husband, or Philipp, his mother's stepson. My contention is that Freud encoded this persistent personal dilemma in his writings and that he most likely experienced these uncertainties unconsciously far more than consciously. Nevertheless, they greatly affected his choice of psychoanalysis as a profession and his attitudes toward both religion and death. Indeed, there are indications that as a result of this trauma, Freud suffered from the archetypes derived from early-life predation and the deep unconscious experience of predatory death anxiety.

The strongest evidence for this hypothesis lies with four major origination narratives that Freud presented and explored in his writings:

1. The myth of Oedipus, which deals with the origins of a person's life and the identity of the parents who gave that person life, and thus with an individual's personal identity and who he or she is in terms of his or her familial and social roots. For Freud, this myth also deals with the origin of human emotional disturbances and neuroses.
2. The origins of totems and taboos that pertain to the beginnings of culture, society, morality, religion, and art.
3. The story of Exodus and Moses, which deals with the origins of the Jewish faith and its moral laws.
4. And finally, to stretch a point, this concern is reflected in the beginnings of Freud's writings on dreams, in that the first dream of his own to appear in his writings, which is mentioned in his letters to Fleiss (Freud 1882–1899), was dreamt the night of his father's funeral.

To begin with this last piece of evidence, Freud offered two somewhat different versions of the dream he had the night after his familial father's funeral. The first and more condensed and incomplete version was reported in his letters to his friend and colleague, Fleiss, in 1896. The second and more complete version of the dream, in response to which, however, there is a dearth of associations, is described in his masterpiece, *The Interpretation of*

Dreams (1900). To my knowledge, this is the only personal dream that Freud alluded to twice in his writings, the only dream for which there are two versions, and the only dream that has two simultaneously dreamt parts.

The second version of this dream goes as follows:

> I had a dream of a printed notice, placard or poster—rather like the notice forbidding one to smoke in railway waiting rooms—on which appeared either
>   "You are requested to close the eyes" or,
>   "You are requested to close an eye." (Freud 1900, p. 317)

Freud stated that each version of the dream took him to a different set of associations, but he does not reveal what they were. He simply writes that he was late for the funeral, which he had arranged and kept simple, a decision that could have opened him to criticism from other family members. He also states he sees the death of his father as the most important event in his life and takes that to be the case for all men. His father's death appears to be the death-related triggering life event that propelled Freud into his self-analysis. It was through these efforts at self-exploration that he discovered—or so he believed—that the incestuous aspect of the Oedipus story is at the core of a man's neuroses and furthermore, that his seduction theory of neuroses was in error. That is, Freud became convinced that neuroses did not arise from actual seductions and other traumatic events—that is, from reality—as he had thought, but stemmed from incestuous and other conflicted inner mental wishes—that is, from fantasies and imagination.

Freud's unusual double dream after the death of his father can be taken as indirect evidence that he believed that he had two fathers, one biological, the other social. Notably, the dream seems to ask Freud to close his eyes to this truth.

This thesis finds additional support in Freud's contention that fathers are the most important figures in a man's life, which may well have been the case for Freud personally. In addition, there are suggestions that in the face of a death-related trauma, Freud believed that humans are well advised to turn to and focus on sex rather than dwell on the loss and other features of the traumatic incident. In light of the trauma that I am suggesting that Freud suffered, this position seems to shed light on an unconscious root of his focus on incestuous wishes in lieu of death-related traumas in human life. Another, and perhaps more fundamental, implication of this line of thought is the idea that psychoanalytic investigations and treatment should move away from reality and focus on fantasy—a point that Freud may have made because at the time, quite unconsciously, he was dealing with realities that were too painful to bear in awareness. Among these untenable realities, there is one striking possibility that deserves recognition: If Philipp was indeed Freud's father or even if he only had an affair with Freud's mother, Amalie, Philipp had in fact lived out a version of the incestuous acts carried out by Oedipus. That is, while Philipp had murdered his (and Freud's) father symbolically, he had in reality gone to bed with his stepmother—that is, Freud's mother. For Sigmund Freud, then, the Oedipus myth may well have been more of a reality than a fantasy—a myth come true. As such, it would have created an enormous need in Freud to flee and deny reality and live in a world of fantasy.

Turning now to Freud's writings that specifically focused on origins, the first of these, the Oedipus myth, which occupied Freud's attention from the beginning to the very end of his career as a psychoanalyst, unabashedly speaks for the secret of having two fathers and not knowing who the biological father really is. The quest for the real father is the driving force of the story. The myth can be treated as if it was one of Freud's own dreams, and the background triggering event would have been indications that Philipp could have been or was his father, while the more immediate trigger must have been an incident that had activated Freud's uncertainty as to who his father was. In focusing on the incestuous aspects of the myth instead of its core death-related paternity issue, which actually is a far more blatant and powerful aspect of the tale, Freud was using a common defense that is seen repeatedly in adaptive psychotherapy patients: He concentrated on and consciously interpreted a secondary issue while encoding and keeping unconscious his primary concern, which was death related and far more telling.

Finally, this analysis of the myth suggests that Freud's turn to the development of psychoanalysis and his pursuit and explorations of the hidden, clue-giving unconscious realm were offshoots of, and efforts to sublimate, his search for the answer to the darkest and most mysterious secret of his life: the hidden and true identity of his father. There is in fact no way that we can escape the unconsciously orchestrated fate that our unconsciously experienced traumas move us toward.

As for *Totem and Taboo* (1913), which was Freud's first major venture into applied psychoanalysis, two major themes stand out. The first, which is the subject of the initial of the four essays in the book, pertains to the origins and functions of the totem, which is an object or living entity like an animal that unites a group of people or a clan through a series of explicit prohibitions. According to Freud, the totem serves mainly as the basis for taboos that prevent incest not only between blood relatives, but also between unrelated members of a clan, including mothers-in-law. Violations of the taboo are punished severely by all members of the clan.

It is noteworthy, then, that among the first of Freud's formal efforts to apply psychoanalysis to problems of origins and guilt, totems and taboos against incest and sexual liaisons between unrelated individuals within the same clan loom large. The guilt and punishment, ultimately through death, evoked by violations of totemic prohibitions in all likelihood speak for the rage that Freud experienced unconsciously against his stepbrother Philipp for his forbidden involvement with his stepmother, who was Freud's mother. It also seems likely that Freud experienced murderous wishes against all three parties responsible for his belief that Philipp might well have been his biological father.

The final essay in this book is also relevant to this discussion. It is based on Freud's thesis that in the very early years of human life on this planet, there was a primal father who expelled his sons so he could possess all the tribal women. As a band of brothers, the sons returned to the tribe and rebelled against the father by devouring his body at a totem feast. They then took possession of the women in a manner that Freud links to the story of Oedipus's murder of his father and his incestuous liaison with his mother.

This tale has several mutually compatible implications for my proposition regarding Freud's father. For one, it suggests that Freud viewed his half brother Philipp's usurpation of their father's place with Freud's mother as a murderous act in which Freud imagined himself to have participated and shared as well. Freud's rejection of his father and of the Jewish God with whom the father was identified was therefore an outcome of an unconsciously experienced drama in which Freud's wish to join his brother in the cannibalistic murder of his father seems to have played a notable role. Freud's unconscious guilt over these wishes and over his participation in this violent drama seems to have created within him a deep and abiding need for expiation and atonement, which he seems to have achieved mainly by rejecting the role of violence and death in human emotional life and stressing love in their place.

Remarkably, the two papers that flank *Totem and Taboo* are on the subjects of false recollections in psychoanalysis (1914a) and the Moses of Michelangelo (1914b), which Freud initially published under a pseudonym! In the text of this elaborate paper, Freud expands on his belief that in his painting, the artist had not portrayed the violently passionate Moses of the Bible, but a new Moses of the artist's conception that falsified the character of the man. However speculative, the link to Freud's doubts about the identity of his father and his belief that he had two fathers, one biological and the other social, fits well with these observations.

The final piece of striking evidence that Freud believed that his biological father may not have been Jakob is found in the last original work that Freud penned: *Moses and Monotheism* (1939). This book is generally considered to be the most controversial, badly written, and poorly argued book that Freud wrote—it was as if he had had a compulsion to write it even though it was greatly flawed. We can consider this work as a part of Freud's last will and testament, or as something akin to a deathbed confession. Freud founded his thinking on research material that had been publicly refuted and withdrawn, although there were some historians who continued to adhere to the thesis that he advocated (Yerushalmi 1991).

Freud argued that Moses, the father of the Jews, was not a Jew, but an Egyptian—a position that is reminiscent of the one Freud took regarding Shakespeare, in which he argued that the writer by that name was not really Shakespeare, but Edward de Vere, the 17th Earl of Oxford. In regard to Moses, Freud further argued that the Jews had killed the original Moses and placed a false Moses in his place.

This theme of replacing one leader with another is connected with a major incident that occurred some years earlier when Freud and Jung were waiting to board a ship to go to America. While the two men were talking in a tavern, Jung told the story of a young Egyptian king who had erased the name of his father from all the public monuments. Believing that Jung wanted to murder him, Freud fainted dead away. The eradication of a father by a younger claimant was a terrifying happening for Freud—and in this case there is reason to believe that the symbolic killing of the father was enacted by his half brother, Philipp, rather than by Freud himself.

However tentative these inferences may be, they seem to accumulate into highly suggestive evidence for my basic thesis that Freud never knew who his biological father was and that this uncertainty and the betrayal and rage that lay behind it played a significant, albeit unconscious, role in his turn away from God and religion.

As Freud stated regarding his young patient, Dora, when she denied masturbating but played with a reticule that she wore at her waist,

> He that has eyes to see and ears to hear may convince himself that no mortal can keep a secret. (1905, p. 77)

SOME FINAL REFLECTIONS

Indications are that death and death anxiety unconsciously empowered Freud's life and the development of his psychoanalytic theory and practice. To the extent that the evidence is convincing, it adds to the thesis that deep unconsciously, death drives life—or if you prefer, that life drives us away from death psychologically, but toward it in reality. The reason that so many mental health professionals and lay persons have followed Freud down his death-denying path is that they too secretly live in dread of death and fearful of the death anxieties that deep unconsciously run their emotional lives. It is much like the story of the emperor's new clothes: No one has dared to acknowledge that the emperor is naked, that is, to break the compact of denial and acknowledge that he is vulnerable to death—no one, that is, except an innocent little boy, and in my case, by an accident of my own fate, a not so innocent psychoanalyst.

As for the deep unconscious effects of his unresolved death anxieties, which, like those of Oedipus, must have been existential, predatory, and predator in nature, Freud reacted *against archetypal pressures*. In a manner very similar to that of Christ but unlike Yahweh, who generally conformed to the archetype, instead of seeking murderous vengeance against the offending parents in some disguised or displaced manner, Freud focused on love, however incestuous, and he buttressed his avoidant defenses with explicit efforts to deny the psychological importance of death. His claim that unconsciously, the male child wants to murder his father in rivalry for his mother is a weak rivalrous archetype that is patently evident in the story of Cain and Abel and other biblical tales, as well as in much of everyday life at present. Typically, it is invoked to cover over the far more devastating vengeance archetype that comes to the fore in response to being preyed upon and suffering from extremes of early predatory death anxiety.

The historical Christ's reaction formation against the revenge archetype and his offer of what at bottom was a denial-based kind of love was fundamental to the Catholic religion that was created in his wake. In like manner, Freud's denial-based focus on Oedipal love was the basis for classical psychoanalysis and its latter-day variants. Because the denial of death is so appealing to conscious minds, Christ's denial of death was embraced, often to good advantage by those of faith, yet ultimately it failed to bring peace to humankind. Freud's denial of death created a false foundation for the understanding of human emotional life and human adaptations, and it was embraced by psychoanalysts and others of all stripes. But it too has failed to bring peace to the world. Indeed, classical psychoanalysis has not only had almost nothing to say about death and religion, it also has little of significance to say about the terrible state of the world today.

That said, and now that I have disassembled Judaism, Catholicism, and psychoanalysis, it is high time to offer a positive approach to the issues I have raised regarding all three entities and to offer a more solid foundation for their future. I therefore turn now to the final chapter of the book, where I will attempt to do just that.

12

The Future of Religious and Secular Spirituality

I intend in this chapter to propose some correctives and to show how adaptive psychoanalysis offers a basis on which the third chapter in the history of God can begin to be written—and a sound and meaningful rational or secular spirituality initiated (see Harris 2004). Classical psychoanalysis is a conscious system approach to the human mind, and as such, even if it found a way to join forces with religion, its ideas would be grounded in the kind of mundane knowledge that has failed to bring humankind significant relief from unnecessary pain and suffering. The conscious mind, no matter how ingenious, is too devoted to the denial and the ignorance that God recommended to Adam and Eve to be of much help to us. We must seek answers that come from an understanding that God—or nature—has chosen to locate our greatest mental resources and divine wisdom where it is out of the reach of conscious awareness and thinking—in the deep unconscious mind, which we can access only through trigger decoding.

Where Yahweh evidently succumbed to his death anxieties or responded archetypically, both Freud and Christ used love to deny death. Their approaches to life and death, however different, had great appeal because they are consonant with the ways in which our defense-oriented, conscious minds naturally think and operate. While each has many detractors, they are outnumbered by followers who accept their credos, which, for both, are more matters of belief than evidence. Christ has been the more successful of the two because he intuitively recognized many of the issues humans have in dealing with death anxiety and offered some relief from their detrimental effects. Yet despite his sense of a narrative-based unconscious realm of experience, ultimately his life and teachings were conscious system based, mundane, and devoted almost entirely to matters of faith. Divine wisdom appears to have been embedded in his parables, but it was not trigger decoded and brought into conscious awareness to serve immediate adaptive needs. Adding this kind of trigger-decoded wisdom and morality to his offerings would help him and God enter new realms of understanding and coping. These efforts also can be used to begin to repair Yahweh's offerings as well and used to enhance all existing religious belief systems. Because they reflect archetypal universals, these ideas and approaches also can be applied both to psychoanalysis itself and to secular efforts to find a sound moral base.

A NEW PROFESSION

Accepting the new view of the mind and emotional life proposed by the adaptive approach can change vital features of both religion and psychoanalysis. For mental health professionals, it offers a new identity as *adaptive psychoanalysts*. But it also is the basis on which we can begin to think of and apply psychoanalysis as a biological science—*the science of emotionally charged cognition and adaptation* (Badalamenti and Langs 1992, 1994). In formal research carried out with the mathematician Anthony Badalamenti, it has proven possible to measure—to quantify—aspects of emotionally charged human communication in a truly meaningful manner (Langs, Badalamenti, and Thomson 1996). On that basis, we have shown that there are deep, mathematically identifiable, universal laws and regularities of communicative expression that are similar to, and as consistent as, the laws of physics. And among our many findings, we unearthed a quantitative distinction between mundane and divine expressions—essentially that narrative tales fraught with divine wisdom require far more measurable communicative mental energy for their expression than do mundane intellectualizations (Langs, Badalamenti, and Thomson 1996).

All of this points to the need to establish a new science and profession that can effectively unite psychoanalysis with religion, and clinical and quantitative scientific data with matters of faith and belief. I would call this profession *theological psychoanalysis*.

Those who choose to take on this avocation would have the responsibility to open a two-way exchange of knowledge and wisdom between psychoanalysis and religion. They would need to have a strong theoretical grounding in both fields, but they also would need to develop expertise as adaptive psychotherapists because the therapy situation is, at present, the arena where expressions of divine wisdom and morality are most accessible and best investigated. It will take a very special group of devoted theological psychoanalysts to complete the second chapter in the history of psychoanalysis and help write the third chapter in the history of God.

Lest it be thought that I am proposing the end of prayer, church, synagogue, and religious rituals and beliefs, allow me to emphasize that I am talking about developing a science that embraces and enhances spiritual wisdom, one that can deeply and uniquely inform and strengthen religious convictions and practices. And as I said, because they will be grounded in validatable and therefore refutable scientific observations and touch on universal archetypes, these efforts also can be expected to be a means of developing a set of core concepts that can form the basis for a rational secular spirituality as well. As a basic science, it would strive to identify and explore the death-related and other archetypes and universal mental and adaptive trends that are most relevant to religion, human morality, and the belief in God. There is already a vast religious, psychoanalytic, and death-related literature ready for integrated study, and these efforts can be supported by interactions with researchers and writers from other disciplines. All in all, the basic initial goal would be to develop a wisdom base and morality that are healing and loving with something to offer everyone, believer and nonbeliever alike.

In this connection, I wish to make a small but important point. Classical psychoanalysis is much like a popular recreational board game because patients can make classical analytic interpretations that are as sensible and deceptively convincing as those made by their analysts. One prominent psychoanalyst bemoaned that his patients are better at interpreting their material than he is, and it is well known that as is not the case with nuclear physics, any layperson who cares to do so can stake a claim that he or she is capable of evaluating and criticizing psychoanalytic ideas and practices. This lack of requisite expertise is another indication of the basic uncertainties and inadequacies of mainstream psychoanalysis. Part of the problem stems from the fact that classical psychoanalysis is conscious system based and has not developed the means of validating or refuting its propositions; as a result, just about anything goes.

This is not the case with adaptive psychoanalysis. By nature, extremely rare is the individual who really wants to listen to narratives and engage in a search for their activating death-related triggers so as to fashion trigger-decoded interpretations and enter the forbidding realm of deep unconscious experience. This creates many practical obstacles and natural resistances against learning how to carry out this process and thus limits the ability of outsiders to mount criticisms of its methodology and constructs, despite the inevitability of flaws and limitations. In addition, the adaptive approach includes a method of deep unconscious, encoded validation or nonvalidation that can be applied to its insights and interpretations, so arbitrary and erroneous claims can be readily refuted. Beyond that, this kind of work also requires a great deal of intelligence—we are all natural encoders, but none of us are natural trigger decoders. Very special people with unique needs and gifts of a kind yet to be fully defined will need to be recruited for the field of theological psychoanalysis. Many will be called, but few will be chosen.

There is one more caveat to engaging in this new profession: At least for now, as I said, the basic field of observation must be the psychoanalytic or psychotherapeutic situations first fashioned by Freud. This is the case for several reasons. For one, it is only when someone is dealing actively with a current death-related trauma that he or she will call upon his or her divine adaptive resources and encode them in dreams and stories. Such events do, of course, occur in an individual's everyday life, but there are too many settings and relationships with which a person must cope on a daily basis to allow for the definitive identification of the key triggering event and the resultant deep unconscious reactions. In general, short of an acute death-related trauma that stands out in a person's current life, it is extremely difficult to identify the most critical triggers for the encoded themes in an individual's dreams. In addition, we are naturally disinclined to hold onto and associate to our dreams and to link them to the active triggers with which we are trying to cope. *Self-processing* so as to gain deep unconscious insights is a difficult if not daunting undertaking (Langs 1993); an expert in adaptive psychotherapy usually is needed to aid in the effort.

Another reason for the need to make use of the therapeutic situation in the search for divine wisdom lies with the finding that humans naturally focus their deep unconscious coping efforts on the here and now—that is, on the words and deeds of those with whom they are interacting at the moment. In addition, on this level of experience, they are especially centered on the words and deeds of healers and caretakers. An added advantage of the treatment situation arises from the finding that for psychotherapy patients, their therapists are on the unconscious level the most frequent agents provocateurs for their death-related traumas and experiences. Having created the triggers to which their patients are responding, therapists therefore are in a unique position to be aware of hurtful interventions—of death-related, traumatic stimuli—of which their patients are quite unaware. In everyday life, obliteration of critical traumatic events and hurtful implications, especially those in which the death-related aspects are perceived deep unconsciously, tends to be the rule.

Another factor that favors the use of the therapeutic situation for these researches lies with the finding that the deep unconscious mind is extremely sensitive to ground rules and frames. The therapeutic setting is ideal for exploring these deep unconscious trends and needs, largely because the archetypal ground rules can be identified through validated deep unconscious, encoded, positively toned images that support one rule or another. Indeed, the management of these ground rules by psychotherapists is experienced deep unconsciously by their patients as expressions of their therapists' moral positions and attitudes—a finding of great relevance for emotionally charged experiences in everyday life. Adhering to archetypal frames is seen as moral and ethical, while departures from these ideals are viewed deep unconsciously as immoral and unethical. In-depth studies of conscious and deep unconscious morals are possible only in the therapeutic situation, and these studies can serve as guides to a new morality based on deep unconscious values and ideals that are applicable to both religion and rational spirituality.

OUR INNER GOD

All humans have conscious and deep unconscious systems as constituents of their emotion-processing minds. There are three basic components to each of these systems:

An intelligence or adaptive knowledge subsystem;
A subsystem of morality and ethics;
A trauma- or death-sensitive subsystem.

There are as well a variety of supplementary systems such as those that involve instinctual drive needs like sex, aggression, hunger, relationships, narcissistic supplies, and the like. There also is a basic mental operating subsystem—*a message-analyzing center*—that perceives events and their meanings, and with astounding rapidity, assigns them to conscious or deep unconscious registration and adaptive processing. This activity protects the conscious mind from emotional overload and also enables the two systems to react to very different inputs—in many cases, to different meanings of the same event. This situation arises because the deep unconscious mind experiences the inputs that are denied entry to the conscious mind, the mental mechanism that accounts for conscious system denial and obliteration.

The emotion-processing mind is an inordinately complex, exquisitely designed, enormously compromised miracle of "mental machinery" that has been fashioned by God or evolution to help us to survive the bombardments of stress we face each day. It is configured adaptively to enable us to cope with traumatic, death-related events effectively or with minimal mental and physical disruption, and it does so mainly by protecting the conscious mind from as many disruptive inputs as possible. Much as the immune system deals primarily with the threat of death from external microscopic predators—and secondarily from death-related threats from within the body—the emotion-processing mind deals primarily with external macroscopic predators, mainly other humans and natural disasters—and only secondarily with threats from within one's own mind and body (Langs 1996).

In secular terms, the deep unconscious part of the emotion-processing mind is best seen as a superb adaptive system that is extremely sensitive to death-related issues. It also is a system that possesses insights that the conscious mind is quite unable to forge. The deep unconscious system embodies an awesome, numinescent wisdom that speaks for and reflects the highest possible moral standards and best possible adaptive solutions to existential challenges. The system is a masterpiece of creation and natural selection, even though the overall design of the emotion-processing mind, with its necessarily compromised, overly defensive, impaired conscious system (our practical adaptive instrument), is arguably one of the most flawed evolved adaptive entities in the history of living beings.

Historically, these design problems stem from the likelihood that the sophisticated conscious and deep unconscious adaptive emotional processing of which humans are capable first developed with language acquisition some 100,000 to 150,000 years ago—a minute amount of time on the evolutionary clock. Language capabilities brought with them a significant advance beyond the "event perception" of animals, through which they are limited to coping with past traumas only when in sight of the locale of the threatening incident. The ability to represent and think and reason mentally using language enabled humans to explore and solve problems and deal with threats when away from the site of a traumatic incident. It also enabled humans to think abstractly and to thereby be creative in ways, advantageous and detrimental, that other species cannot match.

Language and the capacity for mental representation also gave humans a strong sense of their individual identities and the ability to anticipate the future in specific detail—and with that an explicit awareness of the inevitability of personal death. This awareness was an enormous asset in that it allowed humans to anticipate sources of harm and danger, but it also was a great—and perhaps greater—liability in that it facilitated the contemplation of the dead (Harrison 2003; Langs 1997) and the certainty of personal death, experiences that sent humans reeling consciously. Having little to choose from, so to speak, and very little time to evolve sophisticated responses to these environmental threats, natural selection—or God—evidently favored minds capable of consciously denying aspects of the reality of death, a defense that evidently allowed such humans to survive better than those who were ever mindful of, and distracted by, their mortality. But the overuse of denial by the conscious mind and the placement of death-related wisdom and the ideals of sound morality in the deep unconscious mind have made humans especially vulnerable to the effects of deep unconscious death anxiety and inclined toward violent and immoral solutions to their deepest, death-related fears and threats. Lest we eventually destroy ourselves and this planet, we need to come up with new solutions to the problem of death and its attendant anxieties. Most certainly, decoding the messages emanating from our inner god, our deep unconscious minds, is one of the best ways to accomplish this vital goal.

From the religious vantage point, we may think of the pursuit of these goals as calling for the beginning of the third chapter in the history of God vis-à-vis humankind. The scenario could run something like this:

God in heaven comes to realize that he must confront the fact that despite his best efforts, he has failed to save humans from themselves and bring lasting peace to the people of the world, individually or collectively. In his incarnation as Yahweh, he tried to do this by favoring one people and religion over all others and by arming them with the extraordinary strength and morality needed to enforce harmony among all tribes and nations, an effort that met with abject failure. He then changed his approach to these daunting issues and incarnated himself as Jesus Christ, adopting a belief system that was open to all comers, one that stressed love, nonviolence, atonement for sins committed, and eternal life for the good and just. But much to his disappointment, humans failed to adhere to this new wisdom and morality and doggedly refused to live in absolute harmony with each other.

What is he to do now?

In casting about for an answer to this gnawing question, God turns to the numinous, adaptive wisdom and pristine morality that he long ago placed in the deep unconscious minds of all humans. He decides to motivate us to learn how to access, appreciate, understand, and make use of this largely wasted divine resource. Having at long last achieved a measure of peace himself in regard to death and death anxiety, he is prepared to modify his efforts to deal with death solely through denial and divine ignorance, and to offer a new approach to the unresolved, archetypal issues raised by human mortality. And herein lies one of the most profound dilemmas God has ever had to face:

Should he continue to promise eternal life to those humans who are more or less free of sin, a preference that dominates the conscious mind, or should he confront humankind with the excruciatingly painful truth, so clear to Gilgamesh, that except for rare and extraordinary exceptions, there is no afterlife whatsoever for humans — a grim realization that sits buried in our deep unconscious minds waiting to be called forth into awareness? Not satisfied with this difficult choice between two options, God also considers a compromise in which he would see to it that humans have no way of knowing what lies beyond the grave; that is, he would neither promise and ensure humans a chance for eternal life nor make it clear that this option is not available to them—that as was the case when he created Adam, he would imply but not explicitly indicate that he alone is immortal and unending.

Such are the dilemmas that may well face God as he ushers in the third chapter in his history vis-à-vis his human creations, one in which he seeks to find an incarnation that can at long last bring eternal peace and love to our much-troubled world. And as he does so, he will try to find stopgap measures to assist us as humans to better manage and curb our inclinations toward violent, immoral solutions to death-related threats. And he will do so mainly by lighting the pathway to the inner delegate of wisdom and morality that resides deep within our souls, no longer objecting to our use of the inner divine wisdom with which he has blessed us. In a sense, then, God, who first came to be with and soon left us, his human creations, and who returned centuries later only to leave us again, has returned once more and taken up residence in our deep unconscious minds. But we must do our part as well: We must turn to trigger decoding his encoded messages as they are activated by traumatic incidents so we may access this divine wisdom and morality in order to forge new solutions to old, unsolved, archetypal death-related problems.

In his new incarnation, then, God may well call on a broad segment of society to help develop schools for teaching theological psychoanalysis. These teachings will be used for both research purposes and to facilitate the offerings of the clergy who meet with their parishioners, enabling them to do so based on God's new, divine ways of understanding and solving the problems created by human death anxiety. And as I have been emphasizing, these same insights can be thought of cognitively by nonbelievers as coming from a gifted deep unconscious intelligence and thereby used as the basis for a newly created moral and spiritual secular knowledge base.

The Features of Our Inner God

When it comes to the design of the emotion-processing mind, the conscious system has a basic archetypal configuration, but its operations tend to be highly individualized; conscious adaptive preferences and choices tend to vary from one person to the next. In contrast, the deep unconscious system, the seat of our inner god, both has a basic archetypal design and is replete with archetypal or universal values and adaptive preferences in responding to death-related and other kinds of triggering events. The existence of these archetypes makes it possible to identify the common features of our inner god and to discover the nature of the ideal, eternal values and morals that can best steer us through life. There are two fundamental, guiding principles in the operation of deep unconscious or divine wisdom:

The first is that this wisdom is adaptive in nature and especially sensitive to, and activated by, death-related traumas. Our inner god is not a god sitting on a throne mouthing wise sayings and passing idle judgments. It is instead a god that has silently accumulated a great deal of wisdom largely by learning from decisive deep unconscious experiences, and it applies that wisdom to immediate challenges and threats. This system is far more sensitive to threat than is the conscious system; it accurately perceives danger in many situations where the conscious mind does not. (Keep in mind that the deep unconscious system's perceptions and responses always are encoded in narratives and that to be brought into awareness, they must be trigger decoded in light of the threat at hand.)

All in all, our inner god is a death-oriented god, and this feature speaks for the transcendental God as well. In his proposed new incarnation, God knows full well that dealing with death is the key to life. Thus, the God of predation (Yahweh) and the God of love (Jesus) are being superseded by a God of death (yet to be named).

The second key feature of our inner god is that it is guided in its operation by the values established by the deep unconscious subsystem of morality and ethics. It behooves us then to identify the subsystem's archetypal moral guidelines, which ideally should frame the ways in which we deal with those with whom we interact, with death-related traumas, and with life in general.

Morality and Ethics

There are three crucial and somewhat demanding and disquieting features of the deep unconscious subsystem of morality and ethics:

First, it operates on the bias of a pristine, uncompromising, universal moral code of utmost purity, clarity, and consistency within and across individuals.

Second, the system is highly judgmental and makes fair but incisive evaluations of our own thoughts and behaviors and of the behaviors of those with whom we interact.

Third, the system is both advisory and reactive. It makes and encodes recommendations regarding the moral and ethical qualities of our own intentions and those of others. But the system not only establishes ideal moral standards, it also enforces them. It unconsciously orchestrates a turn toward self-rewarding decisions and actions whenever we adhere to its guidelines, but it also unconsciously arranges for self-harmful, poor choices and self-punishing actions whenever we violate its moral precepts.

As humans, we suffer at times from a measure of conscious guilt over an outright destructive act against someone, but given that we tend to consciously deny much of the harm we cause others, that kind of guilt is less common than usually is believed. The more pervasive deep unconscious experiences of guilt for harm done to others—the source of unconsciously arranged self-punishments—are all but impossible to detect because they operate without conscious awareness. They become evident only by trigger decoding the narrative images activated by the harm we've done. This is another reason why the psychotherapy situation appears to be the only place where these unconsciously mediated transactions can be readily detected, and it is a vital reason why pastoral psychoanalysts will need to develop the therapeutic skills required to work insightfully and effectively with psychotherapy patients.

As for the enforcement arm of our inner god, clinical experience makes clear that the deep unconscious system of morality and ethics is strikingly unforgiving in respect to serious breaches of morality. These ethical violations are seen deep unconsciously as sinful and evil, and themes of that kind appear repeatedly in the imagery from patients who have behaved in this manner. In addition, the subsystem is all but relentless in its arranging, quite unconsciously, for the guilty party to make repetitive self-punitive decisions. This includes such matters as repeated involvements in hurtful relationships, poor job choices, and unnecessary provocations of others that cause the guilty person much punitive suffering. Given that the perpetrator of harm usually is quite unaware of the deep unconscious causes of his or her suffering, they tend to blame bad karma or bad luck for their personal ills, unaware that their own behavior and their own inner god are the moving forces behind their tragic lives. This lack of conscious awareness renders true, deep unconsciously directed penitence, reparation, and atonement impossible to achieve, and often the result is a lifetime of suffering.

Predator death anxiety and deep unconscious guilt are the causes of this suffering. This kind of death anxiety arises unconsciously whenever a deep unconscious moral guideline is violated. And as I said earlier, the ultimate punishment demanded by the deep unconscious subsystem of morality and ethics is the sacrifice of the life of the perpetrator of harm—his or her suicide. While actual suicide is rare but not unheard of—let those who harm others beware—most often these offending individuals find countless ways to destroy themselves and their lives in small increments. There is an awesome quality to the extent to which we as humans can wreak havoc with our lives while being entirely unaware as to why we are doing it and even unaware that this is what we are doing to ourselves.

Serious problems also arise because the deep unconscious subsystem of morality and ethics is not easily assuaged even when the efforts at atonement and reparation are based on deep unconscious insights. Conscious regrets and apologies are not enough—deep unconscious forgiveness must be achieved—and this holds for believers as well as nonbelievers. For believers who seek forgiveness through Yahweh or Christ, the moment of grace must eventually include genuine forgiveness from their own inner god as well, an inner response that is conveyed through encoded narrative expressions. Gaining this kind of inner peace requires a great deal of self-processing and uncompromised trigger decoding.

In this light, I wish to emphasize two startling realizations:

First, that the punitive God of the Hebrews, while of little comfort regarding death anxiety, is more a mirror of the unforgiving inner god with which each of us wrestles from day to day than is the forgiving and loving Jesus Christ of Christianity.

Second, both believers and nonbelievers need to appreciate that immoral acts are punished by their own deep unconscious minds and that, without knowing it, they themselves arrange to pay dearly for their transgressions. We have, then, some compelling reasons for both religious and secular individuals to establish and live by a new, deep unconsciously based morality.

In doing psychotherapy, it is striking to see the extent to which these struggles materialize in patients who have deliberately acted immorally, but it is daunting and saddening to see these happenings take place with patients who inadvertently have been party to an act of harm such as a miscarriage, the birth of a child with a congenital disorder, an accident in which someone else was seriously harmed or killed, and similar unplanned events. It takes a great deal of adaptive therapeutic work to bring the deep unconscious guilt that these patients experience into trigger decoded, conscious awareness so they may initiate a genuine process of atonement. Deep unconscious forgiveness from the system of morality and ethics materializes only after many months, if not years, of this kind of therapeutic work. Typically, the achieved forgiveness quickly recedes and efforts at seeking further insight and making further amends must begin again. This creates cycles of denial and reluctant conscious acknowledgment of the damage done, along with intermittent efforts at reparation. In time, however, it proves possible for deep unconscious forgiveness to be established in a telling and lasting manner, and then and only then does the patient's self-defeating, guilt-ridden life takes a significant, final turn for the better.

It is indeed far wiser to not sin at all than to sin and seek the forgiveness of your inner god. Without adaptive psychotherapy or an effort at self-processing based on adaptive principles, true atonement is seldom if ever achieved—the guilty party pays for his or her sins for the rest of his or her life. All one can hope for under these circumstances is a conscious recognition that a sin has been committed and the achievement of a measure of conscious forgiveness, however inadequate that may be; deep unconscious forces of punishment continue to secretly prevail.

SOME MORAL GUIDELINES

What then are the components of the archetypal, deep unconscious, divine moral guidelines established by our inner god? Here too I turn to the psychotherapy situation, where the deep unconscious system of morality and ethics is especially vocal, much of it because it is extremely sensitive to the traumatic and thus immoral interventions made by psychotherapists. This is especially true in regard to their handling of the ground rules of treatment. On the deep unconscious level of experience, therapy is a rule-dominated, death-sensitive experience. Establishing, accepting, and adhering to the ideal archetypal, deep unconsciously sought ground rules are experienced as moral acts on the part of both therapists and their patients, while departures from these ideals are seen as damaging and immoral.

In ways that have a bearing on everyday life, the pursuit of moral integrity in the psychotherapy situation is not a simple, straightforward effort. Both patients and therapists tend to be fearful of doing therapy in an ideal or secured framework because of its entrapping features, which deep unconsciously arouse their dreaded existential death anxieties. Paradoxically, then, the most morally sound and healing framework for a psychotherapy experience is one of the most dreaded conditions within which treatment can take place. This dread is usually experienced deep unconsciously by patient and therapist, and the conscious mind, prompted by this hidden fear, makes rationalized excuses as to why it is opposed to doing therapy in a secured frame. Along with its other forms, these death anxieties account for the many boundary violations and immoral lapses carried out by clergy over the centuries.

The conscious mind naturally favors modified therapeutic frames because they allow the individual to escape from entrapment and commitment, and generate the false unconscious belief that death and the existential death anxieties it evokes can be sidestepped and denied. The existential death anxieties caused by secured relationships and frames in everyday life are the source of many immoral and self-defeating acts designed unconsciously to escape from the incarceration, however healing, caused by secured frameworks. This is the kind of insight that can be developed only in the therapeutic setting and is an example of the divine wisdom that practitioners of pastoral psychoanalysis will be able to offer to the world at large.

God's responsibility to supply present-day humans with a set of effective moral precepts—and comparable efforts by secular moralists—will not be achieved easily. It is possible however to extrapolate into everyday life the deep unconsciously validated, archetypal ground rules and moral guidelines that pertain to the psychotherapy experience. This is what has been discovered in this way to this point:

Yahweh's Ten Commandments, given to Moses as told in Exodus (I leave aside the many additional rules proposed in Leviticus, Numbers, and elsewhere in the Bible), and Christ's preachings offer a series of conscious system moral guidelines that are mostly self-evident. The Ten Commandments include religious instructions along with admonitions to honor thy father and mother, and to not commit murder, adultery, or theft, and to not bear false witness or covet thy neighbor's house or wife. Christ offers many other moral precepts including sacrifice for others and ways of avoiding violence.

All of these conscious system guidelines also hold for the deep unconscious system of morality and ethics that has elaborated on these tenets. For example, the admonition against murder is expanded to include harming other humans both psychologically and in any lesser physical manner, as well as destroying property and other living beings such as animals. The prohibition against adultery is extended deep unconsciously to include all kinds of inappropriate sexual liaisons such as those that are incestuous, that match adults with minors, and that are perverse and exploitative in any manner. The commandment against theft extends to all kinds of dishonesty and cheating. It blends with the tenet that speaks against lying, for which the broader prohibition is against any form of duplicity, deception, exploitation, misuse of one's position or authority, illicit acts, manipulations, and the like. Finally, the admonition against coveting one's neighbor's house or wife extends to all forms of envy and warns against acting on such impulses.

This list of deep unconsciously experienced immoral acts is long yet incomplete. It is, however, sufficient enough to provide us with a sense of their range. Many of these feelings and actions are not recognized as immoral by the conscious mind even as the deep unconscious subsystem of morality and ethics sees them in that light—and moves into action accordingly. These uncompromising deep unconscious perceptions and values are reflected in our dreams and in the stories we daydream about or become fascinated with in movies, books, newspapers, and such. Yet it is the rare and exceptional person who catches on to what they are going through—who gets the joke, so to speak. The turn to trigger decoding to realize consciously that one has behaved immorally is exceptional and seldom made. But this kind of insight is an essential step toward recognizing what needs to be done to undo the harm caused by moral violations and to begin broad efforts at reparation.

There are other moral guidelines suggested by observations of patients in psychotherapy. For example, the subsystem of morality and ethics calls not only for children to respect and honor their parents, but for parents to act in ways that deserve such respect and honor. Parents and caretakers have the moral responsibility to offer secure, stable settings and clear ground rules and regularities to their children, and to manage the family situation with consideration for each person's personal needs and with full respect for the aspects of privacy and confidentiality they deserve. Commitments need to be kept, and agreements, pacts, contracts, and the law of the land should be honored in full.

Many archetypal moral standards involve interpersonal or physical boundaries. The requisite to respect and honor necessary boundaries is very prominent in the deep unconscious lexicon of moral behaviors. Boundary violations are experienced deep unconsciously as assaultive, violently harmful, and overly seductive, and as predatory acts that call for self-protection and appropriate efforts to rightfully retaliate against the invader. These principles apply to individuals, families, groups, political entities, cities, states, countries. Those who intrude into other people's territories without provocation are legitimate targets for revenge, which often is carried out without regard for moral rules of conduct—boundary and frame violations beget boundary and frame violations. The history of this world would be very different today if these deep unconscious principles were better known and respected by world leaders.

Finally, I want to stress again that these deep unconscious ground rules are not easily adhered to or enforced. As humans we are strongly inclined to violate rules, frames, and boundaries and to secretly honor those who do just that. This state of affairs arises because death anxiety is so pervasive in our lives, and unconsciously, ground rule violations are believed to be a way of allaying or neutralizing these anxieties—albeit in costly, immoral fashion. In this connection, there are a large number of immoral and provocative death-related archetypes that religions need to recognize and understand so they may find ways of turning these archetypes into creative, peace-loving gestures.

FRAME-RELATED ARCHETYPES

As I have said often enough, divine wisdom is sought in response to, and organized around, death, death-related traumas, and the death anxieties that they evoke. There are many basic archetypal responses to death-related events, and many of them cause far more harm than good. These ultimately self-defeating archetypes need to be recognized and the means discovered through which they can be replaced by more constructive responses. At the very least, knowing what they are can prepare us for and keep in check inappropriate and irrational urges to retaliate against others who have threatened or harmed us, acts that can only cause unneeded damage to all concerned.

One group of archetypes involves responses to the three forms of death anxiety that prompt the earlier-mentioned turn to frame violations, which then arouses needs for self-punishment in the perpetrator and causes much suffering for his or her victims. *Predatory death anxiety* typically evokes both defensive and attacking responses by an endangered individual and a turn to rule violations that involve poorly rationalized deceit and dishonesty. *Predator death anxiety* tends to lead to frame violations that are carried out in ways intended deep unconsciously to obtain punishments from others. Finally, *existential death anxiety*, which is based on feelings of entrapment in ideal or secured frames because they are limiting and restraining, usually prompts frame violations in the service of escaping from the secured-frame death anxieties it evokes. While we may at times consciously welcome safe, secured conditions for our job and other relationships, these frames tend to arouse existential death anxieties that unconsciously cause us all too often to undo what is truly best for ourselves and our lives.

All of the detrimental reactions that I have alluded to are unconsciously driven, conscious system responses to death-related triggering events. By and large, they are not held in check by mundane knowledge, but they could be restrained and sublimated through access to divine, deep unconscious wisdom garnered through the process of trigger decoding the relevant encoded narratives. In general, we are at a loss to deal with death and death anxiety without divine insights; our conscious minds often respond to danger in dangerous, self-defeating ways.

DEATH-RELATED ARCHETYPES

There is an additional series of archetypal reactions to particular kinds of death-related traumas. For example, there is the archetype of the wounded child who has been abandoned or harmed psychologically or physically by one or both parents. The historical Christ, Freud, and Oedipus experienced this kind of early trauma, which is a driving force that can lead to enormous bursts of creativity or, on the other hand, severe neuroses, depending on a host of relatively complex factors. The archetypal reaction to this kind of trauma is the unconsciously driven search for vengeance by symbolically, or more rarely actually, murdering the offending parents, usually at great cost to oneself. Oedipus lived out this archetype, while both Freud and Christ ran counter to its thrust and turned to love rather than revenge, defending against expressing the archetype through a type of reaction formation.

Another common archetypal response arises with the death of a loved one or someone with whom there has been a close relationship. As we saw, archetypically, the person who experiences the loss holds himself or herself accountable for the death, and then suffers from predator death anxiety and deep unconscious guilt and needs for punishment. There also are elements of *survivor guilt* in these situations, some of it conscious and relatively self-evident, and it too adds to the deep unconscious need for self-castigation. This was the case with the proposed version of the story of Cain in which he did not actually murder Abel. It also was seen with Augustine when his baptized friend died suddenly. Exceptions to this archetypal reaction are all but unheard of, and this universal archetype can cause the bearer much emotional pain and prompt unneeded provocations designed unconsciously to have others punish the self-accused party for sins not actually committed.

Finally, there is the aforementioned archetypal response to being preyed upon by turning to retaliatory predatory measures of one's own. This creates vicious cycles of being assaulted and assaulting the assaulter in return. Both parties suffer greatly for the failure to overcome this vengeful archetype and for not being able to find a peaceful solution to a resolvable conflict.

Each of these basic death-related archetypes operates deep unconsciously and tends to create a sense of inner turmoil in the person who experiences it, even as its true sources go unrecognized consciously. Rather than serving peace and harmony, these tendencies almost always promote conflict and war—individually and on a larger scale. Finding the means of blocking the turn to these devastating archetypal responses depends on understanding how death anxiety affects us and on making a firm commitment to follow the archetypal moral guidelines offered to us by our inner god. Morality must trump immorality, and life must—at least temporarily—triumph over death. If it does not, all is or will be lost.

LAST WORDS

I have done little more than identify some of the new challenges that need to be met by religion and new ways that God needs to be configured in order to buttress humankind's faith in God and greatly enhance our ability to live satisfying moral lives. Even those who believe in a transcendental God need to be shown how to turn to their inner god for divine guidance. In a sense, we are all God's angels and messengers, all prophets in our own time. The problem is that even though we utter words of divine wisdom most of the days of our lives, rather than being stated and experienced directly, this knowledge is encoded in our dreams and stories. The true prophet among many who are false is the one who is able to properly trigger decode these narrative messages so as to bring forth this divine knowledge and bring it into our conscious awareness, individually and collectively. Once this wisdom is established and fixed in our conscious minds, it can be used to help us to live our lives more effectively, replete with personal satisfactions, and with a minimum of unneeded emotional suffering. On a broader scale, this realized wisdom also can be recruited to serve peace the world over.

Religion must not only add divine psychological wisdom to its belief system, it also must be able to find gentle but firm ways to enforce our deep unconscious moral guidelines. Evil must get its due. If we are not appropriately punished and do not suffer for our sins, humankind, driven by death anxiety, will continue to run amok with wanton, evil destructiveness—much as it has for centuries now. For the new religion, this much-needed moral enforcer should be modeled on our own deep unconscious system of morality and ethics. Thus, we ourselves and our deep unconscious, inner god are the first guarantors of personal moral integrity. Both people of faith and those who do not believe in God need, as I said, to fully understand that there is no free sin, that they themselves extract a huge price from themselves in pain and suffering for the evil acts that they commit. Showing humankind the grim reality of such unconsciously orchestrated punishments is likely to be one of the most fearsome messages delivered by the new version of God to which this book is pointing.

Individually and collectively, the ultimate goal for humankind must be achieving peace on earth for all living beings—a divinely informed, inspired return to Eden if you will. This elusive archetypal quest for a benevolent, deeply grounded, effective morality is a search that, despite everything to the contrary, should unify believers and nonbelievers, religion and psychoanalysis, spiritual and psychological understanding, and mundane and divine wisdom. To this point in our beleaguered history, we have had only minor moments of success in this pursuit and countless, horrendous failures. While there is no knowing how and when this goal will be achieved—as it must for life on earth to persist—it will help matters greatly if all concerned recognize that secularist attacks on religion for its failures are as pointless as religious attacks on nonbelievers for their evident deficiencies. Be it by God or nature, as a species we have been given the gift of language and with it the responsibility for life on earth. There can be no doubt, however, that we have failed miserably to live up to that responsibility through either secular or religious means. For countless reasons, some of them presented in this book, the challenge before us is overwhelmingly difficult to deal with and, for this reason alone, all concerned need to join forces against the common enemy which is, of course, ourselves. There are reasons to believe that faith-based solutions to this most fundamental menace may have as much or even more to offer than those that are secular in nature. But whatever the hoped-for final solution, we will not achieve it unless we have a unified front in this grim battle for survival. May God, nature, and, to speak anthropomorphically, our unique capability to overcome the damaging mental compromises wrought by natural selection in its all too brief and largely unsuccessful struggle to help us cope with death and death anxiety enable us to find the means to make this happen.

References

Akhtar, Salman, and Henry Parens. *Does God Help? Developmental and Clinical Aspects of Religious Belief*. Northvale, NJ: Jason Aronson, 2001.

Anzieu, Didier. *Freud's Self-Analysis*. Madison, CT: International Universities Press, 1986.

Armstrong, Karen. *Muhammad: A Biography of the Prophet*. San Francisco: Harper-Collins, 1992.

———. *In the Beginning: A New Interpretation of Genesis*. New York: Ballantine Books, 1996.

———. *Buddha*. New York: Penguin Books, 2001.

———. *A Short History of Myth*. New York: Canongate, 2005.

Augustine, St. *City of God*. New York: Doubleday, 1958.

———. *Confessions*. New York: Penguin Books, 1961.

Badalamenti, Anthony, and Robert Langs. "The Three Modes of the Science of Psychoanalysis." *American Journal of Psychotherapy* 46 (1992): 163–182.

———. "A Formal Science for Psychoanalysis." *British Journal of Psychotherapy* 11 (1994): 92–104.

Barnstone, Willis, and Marvin Meyer (eds.). *The Gnostic Bible*. Boston: Shambhala, 2003.

Becker, Ernest. *Denial of Death*. New York: Free Press, 1973.

Bernstein, Richard. *Ultimate Journey: Retracing the Path of an Ancient Buddhist Monk Who Crossed Asia in Search of Enlightenment*. New York: Alfred A. Knopf, 2001.

Bion, Wilfred. *Elements of Psycho-Analysis*. New York: Basic Books, 1963.

Brown, Peter. *Augustine of Hippo: A Biography*. Berkeley: University of California Press, 1967.

Chilton, Bruce. *Rabbi Jesus: An Intimate Biography*. New York: Doubleday, 2000.

Dawkins, Richard. *The God Delusion*. Boston: Houghton Mifflin, 2006.

Dennett, Daniel. *Breaking the Spell: Religion as a Natural Phenomenon*. London: Viking, 2006.

Edinger, Edward. *The Bible and the Psyche: Individuation Symbolism in the Old Testament*. Toronto: Inner City Books, 1986.

——. *The Christian Archetype: A Jungian Commentary on the Life of Christ*. Toronto: Inner City Books, 1987.

——. *Ego and Archetype: Individuation and the Religious Function of the Psyche*. Boston: Shambhala, 1992a.

——. *Transformation of the God-Image: An Elucidation of Jung's Answer to Job*. Toronto: Inner City Books, 1992b.

——. *The Aion Lectures: Exploring the Self in C. J. Jung's Aion*. Toronto: Inner City Books, 1996.

Freud, Sigmund. *Extracts from the Fleiss Papers*. Standard Edition 1, 1892–1899.

——. *The Interpretation of Dreams*. Standard Edition 4 and 5, 1900.

——. "Fragment of an Analysis of a Case of Hysteria." Standard Edition 7:3–122, 1905.

——. *Totem and Taboo*. Standard Edition 13:131–161, 1913.

——. "False Reconnaissance (Deja Raconte) in Psycho-Analytic Treatment." Standard Edition 7: 201–207, 1914a.

——. *The Moses of Michelangelo*. Standard Edition 13:211–244, 1914b.

——. "Thoughts for the Times on War and Death." Standard Edition 14:274–302, 1915.

——. "Introductory Lectures on Psycho-Analysis: Part III. General Theory of Neuroses." Standard Edition 16:243–496, 1917.

——. "From the History of an Infantile Neurosis." Standard Edition 17:3–123, 1918.

——. *The Ego and the Id*. Standard Edition 19:3–66, 1923.

——. "The Dissolution of the Oedipus Complex." Standard Edition 19:173–179, 1924.

——. "Some Psychical Consequences of the Anatomical Distinctions between the Sexes." Standard Edition 19:243–258, 1925.

——. *The Future of an Illusion*. Standard Edition 21:3–56, 1927.

——. *Civilization and Its Discontents*. Standard Edition 21:59–145, 1930.

——. *Moses and Monotheism: Three Essays*. Standard Edition 23:3–137, 1939.

——. *An Outline of Psycho-Analysis*. Standard Edition 23:141–207, 1940.

Gay, Peter. *Freud: A Life for Our Time*. New York: Norton, 1988.

Gilbert, Sandra. *Death's Door: Modern Dying and the Ways We Grieve*. New York: Norton, 2006.

Grotstein, James. "Why Oedipus and Not Christ?: A Psychoanalytic Inquiry into Innocence, Human Sacrifice, and the Sacred—Part I: Innocence, Spirituality, and Human Sacrifice." *American Journal of Psychoanalysis* 57 (1997a): 193–220.

——. "Why Oedipus and Not Christ?: A Psychoanalytic Inquiry into Innocence, Human Sacrifice, and the Sacred—Part II: The Numinous and Spiritual Dimension of a Metapsychological Perspective. *American Journal of Psychoanalysis* 57 (1997b): 317–335.

Harris, Sam. *The End of Faith: Religion, Terror, and the Future of Reason*. New York: Norton, 2004.

——. *Letter to a Christian Nation*. New York: Knopf, 2006.

Harrison, Robert Pogue. *Forests: The Shadow of Civilization*. Chicago: University of Chicago Press, 1992.

——. *The Dominion of the Dead*. Chicago: University of Chicago Press, 2003.

Heidegger, Martin. *Being and Time*. New York: Harper & Row, 1962.

Hitchens, Christopher. *God Is Not Great: How Religion Poisons Everything*. New York: Twelve, 2007.

Jung, Carl. *Answer to Job*. Princeton, NJ: Bollinger, 1958.

——. "Psychology and Religion." In *Psychology and Religion*. New Haven, CT: Yale University Press, 1966.

——. "Analytical Psychology: Its Theory and Practice." In *The Tavistock Lectures*. London: Routledge & Kegan Paul, 1968.

——. "The Personal and the Collective Unconscious." In *Two Essays on Analytical Psychology*. Princeton, NJ: Princeton University Press, 1972.

——. *The Visions Seminars: From the Complete Notes of Mary Foote*, vol. 1, p. 156. Zürich: Spring Publications, 1976.

——. *Mysterium Coniunctionis: An Inquiry into the Separation and Synthesis of Psychic Opposites in Alchemy*, 2nd ed., trans. R. F. C. Hull. Princeton, NJ: Princeton University Press, 1977.

Kelly, Henry. *Satan: A Biography*. New York: Cambridge University Press, 2006.

Krull, Marianne. *Freud and His Father*. New York: Norton, 1986.

Kuhn, Thomas. *The Structure of Scientific Revolution*. Chicago: University of Chicago Press, 1962.

Langs, Robert. *Empowered Psychotherapy*. London: Karnac Books, 1993.

——. *Clinical Practice and the Architecture of the Mind*. London: Karnac Books, 1995.

——. *The Evolution of the Emotion-Processing Mind, with an Introduction to Mental Darwinism*. London: Karnac Books, 1996.

——. *Death Anxiety and Clinical Practice*. London: Karnac Books, 1997.

—— (ed.). *Current Theories of Psychoanalysis*. Madison, CT: International Universities Press, 1998a.

——. *Ground Rules in Psychotherapy and Counselling*. London: Karnac Books, 1998b.

——. *Dreams and Emotional Adaptation*. Phoenix, AZ: Zeig & Tucker, 1999.

——. "Three Forms of Death Anxiety." Pp. 73–84 in *Death and Denial: Interdisciplinary Perspectives on the Legacy of Ernest Becker*, edited by Daniel Leichty. Westport, CT: Greenwood, 2002.

——. "Adaptive Insights into Death Anxiety." *Psychoanalytic Review* 90 (2003): 565–582.

——. "Adaptive Insights into Death Anxiety." Pp. 275–290 in *The Psychology of Death in Fantasy and History*, edited by Jerome Piven. Westport, CT: Praeger, 2004a.

——. "Death Anxiety and the Emotion-Processing Mind." *Psychoanalytic Psychology* 21 (2004b): 31–53.

——. *Fundamentals of Adaptive Psychotherapy and Counseling*. London: Palgrave-Macmillan, 2004c.

——. "The Challenge of the Strong Adaptive Approach." *Psychoanalytic Psychology* 22 (2005a): 49–68.

——. "Hallmarks of the Adaptive Approach." *Psychoanalytic Psychology* 22 (2005b): 78–85.

————. "Relational Perspectives and the Strong Adaptive Paradigm of Communicative Psychoanalysis." Pp. 223–254 in *Relational and Intersubjective Perspectives in Psychoanalysis*, edited by Jon Mills. Lanham, MD: Jason Aronson, 2005c.

————. *Love and Death in Psychotherapy*. London: Palgrave-Macmillan, 2006.

Langs, Robert, Anthony Badalamenti, and Lenore Thomson. *The Cosmic Circle: The Unification of Mind, Matter and Energy*. Brooklyn, NY: Alliance Publishing, 1996.

Maidenbaum, Aryeh. "Dreams and Other Aspects of Jungian Psychology." Pp. 227–254 in *Current Theories of Psychoanalysis*, edited by Robert Langs. Madison, CT: International Universities Press, 1998.

Meissner, William. *Psychoanalysis and Religious Experience*. New Haven, CT: Yale University Press, 1984.

Miles, Jack. *God: A Biography*. New York: Vintage Books, 1995.

————. *Christ: A Crisis in the Life of God*. New York: Alfred A. Knopf, 2001.

Mitchell, Stephen. *Gilgamesh*. New York: Free Press, 2004.

Murakami, Haruki. *The Wind-Up Bird Chronicle*. New York: Vintage Books, 1998.

Nietzsche, Friedrich. *Beyond Good and Evil*, translated by R. J. Hollingdale. London: Penguin Books, 2003.

Ostow, Mortimer. *Spirit, Mind, and Brain: A Psychoanalytic Examination of Spirituality and Religion*. New York: Columbia University Press, 2007.

Pagels, Elaine. *Adam, Eve, and the Serpent*. New York: Vintage Books, 1988.

————. *The Gnostic Gospels*. New York: Vintage Books, 1989.

————. *The Origin of Satan*. New York: Vintage Books, 1996.

Piven, Jerome (ed.). *The Psychology of Death in Fantasy and History*. Westport, CT: Praeger, 2004.

Rizzuto, Ana-Maria. *The Birth of the Living God*. Chicago: University of Chicago Press, 1979.

————. *Why Did Freud Reject God?* New Haven, CT: Yale University Press, 1998.

Schur, Max. *Freud: Living and Dying*. New York: International Universities Press, 1972.

Shulman, Dennis. *The Genius of Genesis*. New York: iUniverse, 2003.

Taylor, Don (trans.). *The Theban Plays: Oedipus the King by Sophocles*. London: Methuen, 1986.

Taylor, John (ed.) *Ancient Christian Writers. St. Augustine, Vol. 1: The Literal Meaning of Genesis*. Mahwah, NJ: Paulist Press, 1982.

Vitz, Paul. *Sigmund Freud's Christian Unconscious*. New York: Guilford Press, 1988.

Waugaman, Richard. "Commentary of 'Narcissism as a Motivational Structure: The Problem of Personal Significance' Religion—The Last Taboo?" *Psychiatry* 63 (2000): 234–238.

Wills, Garry. *Saint Augustine*. New York: Viking Penguin, 1999.

————. *Saint Augustine's Sins*. New York: Viking Penguin, 2003.

————. *What Jesus Meant*. New York: Viking, 2006a.

————. *What Paul Meant*. New York: Viking, 2006b.

Wilson, A. N. *Paul: The Mind of the Apostle*. New York: Norton, 1997.

Yerushalmi, Yosef. *Freud's Moses: Judaism Terminable and Interminable*. New Haven, CT: Yale University Press, 1991.

Index

Abel, 79–89. *See also* Cain
Abraham, 109–17, 127
Adam, 5–8, 15–18, 23–33, 36–37,
   71–74, 137, 140, 151, 156, 166, 175
adaptive approach, ix–xi, xvi–xvii,
   10–15, 32, 39–40, 52, 70–71, 83–84,
   92–100, 131–33, 158–60, 165–67,
   176–79, 185, 187–88. *See also* Bible,
   approaches to: adaptive
Akhtar, Salman, 155, 193
anxiety, death-related. *See* death anxiety
Anzieu, Didier, 161
archetypes, 52, 59–61, 63–64, 69–71,
   99–100, 102, 119–20, 139–40, 160,
   166–68, 186–90; in Bible, 2–3, 7,
   15–18, 20, 41, 81, 92–93, 95–98;
   counter-responses to, 38, 127–28,
   173, 175; death-related, 87, 89,
   92–93, 115–16, 127–28, 189–90; in
   Jungian thinking, 8–10
Armstrong, Karen, 8, 31, 126, 127, 193
Augustine, St., 20, 35, 54, 55, 89, 101,
   193; Adam's sin, repetition of,
   55–64; Cain's sin, reliving of, 91,
   100–103

Babel, tower of, 48–50
Badalamenti, Anthony, 176, 193, 196

Barnstone, Willis, 25, 133, 152, 193
Becker, Ernest, 162, 193
Bernstein, Richard, x, 193
Bible, approaches to: adaptive, 40–42;
   Freudian, 1, 9–10, 27; Jungian, 1,
   8–10, 29
Bion, Wilfred, 6, 30, 193
boundaries. *See* ground rules
Brown, Peter, 58, 193
Buddha, 126

Cain, 79–89, 137; alternate version of,
   88–89, 95–103; God's role with,
   79–82, 87–88. *See also* Augustine, St.
Chilton, Bruce, 127, 193
Christ. *See* Jesus of Nazareth
communicative approach. *See* adaptive
   approach
conscious system. *See* mind, emotion-
   processing: conscious system of
creation, 48; first, 2–4; second, 4–8

Dawkins, ix, 2, 193
death, xii, xiv, xvii, 5–8, 13–18, 60–62,
   74, 125–28, 140–41, 149–50,
   168–69, 172–73, 180–81; awareness
   of, 30–33, 68, 82; denial of, 149–50,
   162, 175

197

death anxiety, 14–18, 40, 74, 149–50,
165–67, 172–73, 181; and wisdom,
15–18, 43–54, 132–33; deep
unconscious, x, 44–45; existential,
32–33, 37, 49, 68, 79, 85, 111–17,
118, 121, 127, 129, 133–36, 165–167,
186, 189; predator, 61, 63–64, 68–71,
79, 85, 102–3, 114–17, 121, 136–40,
166–67, 184, 189; predatory, 49, 67,
79, 85, 111–17, 118, 121, 127, 138,
140–43, 165–67, 189. *See also*
morality, human: death anxiety and
deep unconscious system. *See* mind,
emotion-processing: deep
unconscious system of
decoding, narrative messages. *See*
trigger decoding
Dennett, ix, 194
Devil. *See* Satan
dreams, 52–54, 99, 168–69; and the
Bible, 20, 91–98; in the Bible, 73,
112–13

Eden, garden of, 5, 15–18, 19–22,
23–33, 36–37, 66–69, 74–77
Edinger, Edward, 2, 8, 9, 10, 29, 76,
125, 155, 156, 194
emotion-processing mind. *See* mind,
emotion-processing
Eve, 7, 16–17, 19–33, 36–37, 42, 43,
65–77, 137, 140, 151, 156, 166, 175;
and her dilemma, 20–22, 24–26,
37–40; and God, 19–22, 23–26,
28–31, 66–67; motives of (triggers),
65–78
events, triggering, 56, 58–59, 60, 65–71,
93–100, 132; death-related, 67–71,
120
evil, 33–35, 85, 101, 106–9. *See also*
morality, human
Exodus, 118–19, 168, 171–72, 187

flood, the. *See* Noah
Freud, Sigmund, 1, 9, 10, 38, 45, 52–54,
74, 98, 155, 156, 161–63, 168–73,

175, 194; dreams of, 52, 168–69;
personal life of, 161–63, 167–73. *See
also* Bible, approaches to: Freudian;
Jesus of Nazareth: and Freud

Gay, Peter, 162, 194
Genesis, 1–8, 15–33, 34–42, 48–50,
63–73, 74–77, 79–89, 98–103,
105–18, 122–23
Gilbert, Sandra, 46, 194
Gilgamesh, 27, 45–47, 60
god, inner, 14, 152–53, 179–88
good, and evil. *See* morality, human
Grotstein, James, 155, 156, 194
ground rules (frames), 7, 119–22,
178–79, 188–89; archetypal aspects
of, 119–22, 188–89; moral
implications of, 120–22; violations
of, 32, 94–95, 120–22, 188–89
guilt, deep unconscious. *See* death
anxiety: predator

Harris, Sam, ix, 146, 175, 195
Harrison, Robert Pogue, 46, 47, 180, 195
Hebrew God. *See* Yahweh
Heidegger, Martin, 46, 195
Hitchens, ix, 195

ignorance, divine, 35, 82–83
immortality, 141–42; human, issue of,
4–6, 31–33, 46

Jacob, 117–18
Jesus of Nazareth, 125–44, 145–54,
156; and death anxiety, solutions to,
133–44, 145; and existential death
anxiety, 140–44; of faith, 125,
128–44; and Freud, 3, 127, 173;
historical, 125, 126–28, 173, 175;
incarnation of, 135–36, 138; missing
elements in, 146–54; and Oedipus,
129; parables of, 130–33; and peace
on earth, failure to achieve, 145–54;
and predator death anxiety, 136–40;
and predatory death anxiety, 133–36,
138; resurrection of, 141–43;

teachings of, 130–36, 143–44;
wisdom of, 128–29, 131–33, 146–54;
and Yahweh, comparison with, 133,
137, 141, 145–46, 153, 156, 185
Job, 119
Jung, Carl, 1, 2, 8, 9, 10, 29, 76, 119,
155, 156, 157, 160, 195. *See also*
Bible, approaches to: Jungian

Kelly, Henry, 25, 33, 76, 141, 146, 195
knowledge, acquisition of. *See* wisdom:
acquisition of
Krull, Marianne, 161, 162, 195
Kuhn, Thomas, 195

Langs, Robert, ix, xvi, 7, 8, 11, 12, 22,
23, 33, 39, 45, 91, 120, 158, 163,
176, 178, 180, 193, 195–96
language, acquisition of, 7, 49–50,
180–81
Lilith, tale of, 73–74
Lord God. *See* Yahweh

Maidenbaum, Aryeh, 2, 29, 196
Maugham, Somerset, xvi–xvii, 161
Meissner, William, 155, 196
Meyer, Marvin, 25, 133, 152, 193
Miles, Jack, 2, 8, 125, 196
mind, emotion-processing, ix, 11–15,
159–60, 179–90; conscious system
of, ix, xv, 12, 159; deep unconscious
system of, ix–x, xv, 13–15, 160
Mitchell, Stephen, 27, 46, 196
morality, human, 34, 62, 68, 147–48,
151–54, 177, 179, 183–88; death
anxiety and 19, 33–36, 75–76,
184–88
Moses and Monotheism, 168, 171–72.
See also Exodus
Muhammad, 126–27
Murakami, Haruki, 47, 196

nakedness of Adam and Eve, 25–33;
and awareness of death, 30–33; and
individuation, 29–30; sexual

meanings of, 27–29; nakedness of
Noah, 108
narratives, as communicative vehicles,
11–12, 131–33
Nietzsche, Frederick, 161, 196
Noah, 48, 106–9

Oedipus, myth of, 50–52, 129, 163–73;
death anxiety in, 51–52, 165–67;
divine wisdom in 51–52, 129, 151,
166–67; Freud's position on, 50–51,
156, 163, 170
Ostow, Mortimer, 155, 196

Pagels, Elaine, 8, 15, 25, 33, 133,
152–53, 196
parables. *See* Jesus of Nazareth:
parables of
Parens, Henry, 155, 193
Paul, 139, 142, 146
perception, unconscious (subliminal),
xv, 12, 59, 132
Piven, Jerome, 162, 196
psychoanalysis: and Bible (*see* Bible,
approaches to); and failure to aid
religion, 155–56; and proper alliance
with religion, 156, 176–79; classical
(Freudian et al.), xiv–xvi, 155–58;
theological, 176–79

religion: beliefs, failure of, 145–54, 191;
future of, 180–82; new perspectives
on, 175–91
Rizzuto, Ana-Maria, 155, 161, 196

Satan, 34, 40–41, 82, 119, 151; and
Jesus, 128–30
Schur, Max, 162, 196
serpent, 19, 21–22, 25–26, 36, 72–76;
adaptive therapists as, 22–23, 39–40;
and divine wisdom, 21–22, 37–40; as
Satan, 40, 41, 76. *See also* Yahweh:
and the serpent
sexuality, xiv–xv, 9, 26–29, 46–47, 51,
58–60

Shulman, Dennis, 8, 41, 196
sin, 35, 50, 56–58, 60–61, 68, 72–73,
    81, 82, 85, 100–103, 112, 117, 140

Taylor, John, 56, 196
Taylor, Don, 51, 163, 165, 196
Ten Commandments, 24, 72, 121–22,
    187
Thomson, Lenore, 176, 196
Totem and Taboo, 168, 170–71
transference, xv, 98
trauma, death related, 59–62, 68–71
tree: of knowledge, 5, 16, 19; of life, 5,
    16, 31–32
trigger decoding, ix, 11–12, 14

Vitz, Paul, 161, 196

Waugaman, Richard, 155, 196
Wills, Gary, 15, 20, 35, 55, 91, 101,
    128, 139, 143, 196
Wilson, A. N., 142, 143, 196
Wilson, A. O., 62, 196
wisdom: absence of, divine, 38, 42, 75,
    84, 85; acquisition of, 166–67; in
    the Bible, 1–2, 15–18, 28–30, 38,
    75, 82–83; choice of, type, 37–40,
    43; and death anxiety (*see* death
    anxiety, and wisdom); divine, xvi,
    75, 82–83, 129, 151, 182–83;

divine, in humans, 4, 6–7, 14,
    28–30, 35–36, 38–40, 43; of Jesus
    (*see* Jesus of Nazareth: wisdom of);
    mundane, 75, 83, 151, 153;
    mundane, in humans, 6–7, 14,
    37–38, 43, 57–58; in psychoanalysis
    and psychotherapy, 22–23, 39–40;
    psychological, 129, 147–54; secular,
    151; spiritual, 129, 151–54

Yahweh, 2–8, 25–26, 105–23, 145–46,
    175, 185; and divine wisdom in
    humans, 6, 14–18, 21–22, 24–25,
    34–36; and Freud, 38, 175; and
    Jesus, comparison with (*see* Jesus of
    Nazareth: and Yahweh, comparison
    with); influence, on human death
    anxiety, 34–37, 40–42, 76, 80, 105,
    107–17, 123; influence, on human
    violence, 88, 107, 110, 123; moral
    uncertainties of, 82, 88, 110, 117,
    118, 119, 121–23; predatory features
    of, 48–50, 106–9, 110, 114–17, 119,
    122; punishments by, 28, 30–33,
    36–37, 48–50, 72–73, 86, 88, 106–7,
    113, 119; and the serpent, 19, 25–26,
    38, 41, 72; unresolved death anxiety
    in, 34–37, 76, 80, 88, 107–9, 115–17,
    119, 122–23
Yerushalmi, Yosef, 172, 196

About the Author

Robert Langs, MD, is a practicing psychoanalyst who has forged a new, adaptation-oriented approach to the study of the human mind and emotional life in which unconscious perceptions of traumatic, death-related realities play a crucial role—both creatively and disruptively. He is the author of forty-five books on psychotherapy and psychoanalysis that focus on the evolution and design of the emotion-processing mind, dreams, archetypes, death anxiety, the therapeutic process, the science of the mind, the application of psychoanalytic ideas to other fields, and much more. He is a visiting fellow at the School of Psychotherapy and Counselling at Regent's College in London.

33206924R00125

Made in the USA
Lexington, KY
17 June 2014